"A tremendously entertaining (
only a witness (and a good wr
The New York Times

True Stories

Portraits from My Past

Felice Picano

"Compelling and engrossing, it will conjure up memories of everyone's adolescence, straight or gay."
Out Magazine

"His glints of flashing wit and subtle hints of dark decadence transcend clichés."
Library Journal

From author Felice Picano, co-founder of the path breaking Violet Quill Club, comes a new collection of memoirs, many of which have never appeared in print. Picano presents sweet and sometimes controversial anecdotes of his precocious childhood, odd, funny, and often disturbing encounters from before he found his calling as a writer and later as one of the first GLBT publishers. Throughout are his delightful encounters and surprising relationships with the one-of-a-kind and the famous—including Tennessee Williams, W.H. Auden, Charles Henri Ford, Bette Midler, and Diana Vreeland.

True Stories

True Stories

Portraits from My Past

Felice Picano

Chelsea Station Editions

New York

Cover and book design by Peach Boy Distillery & Design
Cover photo from Queerstock

Published as a trade paperback original by Chelsea Station Editions, 362 West 36th Street, Suite 2R, New York, NY 10018
www.chelseastationeditions.com / info@chelseastationeditions.com

ISBN: 978-0-9844707-7-8
Library of Congress Control Number: 2011921419

First U.S. edition, 2011

These portraits are the product of the author's recollections and are thus rendered as a subjective accounting of events that occurred in his life. Portions of some of these portraits appeared in earlier and different form in the author's *Men Who Loved Me: A Memoir* and *Ambidextrous: The Secret Lives of Children*; the anthologies *On the Meaning of Friendship Between Gay Men, The Man I Might Have Been: Gay Men and Their Fathers, Loss Within Loss: Artists in the Age of AIDS,* and *A Loving Testimony: Remembering Loved Ones Lost to AIDS*; the periodicals *Fab* and *Art & Understanding*, and the Web journal *Blithe House Quarterly*, and are all copyright © by Felice Picano and are used by permission of the author. Portions which appeared in the author's *Art & Sex in Greenwich Village: A Memoir of Gay Literary Life After Stonewall* (copyright © 2007 Felice Picano) are reprinted by permission of Basic Books, a member of the Perseus Books Group.

To Rob Arnold

Contents

Preface

I've repeatedly said in interviews old and new that what made me a writer was the amount of very interesting people *around me* from early on in life. *They* were the ones with the stories, *they* were the ones who acted; *they* were the ones who were famous, or if not famous than weirdly funny, or odd, or perverse, or utterly unprecedented, or simply fascinating. Whenever I read my memoirs, to me they always read like the story of this pretty ordinary guy who came into contact with a bunch of strange, wondrous, or simply nutty people.

So this volume is in a way a continuation of them and also of my history/ memoirs, *Art & Sex in Greenwich Village* and *Nights at Rizzoli,* and like them, most of the pieces included here are essays; they're much more clearly about that person or couple, much less about me.

I suppose this might be called an *autobiography in negative*: showing me, by showing those I related to, over the years. I've already written of many people (and animals) in my memoirs. But here *other people* take center stage.

I've arranged them alphabetically. I've taken no liberties with truth; these are all (as well as my good memory and my many volumes of journals could provide) "true stories" and usually I wrote them up because they made what I felt were in fact complete stories with beginnings, middles, and ends.

Some of these pieces have appeared in print, in anthologies, literary quarterlies, and online magazines. Others are sections omitted from or totally reworked from my memoirs, with tons more detail. Some are published here for the first time.

Of the people rendered here: A few are famous; a few even infamous— from W.H. Auden and Charles-Henri Ford, to Bette Midler, Diana Vreeland,

and Tennessee Williams. The rest are not known to today's public. But in each case, I was blessed with some kind of really intimate, in some cases quite brief, if inexplicable, and always unexpected connection.

As virtually all the wonderful people written of here are dead, I'm forced to recall the words of the nameless witness to the destruction of the Biblical Patriarch, Job's family and home in the Old Testament:

"And I only am escaped to tell thee."
Job 1:17

Felice Picano
February 2011

"Look for a long time at what pleases you, and even longer at what pains you..."
　　　　　—Colette

The British Auntie

W. H. Auden

Because he worked at night when he was working and like most actors wasn't working or rehearsing for varying stretches of time, George Sampson had developed the habit of going around town and "dropping in" on people he knew during the afternoon.

The first time he did this to me, we were both surprised I was in. I'd awakened with a brain-stunning migraine/sinus headache that morning (they affected my entire time living on the East Coast) and as usual it had taken me most of the day to get rid of the headache and clear my mind. It was close to three p.m. when George rang my bell and I looked out one of the two studio windows onto Jane Street, down four floors to see George waving up, with the kind of expansive gesture Mercutio (who he was planning to portray) might make just before taking a bow and/or thrusting a foil into an opponent's heart.

"The Sherpas abandoned me somewhere below in the foothills," was George's snide comment on the long walk up the stairs, as he sailed into my tiny flat, took in what there was of furniture and decor in a single glance, parked himself on my rocking chair, and pulled out a small pipe that he immediately filled with marijuana. "As you are at home, I thought we'd have a smoke and walk over to Fourth Avenue to look through the secondhand bookstores."

Since part of my therapy for headaches has always been liberal amounts of caffeine, by this time I was already quite jazzed up and restless enough to walk over to Fourth Avenue in some adjoining city. I flaked some of my hashish onto his grass, and this "cocktail" was enough to induce a mild buzz which in turn helped propel us out of the flat, and building, and into the Village streets.

I don't remember our conversation except to recall that it more or less picked up from where we had left it off at our first meeting. George had thought the architect Palladio might have built outside of Italy and wanted to prove or disprove this thesis for himself. Also, he loved the musty old bookstores; I was at the time still unfamiliar with them and simply wanted to hunt through them for the hell of it. I do remember that as we walked, George referred to people and places we passed as though they were old acquaintances, seeming very sophisticated to me, and that he mentioned that he'd studied at HB Studios on Bank Street, an actor's Mecca, under Bill Hickey, whom George assured me was "one of the best unknown actors of our generation." Hickey has since made a name for himself playing character parts in Hollywood films, including *The Godfather*, garnering praise and awards, justifying George's evaluation.

In those days, from Fourteenth Street down to Cooper Union, dozens of secondhand bookstores of various shapes and sizes abounded. A few were mere holes-in-the-wall, others storefronts that could adequately house small delis or flower shops. but several of these bookstores had been rather grand in their day, a half century before, with upstairs balconies curving around two and sometimes three-story open courts, reached by now perilously dilapidated stairways.

No matter their size or pretensions to past glory, every inch of these shops appeared to be covered with books of various ages, and of even more varied literary quality. Some were arranged more or less by subject. Others simply tossed in heaps onto huge, rickety trestle tables that were carried out to sidewalks on sunny days. Still others had been stacked up, who knew how many years ago, in the same dusty cardboard boxes they'd been shipped in from someone's basement or library.

George said he'd spent many an afternoon in these bookstores and had found books on arcane topics—French carriages of the seventeenth and eighteenth centuries; the gardens at Nymphenberg; Atlantis, the Antediluvian World; secrets of the Babylonian necromancers. Since the books ranged in price anywhere from a quarter to ten dollars (for the glossiest and most arcane of art and picture books), I soon found that I, too, could afford to lurk in these musty volume-filled alcoves hours at a time on rainy afternoons and manage to find inexpensive hardcover books to begin to build a real library.

That afternoon, we were both too restless to spend more than fifteen minutes per shop or to buy much—I located a first edition of Conrad's *Mirror of the Sea* for a dollar, George picked up a photo book on Greta Garbo for five-fifty—and we ended up a few blocks west, on St. Marks Place, in search of a cafe specializing in a type of Viennese coffee—"With a dollop of *schlag* sprinkled with grated nutmeg, a virtual nectar and ambrosia in one!"—George said, swearing it was the best he'd ever tasted.

Somehow or other, we missed the cafe, or passed it, or it was no longer in business. We'd just turned around and were in the middle of the block about to cross the street and ask a likely-looking neighborhood type, when a flowerpot fell between us, its ceramic shattering on the sidewalk.

"Oh, my *Gawd*!" we heard someone expostulate above us.

We turned to look up to the third floor, where an astonishing head was peering out a window over a small parapet at us.

"I hope I haven't *killed* anyone," the head said.

"What?" I asked George: "Is that?"

"That," George answered, sotto voce, "is a British Auntie of a certain age and of indeterminate gender."

"You're quite certain neither of you two delightful young lads aren't in some way injured?" the possessor of the remarkable head asked.

"We're fine," I called up.

"Your geranium looks fatally injured," George called up.

"I feel simply awful," the Auntie insisted. "I might have dashed your brains out."

George and I looked at each other.

"It speaks," said I, "in blank verse."

"As," George replied, "The Chimera was said to do."

"Might I?"—all the while the Auntie was shouting down to us—"Might I right things again by the offer of a cup of tea?"

"Definitely British," I said, I then shouted up, "No thanks."

George pulled at my arm. "This could be fun."

"Fun?" I questioned him.

"Cultural fun. High-toned fun," George then called up. "Yes, thanks. We'll bring up your plant. What's left of it."

"Oh good," the Auntie said, and vanished from the window.

The stairway turned several times, each tiny landing at a wildly different cant to the last. We arrived at a small foyer of one of the oddest, most overfilled, and most disorderly apartments I'd ever entered.

The British Auntie, it turned out was male, and was clad in overlarge, worn, corduroy trousers of the palest blue, cinched by a makeshift belt made of two knotted together neckties. His wide torso was sheathed in a summery, short-sleeved shirt with a haphazard pattern of tiny scarlet biplanes against a background, possibly once ivory, now grimy gray. On his veinous bare feet, he wore a pair of beat-up canvas slip-ons, called espadrilles in Essex.

But if his costume was curious and his apartment a horror, the man himself—only partly glimpsed from the steep angle of thirty feet or so below, was something to behold. He possessed the largest head I'd ever seen on a human: an almost perfect cube of a head, topped by a mop of graying reddish-brown hair. His face exposed its features slowly—puffy lips, bulbous nose, eyes hidden within fleshly overslants—because of its enormous, and much wrinkled surface.

His voice, on the other hand, was smart and bright, if slightly querulous.

"Poor loves! And you are a pair, aren't' you?" he gushed. "I doubt that two such young lovelies have been between these sad walls in a decade. Yes, yes! Just what Mother needed as a pick-me-up today."

He all but spun around in pleasure and enthusiasm, and ended up facing George, who held out part of the geranium and its former domicile.

"Dash the geranium!" the Auntie insisted. "But of course, it's already sufficiently dashed, isn't it?" he added, "Now for a nice pot of tea!"

The Auntie pointed vaguely to what we took to be a living room: chairs and a table littered with papers and books of various decrepitude and a cracked-frame love seat missing one clawed leg. Before we could say a word, he vanished, we assumed into the kitchen.

We guessed it was the kitchen because we soon heard assorted crashes and bangs and sudden clatterings potentially indicative of tea being prepared.

George and I discovered a months-old *Times Literary Supplement* and dropped what was left of the plant on it. Then we looked at each other.

"You're certain about this?" I asked George.

He shrugged.

"Darjeeling!" our host announced, and arrived a minute later, balancing a battered, once-painted, now much chipped metal tea tray, a sufficient number of utterly unmatched cups sans saucers, several irregular cake plates, assorted pieces of silverware, a creamer, lemon slices, and a sugar bowl almost as large as the lovely, old Wedgewood teapot. A package of Peek Freans had been torn asunder, its butter biscuits artfully dominoed out. George and I moved a variety of objects off the love seat and settled in.

"I'll be *Mother*," the Auntie said, pouring. "But then, I'm *always* Mother."

Between sips and bites, we answered a barrage of questions from our British interlocutor. Did George know that type of leather vest he was wearing was called a jerkin? (he did); did we think that wearing tight denims caused sterility, as some said, or instead, did they caress the genitals and cause lubricity? (The latter, we opined). We were so attractive, were we actors? (One of us was, yes). Did we ever go to the Electric Circus on the next block? (George had, not I, yet). Did we ingest large amounts of hallucinogenics? Did we object to being called beatniks? Or were we merely individualists? Were we interested in politics at all, or had we completely given up on all that? Did we think socialism was utterly passé? Did we have group sex often? With each other? Might an older, non-participating stranger ever be invited or tolerated? Was that Conrad I was reading? Did we think Conrad was a repressed queen, so many sailor writer types seemed to be, like Melville writing about his marinated boyfriends, then making an ass of himself over Hawthorne who must have been completely uptight? And Jack London, that old bestialist? Or did we think Conrad was merely to out-dickens Dickens?

We attempted to answer his questions as well as we could; in return, he told us virtually nothing of himself over two pots of Darjeeling in what might have been more than two hours. But we came to feel more comfortable with him, and amused by his interest. His obvious attempts to refrain from touching us, oddly, touched us. His general air of being either incisively probing or utterly at sea, though in his own apartment, and his constant referral to himself in the third (usually quite maternal) person, also tickled us. He was definitely a character.

When George asked about the café we'd been searching for, the British Auntie told us that it had shut its doors some months before, then he waxed rhapsodic about Vienna, his favorite city in the world, he said, and went on to mention in passing that Iceland was the newest country on earth. "Did you know that Iceland grows five yards daily?! It does! Because of tectonic activity," he assured us in perfectly enunciated dactyls, and took five minutes to locate and show us some rather technical-looking tomes in German on the subject of North Atlantic topography.

Finally we said he had to leave. It was already dark outside and George had a performance that night.

The Auntie said we'd been the nicest thing that happened to him in months. Perhaps we'd come visit again. Or should he simply toss geraniums down at attractive youths on the sidewalk? And couldn't we stay only a minute more?, but oh, he was getting late himself for a dinner appointment.

He stood there, short and squat in his down-at-the-heels espadrilles, face wrinkled like a Shar Pei, and shook our hands and said we'd been so kind, and so good-looking, and so very interesting to talk to.

George waited until we'd crossed Fifth Avenue and were safely on home turf before commenting, "*There*! Wasn't *that* different?"

Δ

"Now, Phil," Bob warned, "you've promised that you won't talk about the war in Vietnam and you won't say a word about drugs and you won't go on about the U.S. government or anything else you think you know so much about but don't really."

That last because I'd told my older lover that I'd bumped into a former high school classmate, Mario Savio, and promised to join him and the rest of the gang in the SDS in demonstrations that coming August at the Democratic National Convention in Chicago. What I hadn't mentioned was that I'd known Mario briefly in high school, when he'd been a Young Republican and had worn a suit and tie and carried an attaché case and called himself *Bob* Savio, because his given name was "too ethnic."

"Don't worry," I told my lover, "I'll pretend that I'm a deaf-mute."

"Now see, Phil! That's exactly the attitude I'm talking about."

"C'mon, Bob," his friend and upstairs neighbor, Ken growled. "Lay off!" He was getting as irritated as I was with Bob's constant lecturing at me.

"If he's got to come along at all, he's got to act like a civilized human being."

"Orlan *has* gone to a lot of trouble to arrange this gathering," Ken admitted.

The gathering was the prophesized—from my point of view, foredoomed—meeting with the great poet, W.H. Auden, who was a friend of Orlan Fox's. We were to meet with him for no more than two hours at Orlan's apartment, at which time Orlan would whisk the bard off to dinner, *à deux*, and we'd be left to our own devices, doubtless too stunned into contemplative silence by the experience to do much of anything. I considered Auden, like every other figure of authority or importance in the world at that time, to be a fraud and of no importance. I had no interest in putting on a jacket and tie and sitting amidst adorers hanging on his every word.

"I promise," I repeated, just to make peace.

Bob was re-knotting his tie in the mirror. "I just know this will end up a disaster," he commented.

Finally he was ready and the three of us got into a taxi and sped to Orlan's Chelsea apartment.

My first surprise was that other people were present: Kenneth Libo, whom I'd met walking along a Village street the week before with my friend Joseph Mathewson; and James Wilhelm, a pale, thin, high-voiced, but altogether nice and very intelligent man who'd taught the Dante and His Times seminar I'd aced in my last term at Queens College. I never discovered how they knew Orlan.

What was obvious was that they were all quietly excited about meeting Auden. Jim Wilhelm, my former professor, could barely keep his eyes on me as he talked about his current project, a translation of Catullus, which he said would be "A bit shocking, as I plan to translate every word and connotation."

I was pumping him on exactly what those connotations could be—were they homosexual? I thought perhaps some were—when I noticed everyone standing up. I turned and vaguely, and only partly, given the bad angle I was at, saw someone come into the apartment, give his coat to Orlan, then repair to the kitchen. Auden had arrived.

I was still pumping Jim about Catullus when Orlan and Auden came into the room, our host carrying what looked like a lemonade pitcher, which he placed on the table at the far end of the long living room. Auden sat down there, waved a general benediction in our direction and proceeded to pour and drink three good-sized glasses of the stuff.

"Carry on," Orlan said to us in a stage whisper, "As soon as Wystan has had his three martinis, he'll join us."

During this interim, people tried to pick up their previous conversation, but it couldn't help but be strained.

I was shut-mouth silent. The great poet, W.H. Auden, who sat not ten feet away, sipping martinis, was the same dizzy British Auntie who had almost killed George Sampson and me with a flowerpot on St. Mark's Place.

After some time Auden wiped his mouth with a handkerchief, then turned toward the room.

"That's better!... Orlan, you'll introduce your friends?"

One by one we stood up and were brought over to meet him. I held back as long as possible, uncertain what to do or say. When we were introduced, he gave no inkling at all that he recalled our encounter. Fine with me.

About an hour had gone by, during which Auden had moved to an armchair in the center of the room and had imbibed another martini or two and was speaking—a bit pompously, I thought—about something or other, while everyone listened in rapt attention, when he suddenly stopped, propped himself up, and stared at me closer.

I thought, *He does remember me.*

But since he went on speaking as before, I supposed he didn't want our previous meeting mentioned.

About ten or fifteen minutes passed. Then Auden excused himself from the room.

Amidst all the sudden, pent-up and now released chatter, Orlan Fox came over to me, puzzlement all over his face, and said, "Would you mind coming with me a minute?"

Auden was in the kitchen, seated at a table. He motioned me to come closer. When I was inches away from his huge, square, infolded and wrinkled face, he said, "Why, you naughty young man! I know you!"

"You certainly do," I said, bold as brass. "And I know you too!"

I could hear Orlan groan behind me. Bob's lectures had reached as far as him.

"You and I spent a lovely afternoon together. With... that lovely, faunlike young man."

"My friend, George."

"How is young George?"

"He's going to London to make a film with Franco Zeffirelli."

"And you weren't going to breathe a syllable. Were you?" Auden asked.

"Not a diphthong."

"You're very naughty. Why not?"

"I thought you'd forgotten."

"How could I possibly forget?"

"I'm sure you've got plenty on your mind."

"Why, that same evening I told Vera and Igor all about you!" They wanted to know why I hadn't brought you two along for dinner. You should come next time," Auden said.

"Stravinsky?" I asked.

"They're lovely people. She more than he lately. Poor health has drawn him back into the capacious fold of Mother Russia in the form of the Orthodox Church. Quite disturbing, in my opinion," Auden declared. "Orlan! This is the young man. Or one of them, I told you about." Auden stroked my hair. "How beastly clever of you to find him for me again."

He dismissed Orlan and insisted I sit by him. "What was that clever riposte of young George? Ah, yes. Someone had told him he was most edible. And George replied, 'Fifty bucks, before you put the bite on me!'"

We talked and laughed for another ten minutes, until Orlan made an appearance and Auden realized he had to return to his other guests.

"Now that I've found you again, you shan't escape quite so easily," he told me fondly.

We all left Orlan's apartment together. Orlan and Auden got into a cab headed uptown. Bob, Jim, the two Kens and I wandered through Chelsea until we found a restaurant Ken Libo knew.

Throughout dinner, I was a sphinx about what had happened in the kitchen. Torture wouldn't have made me breathe a word about it to Bob or Ken; not that night nor later.

Auden did get my phone number and did call and we met several times in the next year, usually at his St. Marks Place digs, before he made what turned out to be a fatal decision to leave New York and move back to Europe. He was always sweet and open and a little dizzy with me; not the great poet and scholar he'd been with strangers at Orlan Fox's place, but the British Auntie he'd been the first time we'd met. We never spoke about poetry or literature except in the most glancing manner; in fact, we talked of little but silly, superficial matters and we thoroughly entertained each other. I suppose because of Orlan's interest in the leather scene, Auden was fascinated by it. He sent me to Keller's Bar and to the Eagle's Nest and he listened to my reports with many questions and we once fantasized dressing him up in full harness and chaps and entering him into the Mr. Leather contest.

In a more serious mood, he once told me, "I was wrong, you know. I wrote that poetry doesn't mean anything in the real world. But I found out that wasn't true."

He went on to tell me of a trip he'd taken in an American Air Force plane near the end of World War II. German-speaking and a known pacifist, he'd been asked by the U.S. government to be involved in some secret business that he never adequately explained to me. As he told it, he was the only civilian passenger in a small plane designed for parachutists. It had been a bumpy and stormy nighttime ocean crossing and, as they approached the coast of Ireland, two German planes appeared and began harassing the U.S. plane. The American pilots didn't want to endanger Auden, and opened up a radio channel to the German planes. But they didn't speak German, and the Germans didn't speak English.

"Mother was *completely* terrified of dying in the o-cean," Auden told me. "And I could hear them all speaking, as there was no wall between the cockpit and what there was of a cabin. We were *doomed*! Mother flung herself toward them, grabbed the radio phone, and shouted, "*Ich bin Auden. Der Beruhmte*

Dichter!" telling them in German, you see, that I was Auden, the Well Known Poet. Odd, that in that total panic, Mother counted on that to save her skin. And it worked. The Germans have *such* respect for poets. We conversed another minute or so and they let us go. Mother threw herself back onto the tarpaulin and promised she'd do something to pay back those sweet German pilots."

Which he had done, he said, when he translated Goethe's *Italian Journey*, several years later.

In the few years Auden was away in England, we exchanged only one letter. His missive bemoaned the irony of having lived in high-crime Manhattan for decades in perfect safety. Whereas in one week in Oxford, his apartment had been burgled.

Then I heard he'd died, in a hotel in Vienna.

Some months after Auden died, a great literary establishment commemoration was held for him at Riverside Church, in Manhattan. I guess because my name was in his address book, I received an invitation. But by then I was working on the night shift at a fancy midtown bookstore and couldn't get away for it.

As I waited after midnight for the E train home, I found that I missed Wystan terribly. Using the inside blank page of the paperback I was reading, I sketched out the lines:

No solemn music
in uptown cathedrals
suffices...

After much writing and rewriting of the rest of the poem over the next week, those words would stand as written, opening the third part of my "Elegy for W.H. Auden," later to be published in *The Deformity Lover and Other Poems*.

I always wondered what Wystan would say if he'd lived long enough to see me end up becoming a writer. I'm not sure he'd be too pleased. He never thought it was a reputable vocation.

Mr. Broadway

Jerry Blatt and Bette Midler

In the winter of 1969 Jerry Blatt entered my life. Or rather he re-entered my life. I met him on a chilly walk on the Morton Street Pier in the far West Village, the day after Ed Armour left town. Jerry was riding a bicycle and suddenly swerved toward me. I'd seen him in the Village over the past few years and I'd thought he looked familiar, but I could never exactly place him. Several weeks before, when Ed and I were walking along Christopher Street, Ed had said hello to him in passing, and afterwards I asked his name.

"Jerry Blatt," Ed told me. "He's a composer."

"Then it must be him," I replied.

"Do you know him?" Ed asked.

"I used to. He's so built up with muscles now and his haircut is different and he's got a beard so I wasn't sure!"

I told Ed about how during my junior year of high school our family had moved to the house my parents still resided in at Twin Ponds, a strip of New York City only a three blocks wide and twelve blocks long between Laurelton in Queens County on one side and Valley Stream in Nassau County on the other. The spring before the move, my mother had lost her second baby in three years and she was distraught. Although my father and she had sat us all down and explained why this move was necessary to my mother's mental health, I remained pissed off. During the summer I'd misbehaved so badly, so often, my parents sent me to Rhode Island, to spend August with her older sister, my Aunt Lillian and Uncle Bert, supposedly my favorite relatives. I'd enjoyed their company and they mine. Even so, I'd returned to the brand new split-level house on Brookville Boulevard — a nice enough place in a great setting, surrounded by large amounts of park land enclosing the Cross Island Expressway — including the eponymous twin ponds — in a foul mood about leaving all my friends and having to change schools. I'd attempted to get into Valley Stream High but my brother and sister were also changing schools and their credits would only be good in city high schools. Since they were seniors, about to graduate, it was crucial that they be able to transfer to where they could use all of their credits. So I was forced to join them in attending Jackson High.

Jackson High turned out to be a great school, better academically than Van Buren, with more advanced classes and a terrific student body. In fact, those two final years of high school ended up being among the happiest of my life. But I couldn't know that at the beginning, and I was so very grim and silent those first few weeks at Jackson, that all my teachers noticed and eventually the Dean of Students called me into his office and asked me to explain my morbid attitude. I told him I hated the school and proceeded to go into a half hour of precise details of exactly what I hated about it. When I was done with this comprehensive listing, the Dean seemed both cowed and depressed. I might be an A student but he made it clear he thought I was headed for suicide. He and my mother spoke on the phone that afternoon while I was in class and that evening she told me of the phone call and of their decision to add a college level, extra credits, advanced English class to my program — and so I would meet new people, I'd have to go out for a team — of my choice — as well as get involved in some extra-curricular activity. The school newspaper and yearbook were already filled out, but there was always "Sing."

It was a breathtakingly grumpy fourteen-year-old me who reported to Bernie Cohen's literature class that following afternoon, and who groaned aloud at the two page "recommended reading" list; a completely irritated me who appeared in the track team's locker room, gazing with undisguised disdain at the dozen sleeker, more muscular members of the team I was supposed to join and emulate; an impossibly grouchy student who that Friday sat in the balcony of the auditorium where a teacher met the juniors who would be in that year's "Sing."

In later days, Jerry Blatt always insisted he invented "Sing." He scorned any competing accreditation to Midwood High in Brooklyn. And from what I understand, the two productions were somewhat different. Essentially both "Sings" were on-stage competitions in entertainment between the three top classes of the school. The evening would be briefly introduced by a handful of freshmen, and each of the other three grades would then put on a forty-five minute long "show" of its own devising.

What made Jackson's "Sing" different was that it used a mass of students seated on three tiers of bleachers as a chorus. Individual acts by singers and dancers were few, keyed into and often in dialogue with this chorus, which supposedly represented say every sophomore in the school, and so was to be seen—as in a Greek Chorus—as a single character. Jealously guarded themes were developed for each grade—the sophs go to Paris: the juniors at Summer Camp—that determined not only scenery and costumes, but also music and lyrics.

Since the concerns of each grade varied, these differences were emphasized humorously. Given our staggered time schedules for the grades, lowerclassmen often didn't arrive home in winter 'til quite late, so they sang "In the Still of the Night." While seniors, facing the choice of work or college, were told to "Get a Job!" Often satirically apposite lyrics were written onto current pop and rock tune favorites, mentioning the well-known predilections and foibles of certain teachers or other school personalities.

All this was explained to us newcomers by the music teacher on that auditorium balcony. I soon discovered why I'd been shoved into "Sing." In junior high I'd sung in the glee club and eventually been prodded (kicking and screaming) into a production of *H.M.S. Pinafore*, in the role of Sir Joseph K.C.B. This group of Jackson High juniors was four-fifths girls. They needed male voices.

But as soon as other jobs in "Sing" were mentioned, I put up my hand. Yes, I did want to be in audio-visual. Too late. The music teacher chose the boys who'd done it previous years. But I was selected for the art committee that would make the scenery. This was to consist of a single painted backdrop across the back of the stage, with several movable pieces. I would still have to rehearse the songs along with the chorus, but at least I'd be doing art, which I thought was important to me at the time.

When the music teacher was done delegating, she introduced a slender, dark-haired boy whom she told us was to be our director. He began to speak. Although he was only a few years older than me—sixteen, seventeen at the time?—he spoke as though he'd been in Tin Pan Alley all his life.

He'd been directing "Sing" for two years. "Sing" was "his baby," he told us. Also he wanted this year's "Sing" to be bigger and better. He said that last year's "take" for three weekends of shows had enabled the school's Drama Department to buy new theatrical lights with spin gels and pin-spots as well as to upgrade their sound system. His audio-visual squad would be trained in a Manhattan theater. A friend who worked at the Schubert Theater would help them. Our director told us that he played piano, wrote books and lyrics to shows, and composed music. Thus he would be able to help each grade with our show. He would also overlook all the artwork and costumes. The previous year he had briefly tried rapid onstage costume changes for the chorus and thought those, with greater lighting variety, would be effective.

He kept using the words "Broadway" and "professional" as well as many other words I could only guess at. He would be happy to audition anyone with a special talent: singing, dancing, juggling, tightrope walking, and try to get them into "Sing."

Oh, and his name, he remembered to say at the end, was Jerry Blatt.

"Sing" wasn't until early June, but we began work the second week of the autumn term and Jerry worked us hard. There were book sessions, art sessions, art and lighting sessions, art and costume sessions, then around March, the chorus was given its parts and rehearsal began. It was excruciating, endless. Especially once we were given elaborate lighting "cues."

Jerry was everywhere that year. Everywhere, I suspect, but in class. He was tirelessly inventive, solving problems as they arose, inventing new problems most of us couldn't even perceive, working them out, drilling us, pep-talking us, occasionally breaking down, then snapping back. If any of us complained we couldn't do something, Jerry always retorted "They do it on Broadway!" It turned out that he had seen every Broadway show in the previous ten years. Mind you, those were the glory days of Broadway—in a single-year period you could easily see, as I had, the original casts of *My Fair Lady, Camelot, Flower Drum Song, West Side Story, No Strings,* and *The Sound of Music*—so this meant

30

real professionalism. Clearly that was his aim, to go directly to next year's hit on the Great White Way.

To his credit, it worked. My own small contribution was helping to paint a gigantic mural piece by piece in various basements across Laurelton. Our class won that year as well as the next year, when Jerry actually returned from college to help direct "Sing" a fourth time.

Two years later, I again saw Jerry on campus at Queens College, hanging out with the hippest people there. When I became friendly with a group of Bohemian wannabes who hung out in the tiny, old, "Little Caf" rather than with the hoi-polloi at the huge, modern new cafeteria, I saw Jerry more often, but usually from a distance. His pals included all the beatnik types from the theater and music departments, including songsters Carole King, Paul Simon, and—visiting after class from City College of New York—Art Garfunkel—who besides being City University students were already recording artists, going under the name of Tom and Jerry.

Since I was an art major at Queens College, I had little reason to be in Coleman Hall—the music and theatre building—and so saw Jerry rarely in class; once he left a book under my seat in a French lit classroom and came to retrieve it. If he remembered me from Jackson High and "Sing" he never once let on.

Now, however, on the Morton Street Pier in Greenwich Village, with his bike and his brand new muscles exposed by flimsy upper garments in even the coolest weather, Jerry approached, said hello, offered and shared a joint, and told me that he did remember me.

The past, however, didn't interest him at all. In an offhanded way, he asked, "Don't I usually see you with Ed Armour?"

I told him Ed was out of town for the holidays.

Jerry turned out to be direct: "And he didn't ask you?"

"It's some sort of family powwow."

He looked unconvinced. Jerry had the disturbing habit of constantly looking around at men walking along the pier rather than directly at me, and once I got to know him better, an even more disturbing habit of breaking into a conversation by saying things like, "Doesn't that boy have the most beautiful ass you've ever seen?" Not knowing me well enough that first meeting on the pier, he withheld these thoughts, but he sure kept looking.

"I guess you know Ed from the neighborhood?" I asked.

"That too. Are you two lovers?"

As though that would decide what he said next.

"Not really," I replied. "Otherwise I'd be with him at the family powwow."

"Maybe," he replied cryptically, then, "You might as well know. You'll find out anyway. Ed and I made it once." He peered at me for a reaction. When none was forthcoming, he added. "It was a disaster!" He laughed.

Graduated only seven years from college, Jerry already had a checkered career in theatre and he was always working on three or four projects with his partner, a young woman named Lonnie.

He stopped himself in mid-sentence, "I thought Ed was dating someone else. I used to see them together all the time."

"Ben?" I suggested, "Light brown curly hair and beard? Always dressed in blue? He's just a friend."

"Not Ben. I know Ben," Jerry described someone else.

I was about to ask detailed questions when Jerry suddenly said, "I've got to catch up with that guy. See him? I made a bet with myself I'd get him in bed by the end of the year."

"The blond with tattoos?" I asked.

"You're right! He's trash!" Jerry shrugged. He then hopped on his bike and sped off anyway.

I watched him approach the youth, slow down and circle him in bicycle riding rings that got smaller and tighter.

Δ

Some months later, I'm headed for the pier one afternoon when I bump into Jerry Blatt. As we're catching up, the weather suddenly turns: it begins to snow and Jerry invites me back to his flat on Morton Street. There we smoke grass and after a while I begin to tell him about the *ménage à trois* among Ed, Dennis, and myself. I'm expecting to scandalize him.

Jerry brushes me aside. "That's light stuff compared to some of the sick scenes I've been in. Do you know what it's like going into your boyfriend's bureau drawer and finding a set of works? You know a hypodermic needle for shooting up heroin? Especially when the week before he swore up and down that he'd given up Horse? It's like being in a B movie, that's what? I swear you *become* Lana Turner! You hear the cameras whirring! You check your hair and your hem line. And if you'd want to discuss how truly hu-mil-i-a-ting a relationship can get, get this! In college I had this straight friend who let me blow him, right? Ignored me completely. Looked at *Playboy* or covered his eyes. Then he began giving me a certain time to get him off. I was such a jerk!"

Jerry's flat, on the third floor, had a small, crowded living room, made even more unlivable by the bicycle sitting amidst the few pieces of furniture and the old black, never perfectly-tuned, spinet piano. A tiny kitchen was such a jumble that I believe I looked into it only that once and thereafter never stepped near it again.

No matter, because the single bedroom was quite large and with the best view of Bedford Street, which curved and opened to a school playground and parklet and was quite picturesque. The bed dominated, but the side walls were filled with books I recognized from Queens College English and Comparative Literature classes. He had row upon row of LPs, more than I owned—mostly Pop, Rock and Musicals—shelved or in tottery stacks on the floor, impeding rapid movement of any sort. Did I mention that the headboard was unusually wide? It was, and that's where everything ended up.

So his bedroom was where Jerry more or less lived, listening to his stereo, watching TV—the first I'd ever *seen* in a bedroom rather than in the living room—as well as eating, and, of course, sleeping and fucking.

After smoking the grass, Jerry fixed us grilled cheese sandwiches and some sort of "Super Juice" of his own concoction. When I'd known Jerry at Jackson High, he'd been slender and had reached five-foot six tops. To keep the substantial muscles he'd added on, Jerry not only had to work out several times a week at the Sheridan Square Gym, he also had to eat more than three meals a day—and those weren't small meals. He snacked after breakfast, after lunch, after dinner, and often while on his bike. The Haagen-Daazs shop on Christopher Street never had a more loyal customer than Our Man Blatt, except when he was broke. Those times, he'd hang out near it, shirtless, and he hoped sufficiently alluring to finagle free ice cream from passing friends and cruising potential tricks.

That winter and early spring until the weather finally broke after Easter and we could be out of doors most of the day, we spent hours at a time on Jerry Blatt's enormous and all-encompassing bed. We read, watched old movies, listened to music, gossiped on the phone, held court for visitors like Lonnie and Ed Armour, and—when we were really bored—we played "Sonnet."

Sonnet was a game I'd never heard of before, but which was a variation on a game that is usually called Telephone or Rumor. Jerry would write a first line—I recall "Crocodiles love to glide upon the flooded Nile"—and I would have to come up with a second line, say, "They only pause to nibble mice, or sup on baby rhinos." Jerry would add a third, "So delicate of habit, they belch but once a mile," I with a fourth, "And love to pose for artists, hired by King Minos." Etcetera. Meter and rhyme schemes were kept strict, but content within the poem anything could occur based on our whimsy, or more usually, our hapless attempts to get down on paper any *even vaguely coherent* next line. Needless to say the final couplet made little sense except to us, and then only with a stretch.

We passed time together in this way during the next few years, Jerry and I, waiting for our lives and careers to get going. But this first visit and talk over sandwiches, marijuana, and iambic pentameters would make us friends for life.

My friend Susan Moldow, then living in San Francisco, sent me as a belated birthday gift a book containing the selected letters of Emily Dickinson, and I read it avidly, identifying with the Amherst spinster who'd suffered so many restrictions and personal lacks in her life. I copied out the following line in my journal: "The heart wants what it wants. Or else it does not care!"

A few days later, at Jerry's apartment, I repeated the line, and we oohed and aahed over it. Jerry pulled out his copy of Dickinson's poems and we read our favorites to each other. Then I grabbed a pencil and pad of foolscap on which we used to play "Sonnet" and I wrote the words "career... love... money..." on the left side, and above them I marked in the past five years. Then, lying across his bed, with Jerry watching me, I showed him with pencil lines from each of the three areas of my life how activity in all three areas had simply petered out, the leaded lines getting fainter and fainter until they vanished. Jerry was so impressed that in later years, he would often remind me of that afternoon, and of my objective—to him horrifying—graph of my life.

Δ

A year later Jerry had reason to be cheerful. Someone new had come into his life, and being Jerry, he wanted to share that new acquaintance with me. During the time I'd known him, Jerry had already begun writing songs for the successful Public Television children's show, *Sesame Street*. He'd written and produced a children's show, *Thumbelina*, with future opera star Frederica Von Stade in the title role (the show was choreographed by a dancer named Rodney Griffin, who would enter my life in a sideways fashion later as the ex-lover of Bob Lowe), and Jerry and his colleague Lonnie had written a Broadway musical based on Moliere's *Scapin* but were on the lookout for someone to produce it. None of his substantial achievements were "Big Time" enough for Jerry. He was still waiting for his break.

Despite all the time Jerry spent looking for sex, chasing after men, dealing with impossible, in his own words "white trash" boyfriends and lovers, Jerry usually chose women to work with and, because he was good looking, muscular, vain, and self-absorbed, women usually liked Jerry. When my friend Susan finally met him it was in St. Vincent's Hospital where she and I were meeting after work to go to dinner. She'd asked me what he was like and I replied, "Vain in the way a toddler is. Even though you've never met," I told her, "Jerry will show you his appendectomy scar. I'll bet you anything." She clearly didn't believe me, but not five minutes after she walked into the hospital room, he had his shirt up and he was asking her to inspect his new scar which went all the way down to his shaved pubes.

So I wasn't too surprised when he phoned me shortly after I'd completed my first novel and told me he was working with a new woman partner. "We're putting on a show at The Tubs of all places. She's a terrific singer, a very funny comedienne, and pure Show Biz. And," he added, "Like me, she'll do anything, no matter how outrageous."

35

Anyone who has seen those grainy old black and white videos from the Continental Baths will agree those shows were truly outrageous: a few hundred gay men in white towels sitting around, or splashing in the huge pool, while this energetic little red-haired woman entertained—no one had seen anything like it. Obviously she had to be special to keep guys watching and listening when other temptations so obviously called—and she was! Could she sing? Her repertoire ranged from Cole Porter classics and current Broadway hits to torch song ballads, to frenetic versions of Carmen Miranda classics—complete with huge bowls of fruit on her head. She and Jerry had worked out banter with the audience, which she cruised constantly—"See me later in the Green Room, big boy"—and she cracked jokes—"Is that a hair dryer in your towel, or are you planning to get married tonight?" Or "Honey, you wear that towel like Dorothy Lamour!" No one escaped her eye—"Hands off him, he's mine!" she would scream at a couple of guys necking, then more gently, "this next song is for all you young lovers... Hit it, Chopin!" she would yell at her pianist—Barry Manilow on several occasions. Her name—Bette Midler.

I couldn't afford to go to the Baths to see her in those days, which Jerry understood, so he promised to get me in "backstage," even though he admitted there wasn't much of a backstage: "Hell! We've barely got *a dressing room!*" The following night, I appeared at the Seventy-third Street entrance of the Ansonia Hotel, only to be directed downstairs somewhere within the building's innards. There, at last, I was shooed into a back door and from there into a side corridor of the Continental Baths.

"Good! You made it," Jerry sighed, seeing me as he rushed from one door to another. He was shirtless, with flip flops on his feet, his usual skin-tight jeans, a bandanna barely holding in his abundant dark curls. "Take your clothes off. You can use my locker. There's a towel in there to wrap yourself in. Make yourself comfortable. Show starts in a half hour. There are no house seats. There are no seats at all! There's barely a house!" he added, sounding harassed and rushed, before I heard "Jer-rreee!" shouted for from somewhere nearby—and he was gone.

I undressed, leaving my street clothes in his locker, kept on my bathing suit, grabbed the towel, and went looking for Jerry to give him the locker key. Didn't find him, but I did work my way into the corridors of the Tubs:

all cast iron walkways and patterned floors through which you could look up or down two levels, little rooms with wooden doors. Someone snapped my Speedo against my hip, saying "Honey, you're wearing far too much!"

Finally I found the huge pool. There I dove in and hung around with a few people I knew from The Tenth Floor, a private disco in the Flower District which had just opened that year that would become infamous thanks to Andrew Holleran's novel, *Dancer From the Dance,* and which I'd gone to often, thanks to my friend Jay Weiss, who knew Ray Yeates, the club's brilliant deejay.

The floor-show began—at last—and I found a place up front amidst the crowd of men naked but for towels. Jerry must have pointed me out to Bette because in the middle of one number, she came over to me, pulled me to my feet, leaned me against the piano and used me as a prop for a love-song, pretending to feel me up, until I was too obviously excited, at which point she stopped and said, "You're disgusting! Sit down!" to great hilarity before she went on with her number.

Her attention however got me sex directly after the show with one of the Davids from The Tenth Floor whom I'd been talking up before the show. I was in a very pleased and relaxed mood when I drifted back down to the lockers to find Jerry.

Once I'd gotten into my street clothes, I joined him and Bette in a coffee shop around the corner and we all laughed and cracked jokes and talked about how the show had gone.

Bette was the first woman I'd met who could go from total seriousness one moment—"I was so unhappy in high school in Honolulu. I was the only white person... and I was an ugly white person!"—to complete camp the next: "I'll say one thing for this gig: my complexion's become totally fabulous from all the humidity!" She had already been on Broadway in small roles in two shows: most recently as one of Tevye's daughters in *Fiddler on the Roof,* and she and Jerry had big plans: a solo album as well as a one-woman Broadway show he would help her put together and direct. What really amazed me at the time was how comfortable she was, she almost seemed to *be* one of us. Later on Jerry would spell it out, "She's a gay man in a woman's body: she reminds me of myself."

We all grabbed a taxi home and the next day I spoke to Jerry enthusing about Bette and the show. "You told me when you looked at my horoscope I could hitch my wagon to a woman's star," Jerry said to me. "I've got this gut feeling that it's Bette and not Lonnie I should be working with from now on. What do you think?" Terrifically loyal, Jerry was very conflicted. I told him how much I'd liked Bette's personality, and how as a performer I thought she had "a star's charisma."

"Charisma maybe, but she works like a dog," Jerry said, "And she makes sure I work like a dog too!" This was not a point in favor of the new relationship: I knew how much Jerry prized his free time, his cruising afternoons, his sex in the evening, and I had to wonder how—based on all these confusing possibilities—he would decide his future.

Δ

That would take a few years more, and by the time, I visited the Twenty-eighth Street Manhattan studio where Bette was recording her first album, I'd already had my first book published and brought her a copy of the second one, *Eyes*, in its glossy hardcover.

She looked at it and said, "Looks scary. I'm just a down-home girl. *Romance. romance!*" She went back into the studio and put on the headphones again, gesturing that she was ready to start re-recording. We three were supposed to go out for dinner, but Bette wasn't finished with the song they were recording and the two of them were arguing over whether the instrumental background worked or not.

Finally Jerry insisted that the "take" be recorded on a cassette tape and the three of us took it downstairs and into a car parked out on the street belonging to one of the studio musicians. We sat and listened to the song that way about ten times in a row. "This is the way people will hear it," Jerry explained. "On a car radio." It was okayed before we could break for dinner. Although Jerry and I thought "Blue Bird" sounded great, Bette merely sighed and finally said in her most tragic tone of voice, "It reminds me of a trumpet player I used to be in love with... I was such a fool!"

That first album—along with "Light My Fire"—was a hit, and Bette's career was launched. The Broadway show followed a year later, co-produced, co-written, and directed by Jerry, and was an equally big hit. Suddenly Jerry was in Los Angeles every time I phoned. With Bette, or on his own. So it was that the next time that the two of us spent time together was in Los Angeles in 1977.

Jerry had retained his little one-bedroom apartment in the Village, but he had found a boyfriend, Sean, in California, and together they were renting the lower floor of a house located on one of those terraced streets above the Sunset Strip in the Hollywood Hills.

When I first visited it was night time and we had dinner out and then returned to the house. Jerry and Sean turned on the hot tub which was in the middle of a shag rug carpeted living room. We all got into it, and as we listened to Joni Mitchell's *Both Sides Now*, drinking wine and smoking grass, he pressed a button, and the twelve-foot wide living room curtains began to open. It revealed a classic view of Los Angeles lighted up at night; the sparkling grid-work of streets extending seemingly forever. I almost died right there.

Sean turned out to look like all of Jerry's previous "white-trash" boyfriends concentrated into a single, perfect package. He was tall and slender, with muscular arms and legs. He wore his thick, dirty blond hair quite long, sometimes in a pigtail, and he had a Fu Manchu mustache. His face was lazily handsome, with big blue eyes. His manner was easy going and exactly what I would have expected from someone who'd grown up and spent most of his life in Southern California. "But listen to this," Jerry had told me on the phone the first night I'd arrived as I was unpacking my bags and stuffing the closets and drawers of my little suite at the Beverly Hills Hotel, "Sean is nice. He doesn't use drugs. He's got a huge cock. He loves me. And..." I waited, "his family has money. Oil money! Can you believe it? So much money, that his grandmother is sending him to school to take classes in money management!"

I'd arrived in Los Angeles a few days before my thirty-third birthday, meeting with some producers at Brut Productions, who wanted me to write a screenplay based on my novel, *Eyes*. Meanwhile, Jerry and Bette were hard at work, producing her second album and the film, *The Rose*. Jerry would end up directing *all* the music sequences in that movie—including the brilliant scene of Bette in the telephone booth.

Oddly enough, I was with Bette, Jerry, Sean, and Bette's manager at that time, Aaron Russo, heir to a pasta fortune and in love with Bette (who didn't reciprocate his affection), when the idea for the scene first came up. We had driven to the International House of Pancakes on Santa Monica Boulevard, off La Cienega in West Hollywood. It was discussed in some detail—then completely dismissed. A few weeks later, Jerry called and invited me to a screening of the "rough cut" film with the new ending: Which to my surprise turned out to be the same scene that had been mentioned and dropped. The same group as before went to Cantor's Deli on Fairfax Avenue, one of the few places open and serving at one a.m. in L.A., to eat and discuss the new scene.

"It's totally unrealistic. It's totally operatic," one of us said. And everyone agreed. I thought for sure that meant the scene would be taken out. But when the film premiered in New York, months later, I phoned Jerry and told him with relief, "Thank God you kept in!" And, of course, that scene made Bette as an actress and it made the film.

Fed up with all the delayed, postponed, shelved, and fallen through film projects I'd been talked into in Hollywood, by late 1978 I had returned to New York to concentrate on writing novels. Jerry and Bette decided to remain in California. She bought a house in Brentwood, and Jerry and Sean bought one in Silver Lake, a big Spanish style place with patios and lawns and fruit trees high up the hills with a good view of the eponymous reservoir. Often Jerry, Sean, and I spent afternoons time at that Silver Lake house together, and sometimes Bette would suddenly appear—gracious yet demanding—like "The diva I've always dreamed I'd become."

But we sometimes also gathered in New York, although that tended to be far more seldom, and it usually tended to be sudden, and on the shortest of notice. Jerry had become Bette's second hand. He, along with Bruce Villanch, wrote most of the material for her shows. He directed all her shows. He co-wrote the lyrics to half the songs on her second album.

In fact, it turned out to be the show business partnership Jerry had been looking for. And although he wasn't out front, himself a star, he became very much the power behind the throne. And p.s. he also now earned lots of money. So, naturally, Jerry would be protective of Bette. Whenever he would appear in New York and phone me up to arrange a meeting, he'd say something like, "We're going to the Emmy's tonight, but Bette's so nervous, I'm afraid it's only me in the car." Apologizing in advance for not inviting me—although I never once thought to include myself in such glamorous events.

But then there were other times when Jerry would phone me up and say, "Are you busy tonight? Whatever it is, cancel it! Be dressed to the nines and ready at seven forty-three on the dot."

At 7:44 p.m. some gigunda limo would appear in front of my Jane Street apartment building with Jerry and Sean inside dressed in rock music versions of tuxedos and we would drive to Bette's village townhouse. Jerry would spend fifteen minutes prying her outside and into the car headed toward the Grammy Awards at Radio City Music Hall. One time, very late at night, past midnight, Jerry called and asked me to meet them at Reno Sweeny, a small West Village supper club known for its good live music. When I arrived and was checked through two doormen with guest lists at two doors, I joined Jerry and Sean and Bette in the smaller downstairs room where during the final sets from the featured group, Bob Dylan showed up and joined us at our table. Maybe ten minutes later, Bette and Dylan got up on the little stage and they duetted until three a.m. before a surprised rapt, audience.

At the Palace Theater on Broadway rehearsing for her show, *Clams on the Half Shell*, and out in L.A. again in the early Eighties when Bette and Jerry had both signed up with Disney to do songs and films, Jerry was Bette's full time manager as well as her writer. I would appear by invitation and hear the two of them scream at each other over some detail, fight as though they were each other's worst enemies, even throw chairs at each other. They would break up like lovers, make up the next day, and start all over again.

If Jerry had found his life-love, so did Bette unexpectedly find a husband.

To me, it looked as though they were both settled for life and headed nowhere but UP! When Jerry and Sean appeared at Fire Island Pines early in the summer of 1985, they told me they had completely moved out of their New York apartment to live in Silver Lake and part of the year in Amsterdam, which they both had come to love. Bette was filming *Beaches* that summer, and so Jerry had time off for him and Sean to play. We saw each other a half dozen times that summer and enjoyed each others company, and Jerry seemed very little changed from the questing young man he used to be when we would play "Sonnet" together on snowy afternoons in Greenwich Village.

Even so, he and Sean seemed to move at such a speed, as though intent upon filling up every spare minute of their lives with sex and partying, with sub-relationships and complications to those sub-relationships, that I found that despite myself, I kept myself distant from their dizzying vortex of activity.

A year later, when I was in Los Angeles again, this time to publicize my book, *Ambidextrous: the Secret Lives of Children*, I phoned them, and got an answering machine. My message was not returned while I was in L.A., which was not unusual, nor later, which was. When I mentioned that mystery about a month or so after I had returned to New York to a mutual friend, he told me Jerry and Sean had spent the past few months in Amsterdam, mostly because Jerry had begun showing some of the worse symptoms of AIDS. Not too long afterward Jerry developed pneumocystis and, as he'd always been weak-lunged, it killed him.

In early spring of 1990, Bette Midler stood in the Jewish cemetery in Amsterdam, only a yard or two from where Anne Frank is buried, and she sang. Not to a large crowd, but to a small gathering of mourners. After she had sung, she said about the man just buried, "If there were no Jerry Blatt, there wouldn't ever have been a Bette Midler, singer and actress."

It was a generous acknowledgment. From the beginning of her career, Jerry had unquestionably been her friend and advisor, and to a large extent, he'd been the person who more than anyone first accepted who Bette was, then influenced and molded her into whom she became.

A few years later, when I saw the television version of the Jules Styne-Steven Sondheim musical, *Gypsy*, starring Bette as Mama Rose, not only could I hear Jerry Blatt saying—this is your role. You were born to play it, Bette!—I also realized that Sondheim's words about having the guts to go for your dream in Rose's first big number applied to my friend Jerry Blatt (and to myself and all of us who did what we said we would do).

So what if Jerry had used Bette to do what he couldn't as a male do: become a beloved actress and female singer? He made it to the top, anyway, to Broadway and Hollywood too.

Not Quite There

Bobby Brown

During the Sixties and Seventies, it became a commonplace, even cliché, to say of someone you didn't quite understand that he or she was "far out" or "from outer space." I certainly met more than my share of these folks, and indeed to some people, at times I myself was considered "out there" and "far out." In fact, once our little urban commune was going on West Thirteenth Street, our house-mother—and drug dispenser—Margaret D., took to calling me "Phillyyou'resofarout!" smushed altogether like that, so that newcomers thought it was my name, and repeated the entire phrase addressing me until I managed to correct them. But I knew from far out, myself, and among the very many far out people I met during this period, few compared to Bobby Brown. But rather than refer to Bobby as a space cadet or moonwalker as so many others did, I thought of him in terms, not so much of great distance, but instead of deficit, lack, or scarcity, in short, as "not quite there." It was an inadequacy I recognized easily enough, while never precisely comprehending what it entailed. And despite probing, I never quite figured out how it had come about.

I first met Bobby when he was living over a health food store on Eleventh Street off Sixth Avenue in the heart of the Village. My pal George Sampson brought me there to meet his brother and sister, Bernie and Anne Sampson, and we entered while they were all in the middle of a card game called "Hell." This consisted of four- or five-handed Solitaire, played with as many decks as players, with all the cards to be taken off a single giant pile, the participants seated around it on the floor. The object of the game was to complete your lines first. Naturally, everyone grabbing for cards aroused hostilities, since two, sometimes three players, might want a particular card and grab for it; and especially on drugs—methedrine was the drug of choice here—the players could get loud, abusive, even violent. That was, of course, the "fun" of it.

Away from the game, being host, Bobby Brown was a smidgen calmer, though a wire-strung edge ran evident in him from the very first. We'd only just met at his apartment door, when he turned and screeched, "Bernie! Stop cheating!"

I could tell he'd prefer being in the game and we let him go back to it.

A few weeks before Christmas 1970, following two years in which I'd not seen him, Bobby telephoned and said that someone wanted to turn the health food store below his apartment into a two-story health food restaurant. They were buying him out of his lease. But he had to move out quickly: by the end of December. He'd been looking for an apartment in the area and had located a long-leased place. But it wouldn't be vacant until April first and he'd been unable to find a sublet. He knew that George and I were good friends. He also understood—from whom, he'd never specified and George was gone from Manhattan by then—that I was out of work and could use someone to share the rent.

I was and I could. Yet I still hemmed and hawed. I didn't really want a roommate, much as I knew it would financially help me out. I valued—perhaps overvalued—my privacy.

Mistaking my reluctance as hesitation because we didn't know each other, Bobby suggested we meet, I suppose so he could try to dispel any doubts I might have about him. We did meet, in my apartment; we smoked a joint together and drank beer and, looking around the place, Bobby told me he thought he and I had pretty similar lifestyles. He was very easy-going, he said. Sitting there, with his relaxed, lanky, almost muscleless, pale-skinned, East Texas body, his dirty blond hair worn "Dutch boy," and his mellow "country" voice, he actually seemed to be the person he presented to me.

That much established, Bobby more closely looked over my apartment, discussing how he might transform my former-dining-room now-study into his room. He worked somewhere, he told me, although he wasn't crystal clear about it, so I wasn't sure if it was a head shop, a poster shop, or what—from six in the evening until midnight. That meant I'd be alone, free to write without anyone being in the apartment during those hours. I had to admit that was a real plus in Bobby's favor. He thought he might hook a curtain across the open doorway between the study and living room, he said, so I could use the living room to work in, even when he was home.

He was so much calmer and more sedate than when I'd last seen him that I was strongly tempted. The fact that he actually alluded to those card games, made my decision easier. "I don't use speed or play 'Hell' anymore," he assured me, as gravely as his grandpappy might have assured his bride-to-be that he'd stopped cattle rustling and distilling his own "corn-likker."

Even so, again I said I'd think about it. But Bobby phoned two days later and *had* to have an answer. Pressured, broke, I said, sure, he could move in: for three months.

Thus ensued the oddest of my roommates. He arrived with two cats he'd completely forgotten to mention: "Speed" and "Skag," who were twin brothers, Bobby said, *and* homosexual. It only took a single afternoon to appreciate their names. One was hyper and nervous; the other was so idle he might as well be a statue. They ignored each other weeks at a go. Until, that is, they fought. Then they chased each other around the apartment hours at a time, stopping only to hiss, screech, and claw madly. These fights invariably ended with them nuzzling and making up. I would usually remain vibrating for another hour.

Bobby also brought with him cardboard box after cardboard box of undefined stuff which he used—brick-like—to construct a thick, if somewhat unstable, wall between the living room and study, with just enough space for him to pass through, all of it covered by a double curtain. Bobby hung dark swaths of fabric over everything in his room, which, along with the usually dim lighting, meant I could never quite make out what he actually had in there. An opaque shade was fixed onto the window so tightly no light would dream of entering. Another friend, in later years, called his dark bedroom "The Tomb of Ligea," after the Poe story. But Bobby Brown's was the original.

Along with all this darkness and containment, Bobby also brought a reel to reel tape player, tape reels, books, notebooks, marijuana, and who knows what other stimulants. Of all the druggies I knew at that time—and there were a legion—he turned out to be by far the most methodical: he even had the latest pharmacists' "Blue Book" of current prescription pills.

Bobby might have stopped using speed, but he was definitely on something most of the time. He would awaken at two p.m. If I were in the adjoining living room (now dining room and study, too) and I didn't have my stereo earphones on, I would hear him stirring behind the curtain, and some time afterward—often a half hour later—he would draw open the curtain. Sometimes he would reheat coffee I'd made earlier or brew his own pot. He never drank enough of it to account for how strangely wired he quickly became.

Despite my repeated invitations to come out into the bright, sunny living room, Bobby would remain pretty much in that dim little room until it was getting dark out and it was time for him to fix something to eat and go to work. On weekends, he seldom strayed from his room until quite late at night. With his pale appearance, almost colorless blond hair, and thin, nearly boneless body, he might easily have been a contemporary vampire.

Except that Bobby Brown was, in his own weird, completely individual way, touching, funny, and totally endearing. Demons definitely lurked within, even if they seemed to be directed mainly at Bobby himself. His cackling laugh was harshest when he was laughing at some newly revealed flaw in himself or at something he'd said or done. His quiet, intense, completely spelled-out hatreds, which escalated fiercely in conversation before utterly dying away as he lighted another Winston or pipeful of hashish, would eventually return to lodge—and grate—in his own breast. His general demeanor could be best described as world-weary, which I have to admit in those days I found substantially more compatible than if he'd been perky.

But while I and my friends were half play-acting at being cynical and *déraciné*, Bobby wasn't playing at anything. Although he was only a few years older than me and had been out in the world either as long or less than I'd been, he was already utterly fatigued by it all. Then, there were those times, that I'd be speaking on the phone or cooking and I would suddenly catch him looking at me the way an aged grandparent with a fatal, wasting disease gazes at a perfectly healthy grandchild. He possessed a sort of wearied indulgence: he might admire my cheerful naiveté, but he would not think to emulate it.

Bobby moving in with me helped solve the worst of my financial problems and he didn't much intrude on my life. He did provide a bit of companionship—despite the few hours he was awake, or at home with the curtain open. So it was weeks before other, less healthy, aspects of his personality emerged. Maybe there were hints of it all the time but I was then so preoccupied with trying to make work a three-way relationship with two other men that I probably was oblivious to those early signs.

One afternoon, a month after he'd moved in, Bobby said to me in what I had already come to recognize as his most querulous tone of voice, "I never get mail! Since the day I moved in here, I haven't gotten any mail. I put in a change of address. And yet, no mail!"

It was such an obvious accusation and so patently absurd, that I decided to defuse it totally. I replied casually, "You get mail. I burn it."

I thought his eyes would pop out of his head. His voice became a hoarse whisper. At long last, he uttered, "Why would you burn my mail?"

"Excellent question. Why *would* I burn your mail?" I asked back, Socratically I hoped.

He thought a longish time, then said in a more normal tone of voice. "I'll go to the post office and put through another change of address."

"That's a good idea," I replied, casually. End of conversation.

A few days later his mail poured in.

But if that bit of unadulterated paranoia was one hint of Bobby's growing cocaine use, it was by no means the last. Whatever Bobby Brown's own personal demons might be, they had the result of bringing out unsavory effects in the atmosphere immediately adjoining him. For one, my Jane Street apartment poltergeist, which had resided there long before he arrived but had mercifully lain dormant. Once Bobby was in residence, the poltergeist began to act up a great deal—usually with him as victim.

Forget the special-effects movies you've seen: this was the real thing. As a rule both subtle and unobtrusive, it would suddenly come to life, depending upon the person in residence. A few days after I'd first moved in, I was in the bedroom reading *The Guermantes Way*, when I became aware of a constant, even insistent, sound in the living room. It wasn't loud, but it was *invariable* and therefore became really irritating. When I jumped up and went to see what the sound was, it turned out to have a source that was invisible and inexplicable.

I searched the back yard. I listened at each wall for mice. I did everything I could and that anyone else would do to locate the sound. With no success. And, of course, once I was up, the sound stopped. Five minutes later, I was in the bedroom reading again and the noise was back. Subtle at first, then definitely there. It sounded like, well, the closest I could arrive at how it sounded was like sand falling in a tightly closed space. I tapped the walls to see if maybe plaster was dropping. No. Nothing there. But it was awfully irritating! I checked other possibilities. Nothing. Yet every time I went back to my bedroom to read, it started up again.

It happened a fourth time. Annoyed beyond belief, I leapt up, ran into the living room, and shouted at nothing, at no one, nowhere, "Shut up! This is *my* apartment. *I* pay the rent! Shut up! You can make all the noise you want when I'm *out*. When I'm here, you will *shut up!* Do you hear?"

When I returned to my bedroom to delve again into Proust's complex syntax, the noise did not repeat. And I guess it was that instant apparent obedience that confirmed somewhere in my mind the idea that some-thing was actually in the apartment, although it would be years before I even found a name to give it. I also thought about who had lived there before me—poor, stressed-out, hapless Joan Estoup; and I recalled the so-called curse put on her by a witch. Subsequent to this incident, and my screaming, the sound never recurred and so I naturally forgot all about it.

Until that is, Bobby Brown moved in. Suddenly the apartment's revenant was reactivated. First, Bobby began complaining about strange dreams, nightmares in which he was inside the apartment, running for his life, running from something shadowy, menacing.

A day or two days after he told me of the dream, the two of us were on my bed together, lying on our stomachs, looking through *Rolling Stone* magazine, and we heard footsteps along the short corridor from the apartment door to the living room. My bedroom door was mostly shut and I at first thought I'd left the door to the apartment open and someone had walked in. I got up to check. There was no one there. Hmm, I thought, *that's* odd.

Thereafter I'd often hear those footsteps while I was in my bedroom reading or lying awake in bed, hear them step along eight feet of hallway, always going in the same direction. I'd jump up to look. There was never anyone there.

One day I came home to find an opaque new shower curtain had been put up. My transparent one really had needed replacing, it was so streaked and foggy, so I thanked Bobby for this bright new one.

He looked balefully at me and said, "It makes no difference. I took a shower before and I still feel like someone's watching me."

As soon as he said it, I realized that I also felt like someone was watching me whenever I was in the shower; even with the bathroom door closed; even when I knew I was alone in the apartment. In fact since Bobby had moved in, more than once from the bathtub, I would hear a few footsteps along the hallway, then feel right through the closed bathroom door someone looking at me. It was subtle, eerie. In later years, all sorts of friends would volunteer having experienced the same eldritch sensation. One guest of a friend who sub-leased my place for an entire summer month became so terrified that neither of them ended up sleeping there.

"What do you think it could be?" I asked Bobby one afternoon.

He was sitting up in bed, smoking a joint.

He turned with a deadly look and said, "My cats run from it."

"Didn't you go look to see if anything was there?" I asked.

"Hell no!" His eyes huge with horror. "I just hoped it wouldn't come closer." He went on to tell me that it acted up the most when I wasn't home. But, he added, while the footsteps came to within inches of the separating curtain, they never came into the study, explaining why he always kept to that room.

"Yell at it," I said. "That's what I did before."

Bobby said he was afraid his yelling would sound more fearful than furious. "It knows," he whispered as though someone were hearing what we said.

I was more amused than anything. But the poltergeist's intrusion slowly escalated and I found that at last, I had to intervene.

One afternoon there was a phone call for Bobby, and the long telephone wires in the living room had become so twisted through use that they no longer stretched to reach his bed. He stood and talked on the phone, as I attempted to untangle the wires.

The call was an upsetting one for him: either he had to go to work early, or stay later, or work an extra shift. After he hung up, he dropped into my bentwood rocking chair, fulminating, while I continued to kneel to try to untwist the phone wire. A second later, Bobby leapt out of the chair and almost knocked me over trying to get into the study.

49

"Did you see that? *Did you*?" he demanded. "It jerked back the chair! I almost fell out. It's after me!" he wailed. He couldn't be talked out of it.

I lied and said I was going to find a magic spell to get rid of it. A few days later I said I'd done it, exorcised the poltergeist. Bobby clearly didn't believe me and while he didn't complain of it any more, both of us now secretly began counting the days until April first, when he'd be moving out.

Winter suddenly turned nasty, snowy, wet. The little bit of company Bobby Brown had provided dwindled to nothing. After work ended at midnight, he would go out with friends, not get home until six in the morning, then not wake up until shortly before he had to go to work at five p.m. Most of our contact was limited to his increasingly cocaine-assisted levees. And on nicer days, I'd be already be out of doors by the time those occurred and so I came to more and more miss even those peculiar non-events.

Bobby moved out of my apartment and into his own place two weeks early, taking with him half the rent. I didn't realize until he was gone what a small, persistent drain he had been on my attention and on my sense of well being. Once he'd gotten all his boxes out of my study, I tore down the sheets of dark cloth he'd swathed the room in and pulled off the tape with which he'd closed out light from the window. I swept and vacuumed the little room, flung open a window to air it out, and light rushed back into the apartment and back into my life.

And there it might have all ended. Except that Bobby didn't completely vanish. Through infrequent letters and phone calls with George Sampson—our original connection—I discovered that Bobby had not stayed in his new Village apartment for the full length of the lease—his purported intention—but instead moved uptown to a railroad flat in a tenement building in the East Eighties. Through someone else—Miss Sherry maybe—I then heard that Bobby was living with a woman. And from Douglas Brashears or was it Chuck Partridge, I heard the surprising news that Bobby had married her. As I'd never before suspected that Bobby was anything but gay—if indeed he possessed any brand of sexuality, which seemed pretty dubious—this information baffled me as much as it bored me. A few more years passed.

By the mid-Seventies, my life had become relatively different than it had been when I'd first met Bobby. I was now a successfully published author, and

I'd moved out of the little back apartment on Jane Street into a much airier and handsomer Federal Era duplex several blocks further west. I seldom saw many of the people I'd known earlier—mostly their doing as I continued to try to stay in touch. I did spend half of each year—usually all summer—living in Fire Island Pines. Then I began spending winters outside New York City, too—in San Francisco, Key West, or Los Angeles. As a result, my socializing completely altered. After a few years I seldom saw or heard from any of my Sixties friends, except infrequently, or by accident, encountered on street corners or outside theater lobbies. So I was very surprised one summery late March morning in 1979 to get a phone call from Bobby. He was nearby he said, only a few blocks away, and he wanted to talk to me.

His voice sounded a little slurred, but I couldn't think what from at this early hour. (It was ten thirty a.m.) He said he had a nearby appointment—doctor? job interview? I wondered—but would come by in an hour and he would pick up a six pack of beer, he said; was that okay? Feeling curious and a little guilty about having allowed Bobby to disappear so totally from my life, I said, sure, okay, come on by.

Bobby looked the same as a decade earlier. Almost precisely the same. I was aware that I looked quite different than when he'd last seen me. Then, I'd been broke for years on end, and as a result, thin, with a full beard, and longish hair. Now I was well-fed, even muscular, tanned from a winter in Southern California, with short hair, expensive casual clothing, and a mustache. He still resembled a drugged-out hippie, whereas I looked like a Fire Island clone with disposable income—which was pretty much what I was.

I wondered why, on this very warm day, Bobby was wearing a long-sleeve shirt. He looked around my vast new apartment with a certain wry amusement: the fireplaces, the fourteen-foot ceilings, the custom-made bookshelves, the foot-high crown moldings, the Turkish carpets, and hand-made coffee table. Virtually all the older furniture he'd known was gone, replaced several years ago. Only that bentwood rocking chair and a dark wood gate-leg table that served for writing and eating and card games when placed in front of a twelve-foot-long polished oak church pew I'd found on the street remained from the old place—both pieces downstairs in the new apartment. It was the same bentwood rocker Bobby used to sit in, the same one he claimed to have been jerked out by a poltergeist. It now sat unused in a dim corner of my huge new downstairs dining room, while the gate-leg served as a butler's table between the new kitchen and dining room.

When Bobby saw the two old pieces, he decided we should stay downstairs, even though it was dark and closed in, especially compared to the brilliantly sunny living room upstairs with its high windows dominated by the white powered puffs of three flowering pear trees outside.

I opened the downstairs windows an inch while he was in the bathroom, then I pulled up a chair opposite where he'd established his space: the rocker at the table. A nice breeze began to blow, but as he exited the bathroom, he ignored it. He put the six-pack in the fridge, minus one for each of us. During the ensuing hour-long visit, Bobby drank four more beers.

At first, I imagined that it was a purely social visit. Bobby did ask a few questions about me and about my life. He had heard a little bit, from someone or other, about my success: when he'd known me I was just beginning to write. In the decade since, I'd published three novels, with a fourth about to come out that fall. The previous summer, my second book, *Eyes*, was a paperback bestseller: I couldn't go anywhere in the city without seeing someone reading it. Bobby must have seen it, too. He didn't mention that, and not being too egotistical, I quickly moved the topic of conversation from me, to him and his life, saying that I'd heard he'd gotten married.

"That's over," Bobby said. "It's all over. In fact, the reason I came by is..." he rocked in the bentwood and looked at me and sipped his beer, "You know, I'm seeing a therapist. Right here in your neighborhood. Ever since, well, she thinks I should inspect my past and see what the possibilities were then so I can see what they might be."

That explained the appointment that brought him downtown. But despite a handful of questions, I still found what he was saying incomprehensible. Bobby finished one beer, got another, and began on that. When, in the midst of talking, he finally noticed my puzzlement, he put down the beer and rolled up his sleeves. On his wrists were thick bandages.

"Look!" he said in his most familiarly querulous tone of voice. "I tried to commit suicide a couple weeks ago. We had yet another fight and I couldn't stand my life anymore, and I went up to the roof of the apartment building with a big knife, and I slashed my wrists. And you know what? When the blood began to just gush out, to just jet out, I got so scared, I began shouting. And even though I passed out, they found me and took me to the hospital."

I had known three people who'd committed suicide in recent years. I told him so. I also said maybe it was a good thing that he'd stopped himself.

Bobby finished his beer, got another one, popped it open, and drank it down. "No," he said with that country-Texas definiteness I remembered. "I don't think so. I was just chicken-shit. I'm off drugs now. Completely. Totally. And I really *hate* being off drugs. They were the only thing that made being alive worthwhile. I hate being straight and married. But I also hate being queer. I hate working. And I hate doing nothing all day. I just really hate being alive. You understand what I mean, don't you?"

I didn't know how to respond and said so. I told Bobby that I was finally living the kind of life I had wanted for years. I didn't hate being alive. And I loved being queer; although I could understand someone else maybe not loving it. But wait, wasn't there anything Bobby wanted? Wasn't there anything to strive for? To have as a goal?

He lifted one of the bandages to show me the wide, thick, barely healed scars across his veins. He opened another beer and drank it down. He told me he would probably try to kill himself again. And he was coming to see me to tell me, well, he didn't know what it was that he wanted to tell me. He had no idea why he'd called me and why he'd come by today. Except he'd been in the neighborhood, at that therapist's office, and he'd remembered the phone number and he thought it might be a good idea.

He drank the fourth beer, rocking back and forth, the two of us silent, then he got up and left. He hugged me awkwardly at the door. And Bobby smelled, I don't know, somehow like a little boy smells: someone seven or eight years old. Not like a grown man of nearly forty.

I remember thinking about him for the next few days. But whenever I did, it was with that resigned consciousness one has about something that is already consummated. I'd always known something inside Bobby was chasing after him, and I'd come to believe that somehow, because of my apartment, and possibly even because of me being there, whatever was chasing Bobby had coalesced into a recognizable force those few months we'd lived together.

What it was, exactly, and how to get rid of it, I didn't understand, although clearly by now Bobby had alienated himself totally. From me. From his closest friends, George and Anne Sampson. Even from his wife.

I'd known other young men who had killed themselves. But they'd had reasons. One was a handsome young marine, who found out he was gay, went A.W.O.L. after the Christmas holidays, and hung himself from a sixth-story plant hook jutting out from a concrete balcony of the upscale Van Gogh apartment building where he'd been staying with a gay couple who'd befriended him. I'd come home from dancing all night and stepped out of the cab onto the utterly desolated corner of Jane and Hudson Streets at five-ten in the morning and I'd instantly seen him hanging there, his body sort of flapping against the side of the building. I'd known who it was and why he'd done it. The cabbie called the cops. But I was exhausted and didn't wait around until they arrived.

Another handsome, slender young man I knew, who used to date my barber, also killed himself—in fact, spent most of a particular afternoon killing himself—slashing his wrists and neck, trying to hang himself, and finally throwing himself off the roof of the Twenty-third Street YMCA. I'd spent little time with him, but I vividly recalled this reserved, shy, quiet guy suddenly opening up to me one evening as we rode home together side by side on the privately owned Fire Island to Manhattan bus. Even though he had seemingly everything to live for and to look forward to, he told me that he felt like a total stranger, a fake human, an alien. After explaining how enviably ordinary and filled with good things his life had been, he concluded, "But I'm not like other people." He said it with quiet, insistent passion. And when I tried to explain how similar that was to many young people, he answered, "No! You don't understand. This body feels all wrong to me. And the sky—and the water—everything here's the wrong color, the wrong consistency, the wrong odor! I think I was born into the wrong species. Or born on the wrong planet. That's possible, right?"

Nothing so life-defining or life-threatening for Bobby Brown. When he first moved in, I was so perplexed by his nihilistic attitude toward life that I eagerly searched for clues within the scanty information about himself Bobby had told me of his past life and growing up. He'd come from Eastern Texas. His mother separated from his father, who had then moved, following oil drilling west, and never came back. Bobby's mother and he had been close, especially as he was an only child, but she was sickly and they'd moved to her parent's homestead, where she died of tuberculosis. Yet he didn't speak about her death as the tragedy that had ruined his life. He didn't particularly miss his father or older male company either. Bobby had been raised by his grandmother. He had no stories about her or how she'd raised him to suggest that she was particularly kind and loving or peculiarly cruel and monstrous toward him. He had no stories about his childhood at all. I'd tell him about my childhood, and he'd rock in the bentwood and smoke his hash pipe and not have anything to offer by way of reply. Since Bobby was given to instant, thorough, and at times extremely fault-finding analyses of his friends, I would expect him to say something about anyone who had even dreamed of mistreating him while growing up. So I explored his past in our conversation. And I came up with no one and nothing to account for his dark moods. He'd done okay in high school. Had no tales of it to tell. Had no first-time sex stories to relate as a kid. Perhaps his best times had been his first two years in college. He spoke of those days with a restrained sense of pleasure. But all I could figure out as a potential cause was when Bobby first had sex with other guys and got turned on to pot. He'd left college after two years, offering no reason why.

The summer of 1980, following Bobby's inexplicable beer-drinking visit, while I was home overnight from Fire Island transacting business, I received a phone call from his ex-wife. Bobby Brown had finally accomplished something he'd really wanted in life: he'd at last succeeded in killing himself. She said that Bobby had taken sleeping pills and put a plastic garment bag over his head. She sounded distraught, yet hardened too, so I assumed that I must be about the tenth or twelfth person she had called with the news.

His ex-wife promised to call again and let me know when Bobby was being memorialized or buried and where the funeral or memorial would be held. I was visiting friends in Los Angeles for the next few weeks and, if she ever phoned, I must have missed the call.

Perfection of the Man, or –?

Frank Diaz

I believe it was the poet William Butler Yeats who first expressed the question: "Perfection of the Man? Or of the Work?" The implication being that one couldn't have both. Of course, every once in a while someone *does* come along who can have both: Leonardo da Vinci, one of the greatest artists and inventors of the ages, more or less openly gay, was supposed to be the most beautiful man in Italy of his time. Imagine competing with a number like that?

Few of his time dared. And even fewer in our time. But if anyone might be imagined to do so it would be Frank Diaz. When I first heard of Frank he was described as "the hottest Puerto Rican in New York." This being 1975, the phrase could be applied with a rather liberal brush.. But in the very next sentence, I heard the words, "Frank's the Number Three person in The New York State Council on the Arts, just below Kitty Carlisle-Hart." And just as I was absorbing that gloss, my interlocutor added, "He's the number we see dancing at Flamingo every Saturday night, the one with the black panther tattooed upon his huge, right bicep."

Oh!? *That* Frank Diaz!

That very same Frank Diaz phoned me "out of the blue," one afternoon in the spring of 1989, wondering if he could ask me a few questions about the state of gay politics. I knew he was no longer working for La Carlisle-Hart and so assumed it was about some new position. He quickly assured me it was and named the position, which was, as might be expected, Mr. Number One in what was at the time the topmost political Lesbigay group in the nation. Frank said he knew I sometimes wrote for gay magazines and newspapers and that I sometimes hobnobbed with the people involved. He, on the other hand, didn't know any of them—nor the scene itself. Could we meet for a cup of coffee so he could get a feel for the crowd, the place, the atmosphere, and the people?

We'd never known each other very well, and we'd not spoken to each other in a long while, and my feelings about Frank certainly weren't anything special one way or the other, but I agreed to meet him for coffee the next day, mid-afternoon, at a shop near me in the West Village, a concession for him, since he lived much further east. However, I told him to not credit my reputation: I was far less connected than he assumed to any higher echelons of gay power. Despite that, Frank wanted whatever knowledge and advice I did happen to possess.

He looked the same as he always had, when he entered the diner and spotted me, except that this day he was dressed in casual, if pricey, work clothing rather than in a black skin-tight T-shirt, black denims, and engineers' boots I was used to seeing him in. When he arrived at the booth and took off his winter coat, he was only a little less solidly built and muscular than he'd been in his heyday when men literally threw themselves at his feet wherever he went clubbing and Robert Mapplethorpe photographed him shirtless, thrusting a large butcher knife with that panther-stalking arm. Frank's head and face were classically handsome, in the austere rather than lighthearted mode of Roman statuary, with features—large brown eyes, strongly defined nose, nice mouth, good cheekbones—that were not especially Spanish, yet unquestionably Mediterranean. In addition, his demeanor and deportment— except in bed, about which later—were as courtly as though he were a Sevillian *alcalde* meeting royalty.

So, as we gazed through the window at anemic snowflakes failing to survive the filthy Manhattan sidewalk, we talked on the subject he'd asked about. I told him what I knew, which wasn't much, but was a lot more than he knew and it seemed enough to satisfy him. This mostly meant me answering Frank's specific and general questions about the gay group, and being as candid as I could about the internecine politicking—i.e., betrayals and back stabbings—I'd heard of.

I got the impression that Frank thought of it as all somewhat beneath him, but nevertheless, something to do. I had also heard from whoever had gossiped the original news, that Frank had left Albany with a fiduciary "package," which while not quite a golden parachute, still would assuage his fall. I hinted at that and Frank assured me that he was well off financially; for a while, if not forever. As for the new position, now that he was forearmed with what I'd told him, he would look into it and see what they had to offer. He seemed relatively indifferent to the outcome, which eliminated whatever anxieties I still may have possessed.

Frank got up to use the bathroom. When he returned, he had our coffee refilled, and he asked about Bob Lowe with whom he had come into contact even less frequently than he had me, allowing me to boast about Bob's new career as an attorney.

I thought our meeting was over when suddenly Frank began speaking in a far lower and less distinct voice than he'd used so far, forcing me to lean forward to hear him. I couldn't help but notice that the diner had considerably emptied out: Aside from our selves, a waitress on the telephone and a middle-aged man at the far end of the counter reading what looked like the *Racing News*, the place was empty. Despite this, Frank spoke so quietly I had to listen carefully, especially as all the time he spoke, I was quietly but totally astounded by what he was saying. At first, Frank talked about bureaucratic politics at the Council for the Arts: yet another Byzantine intrigue that had overtaken the halls of power at Albany; why he had suddenly felt it was time to leave there after almost twenty years.

Then he changed the subject. It took me a few minutes to see how very much of a change it was: Frank began to intimate how he'd begun going to a really *louche* after-hours place in my neighborhood called The Hellfire Club. He went on to tell me he'd been surprised to find himself going there quite regularly after the first visit, and furthermore going not as a master, a sadist, but instead as a masochist. He told he now went there every weekend to be flogged and beaten and urinated on by strangers: men, women, anyone who wanted to.

I attempted, and I guess succeeded, in trying to appear utterly unshocked by what he was telling me. The truth is I was deeply stunned. Then again, it was ten years into the AIDS epidemic when this meeting occurred and the truth was—after what I'd heard, and witnessed, little could really upset me anymore. Even so, I was dismayed a few minutes later when, having gotten that first news off his chest without eliciting apparent disgust from me, Frank now added that he was seeing a psychiatrist once a week.

He! Frank Diaz, whom I—and everyone else I knew—had always thought of as so sure of himself, so powerful and effective, so assured and self-reliant! The one, totally together gay man! At the time, I wondered and couldn't really know whether he was telling me the truth or not, or if he was once again—as he'd done when we'd first met—testing my reactions, seeing if I would flinch, be revolted.

I wasn't appalled: at least not openly appalled. Nor, thankfully, did I immediately do the opposite and begin to play Social Worker. As casually as I knew how and quite unjudgmentally, I replied that therapy had helped some people I knew and that I hoped he was treating open wounds against possible infection, and other dopey practical stuff like that.

He took my words for a friend's concerns. He explained the steps he took to assure no infection would take hold. He then asked in the most astonishingly un-weaselly manner if I'd ever enjoyed anything like what he was talking about. For a minute I wasn't certain whether he was asking if I was a co-masochist (and if, say, I'd like to join him hanging by the thumbs at Hellfire the following night) or if he was propositioning me, i.e., he was in the market for a steady sadist. When I regained my momentarily lost balance, I confessed I enjoyed fairly vanilla sex, and Frank didn't probe farther along that line of questioning. A few minutes later, we parted, Frank giving me his usual death-grip handshake, with a promise that he'd call and let me know what happened.

Well, he didn't call. And for another six months I was left to wonder why he had *really* phoned me, and what—in particular—he felt he'd gotten out of our conversation. I also wondered what, if anything, he was doing now, since I found out he didn't take—or hadn't been offered—the administrative position we'd discussed.

The night of the first re-encounter, when later Bob had asked about Frank, I'd tried and failed to tell him everything that had been said at our meeting. This fell under the "Bob-is-innocent-and-I-must-protect-him-from-the-truth" mode that I often operated under.

Even so, Bob sensed something odd had occurred, and a few months later, when we were driving upstate for the weekend, Bob mentioned having encountered someone at his gym who used to be out at the Pines when we all were there, who told him of yet another acquaintance coming upon Frank on his hands and knees licking someone's high heels. So at last I could reveal what Frank had said, and the two of us were free to wonder about him, as we often did wonder about people.

What made it all the more surprising, as both Bob and I knew, was that Frank had a reputation of behaving in the manner of a rapist. He'd woo you seductively enough, and romance you in the cab or along the street and into his East Village flat. But once you were inside, he attacked.

He wasn't subtle and he didn't take no for an answer. Resistance, as The Borg on television's *Star Trek Two* used to repeat, was futile. He'd tear your shirt, your undershirt, your underpants right off. And while his foreplay was certainly aggressive, he handled your body as though he'd bought it and could do whatever he liked with it. Worst was if you didn't want him to fuck you. In that case "No" meant nothing to Frank. Once you were on his sofa, bed, or floor carpeting, you were getting fucked, like it or not.

Now I knew about his reputation long before we ended up in the taxi from The Saint that took us to his place, and frankly, that night I was surprised by his lust and by his telling me how long he'd had that lust—a decade or more, since we'd shared a house in the Pines.

Once I accepted that and realized that club onlookers were envious that he was openly necking with me in a corner of the front room while we waited for our jackets, I became totally objective and experimental. Okay I said to myself, I'm ready for this. Let's see this Frank Diaz guy in action!

He did not disappoint me. But with me, as with Bob Lowe some other time, instead of being cold and uncaring after we'd had his explosive brand of very active and only slightly rough sex, Frank had gotten up to fetch us brandies, and we'd lain in bed together another hour, sipping liqueur and chatting. So I guess I never felt victimized as some other guys might have.

Δ

It was at my close friend Dennis' twenty-seventh birthday party, in spring of 1975, that his roommate John began talking about summer plans, and also how it came about that I once again spent time on Fire Island, after being away for years. I didn't know it at the time, but it would end up being one of best and most productive summers of my life, and the summer that I would meet the people who would be crucial to me for the next twenty years.

John was sharing a house on the eastern ocean side of the Pines with two men he'd met through the gym, he told me, pushing me into a corner of his and Dennis' oversized, cheap, located-in-the-depths-of-Brooklyn apartment. Both of these potential roommates were "professionals" John said, vaguely enough. Both, again according to John, were "very hot" and they knew not only "the scene" in the city, but also the scene out in the Pines. The only problem was that John, who'd rented the second bedroom for the summer with these two paragons of male pulchritude, had a week after he'd signed the lease and handed over the money, met Randy—he was at the birthday party, a dark, cute, curly headed guy—and now John and Randy weren't all that interested in the Pines scene. Instead, Randy had planned a vacation in the Pacific Ocean: Samoa, Fiji, places like that, for several summer weeks and John was thinking he'd prefer to be there. In short, John wanted to sell the second half of his Pines share: August first through mid September. Was I interested?

I was interested for several reasons. The first was meteorological: I intuited that this would be an intemperately warm summer in Manhattan and I really didn't want to remain in my Jane Street apartment with nothing but window fans cooling me the entire steamy time.

Second, I had work to do: I was in the middle of writing my third novel, and I thought I'd finish a first draft then bring the work out to Fire Island and live out there a month and a half and finish a second, typed draft.

Third, and best of us, I could actually *afford* to go to Fire Island, thanks to my publisher's cash advance against royalties on the new book. For the first time ever I had enough money to pay both my relatively low rent in town and rent on John's room in the Pines.

Even so, I hesitated. Who were these two guys, I'd be living with? Would I get along with them? And if they were so cool, would they even talk to a stranger? John offered a possible solution to the problem—I could go out the very next weekend, stay at the other Pines' house where Randy had taken a share (he slept in John's room anyway, barely using his own except to store clothing) and I could come visit John's house, meet the men, hang out, and see if we got along.

A free weekend at the Pines sounded fine to me, even if I ended up not liking the men or they me and it led nowhere. So it was two days before the enormous Fourth of July holiday weekend, and the ocean side house Randy had a room in was already full when he, John, and I arrived by Ferry at the Pines, and they dropped me off at Crown and Ocean Boulevard, brought my weekender bag into Randy's room, and in the most casual way possible introduced me around.

Present were five other guys, one I'd met at a West Village bar on Hudson and Eleventh Street called the Roadhouse and slept with a year before, another two I used to see at dance clubs. All of them were about half a step above what Dennis called "ribbon counter queens at Bloomies," a derogatory, if not totally inaccurate description of the shallowness of their interests and mentality, and like Randy before me, I wasn't nuts about them. Even so, I was forced to spend that first Friday night dinner with them, and not at John's house—where I hoped to stay the rest of the summer. There, they planned to discuss the future: meaning me.

What might have been a totally superficial and wasted evening turned out to be quite otherwise when the guy I'd previously had sex with suddenly invaded my room an hour after I'd arrived and initiated a repeat performance of our sexual matinee while his housemates were out—at the Friday "Tea-Dance." Shallow as they might have been, the others were socially acute enough upon their return to the house to recognize that due to this hour of dalliance I was no longer a stranger, but as a result of my activity with their housemate, now part of the family, "one of them." So it was easier, and they claimed to be disappointed that I couldn't "stay and play with them" the rest of the weekend.

Latish the next morning, Randy brought me to the house on Floral Walk between Fire Island and Bay Boulevards with the potential rental share.

The first thing I noticed even before I'd gotten inside, was that although it was at the bottom of a hill, the place was surrounded by decks, and even possessed a small rooftop deck—what might have been called a Widow's Walk in earlier times—overlooking the thick foliage and nearby houses, from which one could sun, watch sunsets over the Great South Bay, *and* see the ocean. Upon a ground level deck outside, two connected bedrooms that I supposed to be occupied by Jack and Frank, I couldn't help but notice worn-looking leather mats upon which were strewn graduated hand-weights, a barbell, and loose black discs of weights.

What would turn out to be my first home in Fire Island was as unextraordinary as it turned out to be beachily practical. Once indoors it became immediately obvious that these guys did not earn their living in Design & Decoration, like so many of our neighbors, nor did they subscribe to *Architectural Digest*. Externally, it consisted of two slanted-roof wings in ginger-colored cedar planking, attached to a central living-dining area. Inside, was the same planking although in a lighter shade. Above the large refectory table, a good sized skylight opened to aid circulation from opposing floor-to-ceiling glass doors. The bedrooms were rectangles just large enough to hold a double bed, with a closet. John's room had its own bathroom with a tall shower, and backed onto the kitchen, and was thus bit more private. Jack and Frank's rooms were in a wing across the spacious center and they shared a bathroom. The kitchen was in dark greens and reds. Functional. Two pieces of art decorated the barely furnished—couch, two rattan chairs, a few lamp tables—living area: a brightly colored parrot-like papier-mâché sculpture upon one wall, and a pop-art painting of a slice of American flag and the right half of someone's face. I later discovered these had been brought out by their creator: house guest number one Jack Brusca. One deck held wooden chairs and a table.

The entire place looked simple and masculine and I said as much to Frank and Jack. They'd evidently been out late Friday night and looked not totally awake when I arrived and they unhelpfully grunted in response.

It was the oddest meeting of future house mates. John and Randy vanished into John's room to fuck, while Jack and Frank ate breakfast, made plans succinctly for the rest of the weekend, and occasionally would ask me a question, although they barely heeded my answer. I found both men to be dauntingly handsome, although in distinctive and individual ways, and ultra-butch. Jack, with his sculptured head, close-cut curling hair, and prizefighter's face—large soft eyes, broken nose, and sensuous mouth—took the breakfast dishes and began washing them. He wore tight fitting shorts and a loose

A-shirt which couldn't help but show off his lithe compact body and catlike movements, his heavily muscled arms. Frank, meanwhile brooded darkly over a third cup of coffee, brushing crumbs out of his luxuriant black beard. He was more muscular than Jack, with a "Draw Me and You Too Will Become an Artist" conventionally dark-eyed beautiful face that defied precise ethnicity. Both men were much photographed later on and Frank's head and torso would be photographed and drawn by David Martin to represent Zeus, king of the Gods, in my retelling of the Ganymede legend, *An Asian Minor*.

For the moment, however, I was made to understand that Frank Diaz was the number three person in the tonily successful New York Endowment for the Arts. While the other roommate, Jack Brusca's art had become so successful, that he'd been commissioned by the government to go to still abuilding jungle capitol Brasilia and put up a hundred-foot sized sculpture.

Though they didn't say a word at the time, later on both privately told me that I fit their idea of a housemate better than my pal John had: Not only being masculine in appearance and attitude, but also being connected to the arts, as they were—since I was a published novelist, and nominated for a prestigious literary award.

Even later, they also told me that despite being hung-over that first meeting, they'd both found me attractive enough so that after I'd gone to the beach with Randy and John, they'd discussed me at length and agreed, "Okay! Neither of us gets to fuck him until after the summer share is over. Okay?"

In Jack's case that turned out to be that very autumn after our summer share; it took Frank several years longer. And in both cases, when they did come on to me, I was astonished by their interest. If I'd overheard their pact at the time it was made, I doubt that I would have believed it. Although only a few years older than me, both men seemed so completely "arrived"—not only in their careers, their looks and bodies, but in their attitude and bearing, their totally assumed manliness—that I felt not only completely out of the sexual running with them, but like a child next to them, determined to carefully, not too obviously, watch and learn.

Jack Brusca laughed when I told him that some years afterward. He reminded me how much he and Frank had teased me that summer, every day recounting ever wilder tales of their sexual activities, sometimes going out specifically so they might indulge in crazy scenes with questionable partners the night before—just to be able to return and relate those tales at the breakfast we always shared over our refectory table the following morning—and to see my reactions. And how whenever I was alone with one of them in the house, Jack or Frank would go out of his way to cock-tease me: wearing the least amount of clothing: the shortest shorts, the smallest Speedos, the tiniest possible posing straps for their workouts, a face cloth barely covering their crotch whenever they'd step out of the shower and come looking for something they suddenly required, which was somehow always close to wherever I might be typing or sitting reading.

Jack reminded me how each of them had ended up in my bed at least once that summer, although neither had broken their agreement, neither had had sex with me—at least not then.

Frank had stumbled into my room naked, bed sheet trailing, early one morning when he knew Jack was sleeping out. Mumbling "Damn Blue Jay is yelling into my window," he flopped into my bed, wrapping himself and his sheet around my astonished self. For his own foray into my bed, Jack pretended to be too stoned to know he was in the wrong room when he fumbled his way in from being out all night, and once in bed next to me, he had done his best to excite me as he undressed himself, until I'd half panicked, unsure what in the hell he was doing, and had gotten up to go to the bathroom, at which he'd relented and left the room.

Yes, they'd had their fun with me.

And while we all got along pretty well that summer, beginning two weeks earlier than planned, since John had taken off with Randy for the South Pacific letting me move into his room before the time I should have, Frank and Jack usually went out together, without me, later at night, or went infrequently to the sunset time "Tea" I frequented.

Frank and Jack seemed to prefer a bar, the newly opened Monster in Cherry Grove, rather than what they called the "twinkie" spots such as the Sandpiper or the Boatel that I frequented. They were the first men I knew who dressed in leather; leather vests over bare torsos or over a tight fitting black T-shirt, sometimes skin-tight black leather pants and crotch-and-ass-revealing chaps over tight denims. And while I had to assume that they each scored a man anytime they wanted, they never brought one home, or if they did, didn't let him sleep over: we were never more than three for breakfast.

It wasn't just the black leather, nor the ultra-restrained low-keyed approach to everything, nor even their closeness to each other that kept me from feeling close to them. What really stopped me was that when we were just sitting around, listening to music, passing a joint, relaxed and they began to open up, an all-pervading darkness seemed to rise and hover around the room. Negativism, a fascination with pain not as something aesthetic but something deserved, with humiliation and degradation, not as an act, theater—which was the only way I would even consider it—but as something so familiar, so common, it must be embraced and accepted. They exuded attitudes I couldn't help but shudder at once I was alone again and which I secretly felt quite beneath me.

I never knew how Frank had come to these ideas. From stoned conversations with a few ex-boyfriends and from Jack, I got the strong impression that Frank had broken with his family when he'd come out; that like many Hispanics, they had disowned him once he made the decision to live an openly gay life. This, despite the fact that he'd gone further, faster, professionally and socially than any of them had ever before dreamed. I suppose the conflict of being accomplished and yet not being able to be honored for it by those he most wanted to honor him, caused the black moods Frank fell into and eventually led to the cheerless beliefs he came to embrace.

At Fire Island, Jack and Frank had many, many acquaintances, but the group of friends they seemed to enjoy most, in a big new house on Beach Hill on the west-ocean side of the Pines, while also handsome and muscular and masculine seemed to be even more attracted to iniquity and creepy shit than they were.

I recall visiting that house one time only, an evening with Frank and Jack where, after dinner, a coffee-table sized volume of the gruesome, oozing-cloaca paintings of Dutch artist R. Giger (who later on designed the movie, *Alien*) and another book of sickly mordant sexually perverted "cartoons' of Tomi Ungerer were passed around, discussed in detail and highly praised. The rest of the conversation was of the suicide of some acquaintances: two successful ones that they spoke of in great, shivering detail, and an unsuccessful one—that they mocked.

Some years later, in a picture book on gay life, I came across a double-page photo spread depicting a dozen men from that morbid house or close friends of theirs I'd met there. They looked as beautiful as I recalled them, as they nakedly played at tug of war. But even before AIDS came along, eight of those twelve young men were already dead, either by their own hand, through overdosing drugs, and in one case, as a result of homicide.

I was never able to ascertain how much really Jack Brusca subscribed to these morbid and thanatalogical interests: I know that while he did go through periodic spasms of depression and uncertainty, his art seemed to carry him through the darker patches of life. As, later on, did a loving companion named Raoul, a stunning looking and sweet Brazilian man.

One time while we were waiting on the coat-check line of some club Jack said, "I didn't know your father and mine were competitors." It turned out that his father and uncle owned a large wholesale produce company similar to my father's and not far away on Horace Harding Boulevard in Queens and they and my dad often vied for new wholesale accounts: airlines, hotels, hospitals etc.

Like myself, Jack had to battle his family's wishes and plans in order to become an artist. That lack of parental support continued to breed insecurity. It galled him, remaining internalized for years, but making every tiny defeat he encountered more bitter, and every step forward more gratifying. Even so, whenever Jack and I met he was always filled with future plans and recent successes—he was doing murals for a ministry in Sao Paolo, he'd had a museum show in Mexico City, he'd just designed the costumes and sets of Roland Petit's ballet corps—filled with optimism, and that is how I best remember him now that he's gone.

However all that flirting with dark forces ended up affecting Frank. But then he also would have far darker life experiences than Jack Brusca, or indeed, than most of us, at the time.

In the decade of the Seventies, from even before I met him to about 1978, Frank had acquired a peculiar reputation: He'd had three lovers die on him, all of them in strange, when not overtly suspicious circumstances. The first lover died in his sleep; Frank woke up to find a corpse in bed with him. The second choked on a chicken bone. The third, after they broke up, returned home to Scotland and hanged himself: All of them died before the age of thirty-five. No wonder whenever Frank appeared at Flamingo's Black Party, people who only knew of his past relationships drew back and repeated his nickname, "The Black Widow." George Whitmore, who visited my Fire Island house the summer that the third death occurred, caught just enough of the gossip to write up a short story using the nickname as title; the story was published in *Christopher Street* magazine, and it couldn't help but discomfort Frank—and me, for his sake.

Some years after that, Frank and I had met for dinner and we were returning to Frank's Manhattan apartment on Eleventh Street east of Fifth Avenue. When we arrived at his apartment door, something was wrapped around the doorknob, some nasty-looking concoction of hair, cloth, and poultry bones, with what seemed to be soot strewn across his threshold. He lurched back, tried to hide his surprise behind a frown. "Santeria!" he murmured. "Voodoo! Someone put a curse on me."

He didn't seem surprised nor even much taken aback. But when he didn't move, I grabbed a magazine I was carrying, scattered the soot from the doorway and knocked the crap off the door handle, kicking it away, and saying, "I don't believe in that and anyway no one put a curse on me! So it's okay!" I could tell Frank didn't one hundred percent believe me, but we went inside for a brandy and a chat. And for weeks after, I heard second and third hand that he mentioned the incident to people that we both knew, perhaps trying to find out who'd done it.

Δ

Not too many months after his confession about becoming a masochist, Frank jumped out of his apartment window and killed himself. I was led to believe he was talking to his therapist on the phone at the time of the plunge. I was shocked of course, despite all the death around me at the time, every new one was still a shock. But given what I'd inadvertently come to know about him, that final detail somehow made a deep kind of sense to me. It didn't so much mean that Frank was asking for help, it meant he was telling the therapist, "You were incompetent; you fucked up bad. Now you pay!"

That he would pay too was assumed. After all, Frank was now less than perfect; he couldn't expect to continue existing.

The Iron Maiden and Mr. Grumbles

Robert Ferro and Michael Grumley

... what to make of a diminished thing.
Robert Frost—The Oven Bird

"To Lou-Lou," the dedicatory handwriting minuets across the title page of Robert Ferro's novella, *The Others*: "with love, across the ages!"

He gave me the book several years after we'd become friends. Published in 1977 by Scribner, it was already out of print when I received it, and we were playing with the possibility of my self-owned and operated SeaHorse Press reprinting the book. That never happened, for several reasons (his current publisher expressed interest in the novella; we couldn't agree on a format, etc.). But throughout my many moves from residence to residence in the years since, whenever—packing or unpacking—I've come across the slender, handsome, little book, I've always stopped and opened it up to the dedication and I've always found myself rooted to the spot.

Seldom has an inscription been so revealing of a person—and to a certain extent—of a relationship. So revealing, and at the same time, so cryptic. Now that decades have passed since his death from Kaposi's sarcoma, I've only begun to appreciate that was the domain of Robert Ferro's life, of his work and possibly also of whatever influence he may in the future wield: to have been the most confidential of strangers, the most arcane of explicators. Luckily, much of this paradoxical quality was caught in his writing and so it is still communicable to those who never knew him personally. It would be nice to see some of his work back in print again.

A bit of explication about that inscription is needed: Lou-Lou is myself. It was a pet name for me of Robert—and of Michael Grumley, his lover and in the truest sense, life-partner. But how does one get from Felice to Lou-Lou? Follow the permutations for a glimpse into the Ferro sensibility. The year is 1982. Several years after we all met, and formed a short-lived but ultimately momentous writing group called The Violet Quill Club. By then, one member of the seven, George Whitmore, had fallen away completely. A second, Christopher Cox, had ended his relationship with a third Quillian, Edmund White, and only I would continue to see him much socially. Edmund seemed already mentally, if not yet physically, in Paris, where he'd live for the next twelve years.

But the remaining four, Andrew Holleran, Robert and Michael, and myself had somehow grown closer after the Violet Quill meetings had ended and we saw each other often. The four of us were spending a late autumn weekend at Gaywyck, my nickname (taken from Vincent Virga's novel of the same name, and blithely appropriated by Robert) for the Ferro family's beach house, sited on an estuary of the New Jersey shore, between the "Irish Riviera" town of Spring Lake (it's Grand Hotel used in the movie *Ragtime*) and the newer, yuppie shore town of Sea Girt.

We were seated outside, on the ocean-facing roofed over porch, in the midst of a typically Ferro-Grumley ritual, tea and muffins, and I uttered something by way of explaining a particular career move. Robert lay a hand over mine and, his large bittersweet chocolate eyes almost melted as he said, "That settles it. You are darker, deeper, and more unfathomable than Lake Louise. No one has ever sounded the bottom of Lake Louise. It is reported to be the deepest freshwater lake not only in Canada but in all North America."

For the rest of that stay I was "Louise" rather than Felice. And later a month or so later, when *Christopher Street* magazine published a portfolio of authors' photos, with Robert Ferro's captions, my photo—of me appearing to touch up with a paintbrush my own reflection in a mirror—was captioned "Poor Louise—mad at last." From "Louise" to its foreshortened "Lou" required barely a year; and was probably due to the fact that among the

Ferro-Grumley retinue, I was insufficiently femme (perhaps also insufficiently "grand") to merit a full fledged drag name. The doubling to "Lou-Lou" took place a few months later, and was clearly an affectionate augmentation and an indisputable sign that I had entered the magic circle of the most inner of their cronies.

For months afterward I tried to discover what had so suddenly endeared me, and when I couldn't, I asked Robert. He assured me it had nothing to do with anything directly beneficial to them, but to the fact that I'd written a dismissive review in the *New York Native* of the stories of David Leavitt, an author whose work Robert wholeheartedly loathed.

And so I had unearthed another aspect to Robert Ferro: what I would come to call his *Commendatore* persona. For if Robert could be the most delightful of one-on-one personal and cerebral communicators, he also possessed another, more forbidding, persona equally critical to who he was and how he wrote: social and intellectual arbitrator, nay, despot, whose judgment was as good as an edict: instant and immutable.

So I put up with a nickname I didn't care for, even though there were times I fled from it: Robert shouting across the half-acre width of a New Jersey garden supplies center where he was purchasing gigantic flower pots. "Where were you?" he stamped his six-hundred dollar, silver tipped, Florentine boot heels at me when I finally deigned to appear, "I was calling you!" He was so irate, I wasn't about to tell him that I'd been busy flirting with one of the employees and would have eaten glass shards before answering to the name Lou-Lou.

Both the Italian made boots and the enormous ceramic pots I just mentioned are further aspects of what were by that time intrinsic facets of his character. Robert's family, he told me, derived from Calabria, the area around Bari known as the boot of Italy, and from Sicily—the ball that boot is kicking— far from my own father's Roman background. Robert was born October 21, 1941, in the New Jersey town of Cranford, and grew up in the tony suburbs of Morris County. After he'd graduated from Rutgers University in 1962, he immediately moved to the city of Florence, Italy. Robert would write several times about this brief era of efflorescence and of his life amid the far more evolved personalities of the tiny, family-like Florentine *pensione*, testimony to how climacteric it had been to his life and thought. The first time was while at the Iowa Writing School, the second in a never completed heterosexual novel he was writing at the time he and Michael went in search of Atlantis. The third and most successful time he wrote of it was in the gay-themed, sixty-seven paged opening section titled "The Bardolini" of his second published novel, *The Blue Star*, a novella-like section some readers consider Ferro's best writing.

Robert remained in Florence until late 1965 when he began a two-year program leading to an MA and MFA at the University of Iowa's Writing School. It was there, in the Midwest, that he met Michael Grumley. Originally from nearby Davenport, Iowa, Michael had by then already been to Hollywood where he'd taken a few small film roles and sufficient body modeling work to live on and had returned home unsure what career to follow: film actor or writer.

At Iowa, Robert and Michael studied with Kurt Vonnegut and Chilean novelist Jose Donoso; among their classmates were the novelists John Irving, Gail Godwin, and Andrew Holleran—a pretty stellar group. After they left Iowa, there were some months in which the two young men, Robert and Michael, moved about and tried to solidify their lives together. They finally did so only by leaving the country and going to Italy. This time their destination was Rome, which in the mid-Sixties was the center of a flourishing, international movie business at *Cinecittà*. I myself was in and around Rome during this same time, and later on we would reminisce about people and places and events we had shared (in ignorance of each other's existence) during those carefree days.

For myself, however, my early visits and finally my stay in Rome—to all of Europe for that matter—was a detour, if a way to recognize how unchangeably American I, and my destiny, actually was. After I left in 1967, it would be decades before I went back.

For Robert and Michael, Rome became home, and in later years, their second home and haven. At the time, it was a perfect place for Michael to find art-studio modeling work and for Robert to become re-acculturated to Europe. They remained American expatriates for another five years, by which time the Italian film business had begun to flounder, taking with it Michael's hopes for a screen acting career.

When they returned to the U.S., it was to New York City. They first lived in a small, loft-like apartment downtown, then moved to what would thereafter become their permanent base of operation in the U.S., a large, sunny, Pre-War apartment on West Ninety-fifth Street, off Central Park. But most of the time I knew the Ferro-Grumleys, i.e., from 1978 to their deaths in 1988, they spent spring and early summers in an apartment high above the *Piazza d'Spagna* in central Rome. It was only following the nuclear accident at Chernobyl, Ukraine, with the venting of atomic radiation all over Europe, that the pair ceased their annual three-month-long Roman sabbaticals.

Even in New York, their art, their furnishings, their clothing, their jewelry, and their accessories all spoke of their life in Italy. For Robert, the most beautifully made example of anything could be found within a few miles delimited by the *Via del Corso* and the *Piazza della Repubblica*: except for leather goods—better in Florence—and cloth—superior if from around Turin. Once prices in Europe began to rise and Robert and Michael found themselves more involved in the New York gay literary scene that they helped create, Italy slowly began to lose its attractions and become more retrospectively appealing, grist for essays and novels. At the same time, it became a great treasure house for Robert to rummage through as he delightedly took on the large task of repairing and updating the Ferro family beach house.

I recall the first time I became aware of both the enormity of this redecoration labor and also Robert's commitment to it. The large first floor living room/dining room area encircled one end of the house, as a bowsprit semi-circumnavigates a seagoing vessel, debouching onto side and back terraces, enclosed porches, foyers, and subsidiary corridors. It boasted nearly two dozen windows in need of being re-curtained. At one point, I—and every other guest in Gaywyck—was asked to offer opinions on the swatch book of favored chintzes. Later on, when a pattern had been selected and work begun, Robert proudly offered this update: "There isn't enough fabric left for the whole place. They have to reprint it at the Italian factory!"

The enormous pots—ten were needed, it turned out—were also for Gaywyck, for a small forest of trees to grace the numerous outdoor sitting areas. And only at long last were they discovered in the befitting silhouette and with appropriate ornamentation, some of them two-thirds as tall as Robert. An eighteen-wheel tractor trailer with an electronic loading gate was needed to deliver them. By then, Robert had redecorated the three upstairs bedrooms (mine, aquatically done up in tones of white and green, was instantly dubbed the "Princess Louise sur Mer Suite"), the two basement ones, the halls, and the maid's room downstairs. He had the entire driveway relocated ten feet to more incisively curve into the property, nearly redefining it as a *porte-cochere*. When a Madison Avenue tycoon moved into the adjoining acreage, Robert panicked, fearful privacy would be compromised, and had an enormous earthen rampart raised between the houses, upon which he installed pine trees, once boasting that it was large enough to be seen from outer space. The neighbor complained to the village that he was losing any view of the water, and the pine trees were removed, and the berm itself whittled down a bit.

Robert's mother, nee Gaetana Panzera, had died in that beach house, not many years before, in the very front bedroom Robert and Michael subsequently slept in. When she'd been healthier she'd governed two houses, the newer, larger one upstate, a home and an entertainment center for her husband, president of his own generic cosmetics firm—and this shoreline abode, originally named Eagle's Nest by its builders and first residents—in honor of the largest of the sea birds that occupied the estuary, as well as for its unobstructed site.

Intensely invested both in his mother's death—a major element of his first published novel, *The Family of Max Desir*—and in keeping her memory alive in the beach house he came to see as her *embodiment*, Robert in effect turned himself into a new family matriarch. Quillians and other big city visitors were welcome, but only off-season.

In the summer, Robert's large family, his two sisters, his brother and their spouses and children, as well as his father and his lady friend, would stay there. Robert seldom wrote during these times, he was too busy cooking, cleaning, keeping house and order. But even off season, he'd hold parties of women—sisters, aunts, and his niece—varied with parties of men—his brother, uncles, brothers-in-law and their sons—at the house for weekend card parties that might have come out of the pages of *Max Desir*.

Robert wasn't at all deceived, he told me, about the reason behind his father allowing him such largess and artistic freedom in redecorating: the expensive beach house was to be tarted-up only to be sold. Gaetana's four children would share the proceeds. Robert's stratagem was to do all the work necessary and then stall for time, possibly until his father died, and he could lay total or partial claim with one other-hopefully easily manipulated sibling to the house, as the rest of the estate was otherwise divided: another example of *Commendatore* Ferro putting Machiavellian precepts into action.

Via George Stambolian, who remained in contact with the Ferro sisters after Robert's death, I followed for several more years the history of the property we had come to know so well and to call Gaywyck. Evidently, early post-mortem plans to sell it dissolved on several occasions for unexplainable reasons—which seemed to belie what Robert's sister Camille Ferro-Burns told me after his death: "If there was any trouble in this family, Robert was invariably its source. It's been so quiet since he's gone!"

It seems that once the decision to sell had been made by the three surviving siblings, the house was after some time acknowledged to be haunted. One of Robert's nieces claimed that her boyfriend was literally stopped from ascending to the master bedroom floor: pushed back down by some unseen force. Bizarre noises and flickering light fixtures became commonplace events. Vases dropped off sufficiently deep shelves and dinner plates self-ejected out of closed cabinets; the eerie become everyday occurrences, all easily attributed to Robert's revenant, since no one could deny that the selection of destroyed objects seemed to so precisely fit his long stated preferences and dislikes.

An exorcism of the house was contemplated and discussed but before that extreme step, another plan emerged: three of Robert's friends, myself, Stambolian, and Steven Greco were delegated to visit Robert and Michael's grave-site high above the Hudson Palisades to entreat him to desist. We made an early June social call, brought flowers, gossiped literary shop talk, picnicked rather well, sunned a bit and, before leaving, danced upon the grave in a ring—three not very lissome Graces—whether to divert or to mollify Robert's refractory spirit was never made clear to me. But possibly in response, or to avoid any further cemetery visitations by the oafish living, the haunting of Gaywyck abruptly ceased. After Stambolian also died in early 1992, I lost track of the Ferro family and had no idea whether the beach house remained in their hands, or continued to be frequented by Robert's phantom. Not long ago I was in contact with Robert's niece and literary executor, Elizabeth Barrett, and she said the house was indeed sold for a great deal of money—unobstructed views on three sides at Sea Girt! Even so, Gaywyck is Ferro family, and because of all our many visits, also Violet Quill Club—history. I've got a postcard drawing of it made by someone in the town, framed and hanging in my dressing-hallway.

If the above paragraph reads rather dottily like something out of a Shirley Jackson novel, it is more than apropos. For while in life (and in the one book they wrote together) Robert played the rational, Renaissance man, skeptic to Michael's greater credulity, the truth is that he allowed the occult, the arcane, the not quite visible and material a far larger than ordinary place in his life, crediting to it much that otherwise seemed inexplicable.

His meeting with Michael, for example, fit into that category Robert called "karmic connections." He told Andrew Holleran, whom he first met in the Iowa writing program and with whom he remained lifelong friends, that until his final book tour for *Second Son* in 1988, he and Michael hadn't been apart but six days in the intervening twenty-two years. And, going back for a second to his dedication to me in his novella, that phrase "across the ages" spoke of Robert's stated conviction that when he and I first met at a preview screening of Helen Whitney's path breaking television documentary of gay life in America in the autumn of 1978 that we had already known each other in former lives, and would do so again in future existences.

Of course, I'd already noticed both Robert and Michael within Manhattan's not that large gay underground a few years before our formal introduction. At private dance clubs like The Loft and an earlier incarnation of Flamingo on Duane Street, Robert's equinely handsome, dark-bearded face, his aristocratic, erect bearing, his slender, well-muscled *Cinquecento* physique and long, straight mane of brown hair made him an immediate stand-out—even in an era of what, in retrospect, seems to be a stunning number of naturally, distinctly beautiful men.

At that time, I recall Robert being referred to as "Max" by my artist friend, David Martin, who had already painted Robert, and later—fittingly—drew him as a centaur, for an invitation to a Black and White Men Together Party, at I believe The Paradise Garage dance club. More solidly built and less aloof than his partner, Michael was then known as "Mickey." At that time, the mid-Seventies, both were deemed prize catches for the night among the mixed crowd of whites, African-Americans and *Cubanos* among whom they danced, and with whom they had love affairs.

So when we first did become friendly, Robert and I, he was already trailing years of glory behind himself. For one thing he was several years older. For another, he'd lived in Europe on and off for years and still did. His first book had been published almost a decade before and was still in print, albeit by then only from a discount reprint house. His second book, the novella, had received admiring reviews in the mainstream media. He and Michael had a substantial history together, which had included months onboard a yacht sailing the Eastern inter-coastal waters and the Caribbean in an allegedly successful search for a newly arisen section of a mythical lost continent. Among their circle of friends were men and women of all ages and occupations, from jazz singer Susannah McCorkle and novelist Julia Markus to landscape designer/gardeners for the affluent. There were also Parke-Bernet appraisers who resided in eccentricity on upper Fifth Avenue, and a smattering of acquaintances who never worked at all, but who occasionally sold some small thing they had inherited at auction or had a travel book published, or lived on "incomes": fast food heiresses, dilatory scribblers of columns on interior decor in hard-covered, coffee table bound, quarterly magazines that only eleven people in the world actually read.

Even for someone like myself who'd by then lived in Greenwich Village a decade, it all seemed epicene and *soignee*.

At those first, elegant, upper West Side "teas," after everyone else had left, and Michael had withdrawn to his studio to sketch or nap, Robert would keep me by his side plying me with Milanese nougat and Pinhead tea while we discussed the current crop of bad novels, the teachings of *I Ching*, recent publishing gossip, problematic Tarot readings, the niceties of Mahayana Buddhism, and the manners exhibited in the most *au courant* downtown sex club. Robert was witty—of a short story writer whose quite bad novel had been trumpeted on the front page of the *Sunday New York Times Book Review* he said, "She's gone directly from mud huts to the cathedral stage without a single intervening era!"

He too was writing a new novel, the one that eventually became *The Family of Max Desir*, his first openly gay-themed book, and he was frankly desirous of having it make a splash. Among the members of the Violet Quill, when we seven first gathered to read and discuss our work, two of us, Andrew Holleran with *Dancer From the Dance* in 1978, and myself with *The Lure*, in 1979, had "hit the big time" in Robert's words: i.e., published unquestionably "out" gay novels with major publishers that had generated publicity, reviews, word of mouth, and especially sales. Robert was candidly curious how it happened. Although he'd known Holleran for years and exchanged letters with him whenever they'd been apart, Ferro found his old pal too flummoxed by success to talk about it; Robert thought for fear of jinxing the next project. I had no such fear, having readied my next, very different novel, *Late in the Season*, for publication, and I was already looking to short fiction and a memoir to outline an even more wayward career course.

I ended up reading much of Robert's novel in manuscript and it was at his urging that I consented to put together what now appears to be the first gay and lesbian literary anthology: *A True Likeness*, which I then published through my own small press in 1981. The high standard of fiction, poetry, and drama in the book, and the contributors involved—most of the Violet Quill members, Bertha Harris, Jane Rule, and Jane de Lynn—guaranteed the book would get attention. It did, including a handful of reviews, an American Library Association citation, and a small grant to SeaHorse from the New York State Council on the Arts.

Within its pages were excerpts from two books that subsequently rocketed into prominence, Edmund White's *A Boy's Own Story* (1982) and Robert Ferro's *Max Desir*, published the following year. Also in its pages was the fragment of a never completed autobiographical novel by Michael Grumley set in Rome, a piece that aside from whatever intrinsic merits it might possess, signaled a sea-change within Robert and Michael's relationship to each other and to the world that the rest of us, no matter how close, wouldn't become aware until years later: one that continues to haunt and intrigue me long after their deaths.

Here I have to retrace steps a little, back to the Ferro-Grumley's first production, *Atlantis: Autobiography of a Search*. In that book, a remarkably readable, personable volume even some forty years after it first came out, first Robert and then Michael alternate, narrating how it was that they became interested in, and then ended up actually looking for "Poseidia" not far from the mouth of the western inlet separating two islands of Bimini in the Bahamas.

It devolved as a result of 1) an Edgar Cayce prediction years earlier that Michael had come across, 2) Michael's own dreams, 3) the loan of the thirty-five foot boat they would use, by Robert's father, as an enticement to woo Robert back to the U.S from Europe. and, finally 4) the predictions of a *Strego*, or male witch, the two young men had come across in their early years in Rome.

"Yaria" is what they call him in the book, but I recall Robert telling me his actual name, something more like Hieronimo. Months before it was more than a notion, the *Strego* assured the two American not-yet-writers they would take the boat journey and fulfill Cayce's prediction of a 1968-1969 Atlantean "discovery." What they—and their teammates—eventually did discover was a to-this-day ambiguous archaeological find, an unexplainable series of huge, regularly shaped stone slabs, forming what resembles an underwater causeway.

Later finds at this same spot by an Italian scientist who'd accompanied them, included other underwater walls set at right angles to the first, along with non-randomly spaced columnar fragments, all deemed to be composed of material found only in the Andes Mountains and dating back over twelve thousand years.

Of the two writing, Michael concentrates mostly on the "mumbo-jumbo" aspects of this story, while Robert's sections deal more directly and straightforwardly with the "action," i.e., problems of handling the yacht, geography, meteorology, the people they met and how the thing got—and almost didn't get—accomplished.

Whatever else besides the book accumulated, once the adventure was over, the Ferro-Grumley's conviction in the *Strego* was consolidated. When I first met them, they continued to consult him and to receive *Auguri* every year in Rome. Thus I learned that he had foretold their deaths, "together, around the age of forty-seven, from some kind of new cancer," a prediction that unfortunately came true, but which a decade earlier seemed pretty implausible.

Since I myself dabbled in astrology at the time, although in its more pragmatic form, I was given their birth data and asked to draw up natal charts to read and investigate. Thus, for anyone interested, Robert was born close to the end of Libra, a sun sign connected to partnership, social issues, jurisprudence, the visual and decorative arts, and in which discernment and judgment seem accentuated. His ruling planet, Venus, ascended in Sagittarius, sign of the Centaur archer—and also known as the Explorer or Wayfarer. (Note: horses—real or as statuary—appear as a leitmotif throughout his books). Mercury and the Moon—representing his thinking and writing ability—were joined in the fixed sign of Scorpio, a martial sign also thought of as the power behind the throne. Robert's horoscope co-rulers are an embattled Mars in active, hot-tempered Aries, in a sector where it emphasized his family and domicile; and a far happier Pluto in Leo, a regal sign, in the astrological sector where it holds sway over foreigners and distant lands, voyages, publishing, the courts, and universities. Beneficial Jupiter was quite solid in Robert's house of marriage and partnership, and it helped expand his circle of friends and assistance from them. Only Saturn, the teacher, the limiter, was equally strong in his birth map, descending in Taurus, tightly bound to the inventive, eccentric, unexpected hijinks of far-out Uranus, unhappily placed in earthbound Taurus.

The last combo seemed to deny him any long term compensation in life and all but insured that he would have to experience difficult to cope with final separations. But that troubled duo of planets was in a positive aspect to imaginative Neptune—the most elevated point in Robert's horoscope— suggesting any art he tried that dealt with death and transfiguration would succeed with the public. Some believe that this pairing also confers repute beyond one's lifetime. which has not come to pass, alas. All of this, I intimated to Robert some thirty years ago; and little of what I said in any way startled him.

Robert's first solo publication, *The Others*, begins with the narrator speaking of surviving a greatly debilitating illness "which changed me." He then goes to say he wasn't certain whether it was "of the mind or the body," and some have read the entire short, often baffling, book as an allegorical charting of the transition between life and death.

The Family of Max Desir, six years later, opens with the onset of a fatal stroke of the protagonist's uncle while driving a car, and quickly segues into the subsequent cerebral seizures of Marie Desir, Max's mother, whose slow death from an inoperable brain tumor forms one well investigated center of this impressive debut novel.

In *Second Son*, published five years later, the illness that comes upon the narrator and then dominates the book is an undefined one, but an obvious correlative of AIDS; the then-inevitable death expected, is transmogrified into a fantasy ascent to a gay planet of complete health.

Of Robert's work, only his third novel, *The Blue Star*, escapes overt thanatologic subject matter, and even that book seems to contain the theme embedded in his elaborate reverie on the hidden Masonic temple beneath the Obelisk in Manhattan's Central Park. By now, we're used to reading about death and dying whether in "self help" books, memoirs or novels, but Robert was one of the first to address it with candor, unflinching stoicism, and all the abhorrence it deserves, both in his books and later on in his life.

Another motif that insistently appears in Robert's writing is that of the seagoing vessel. It's the very setting of the novella, and its layout and decor are described with the lapidary disillusionment of a Kafka fable. In Atlantis, again a boat dominates: this time Ferro Senior's "Tana" is the milieu of most of the book's action. *The Blue Star* is titled after another luxury yacht sailing up the Nile, first helping to cement, then aiding in driving apart the book's two male characters. In *Second Son*, the vessel is divided in two, first the canoe in which the two desperate heroes row across the vacation lake that has become their final refuge and thus the physical gauge of the progress of their declining health; and second the fondly desired spaceship and it's promised escape they eagerly await.

The third most salient of Robert's topics, and the one most crucial to his success as a writer in the mid-Eighties is the relationship of gay men to their birth families, an issue Robert openly grappled with in his life and in his writing as fiercely as the biblical Jacob wrestled the angel. As the third child, second son, of a large, affluent, ambitious, second generation Italian immigrant family, from birth Robert's place and position appeared to be predetermined. Traditionally, in such a family, the first son received all the attention and the bulk of the material bounty, but was then forced to bear the complex burden of continuing the lineage, enriching the household coffers, and upholding the family name. Decades ago, in the "old country" the second son—automatically bereft of power and status—typically accepted his situation, becoming a priest or professor, sometimes a doctor or lawyer, i.e., someone "helpful" to others. When, that is, he didn't turn instead into a wastrel.

The same basic problem held true for myself, born into the exact same family position, but where Robert and I—vocally, sometimes angrily—differed, was that he accepted the fundamental rightness of the system and only sought a greater place within it. Whereas I scoffed at it all—and pretty much abandoned my family to live my own life. Certain of his intellectual and moral superiority, Robert rebelled early and in varied ways, trying to usurp his brother, although he'd never dream of taking the elder's position as active second in command of the family firm or to raise a family, as was also required.

By being a homosexual and by becoming an artist, Robert—again, like myself—doubly betrayed his origins. If the first was acceptable only by a stretch of doctrine that it might be innate—if not precisely "natural," at least not solicited, not chosen (who would be mad enough?)—the second was both unnatural and overtly sought after. To decide to be a writer, painter, composer, in the face of the likelihood of poverty, defeat, and most significantly a built-in lack of stability inimical to family structure, was equal to spitting in one's parents' faces, denying them the fruit of their years of care and sustenance. As an example of this attitude: even when my second published novel was on national bestseller lists, and I barely thirty-two years old with a presumably long career ahead, my mother could only comment, "Your father and I still preferred if you were an attorney." I could ignore their preferences since by then I'd already supported myself half of my life and had even put myself through college without anyone's help.

Robert's parents were far more materially supportive of him during the decades he wasn't yet published and self-supporting. For one thing, they had more resources than my family to do so. Then too Robert never abandoned them as I did my kin, but remained a major player in their intricate familial rivalries. Thirdly, they expected him to fail as an author, and then to fall in line with their rules and wishes. It took Robert an interval to prosper. I recall some hand to mouth years for him after the money from home had ceased, when all prospect of other loans had been used up, when he worked as a waiter for a gay catering service—years that he endured, at times even enjoyed, with a certain noblesse oblige, a well-disposed slumming—but which he afterward shuddered over whenever they were alluded to.

Beyond our differing experience, however, Robert and I disagreed on the role of the family in gay life on a far more essential level. When I'd discovered I was gay, it had been with joy, providing me another potent arrow in the quiver I'd amassed in my attack on all that was rigidly established. I embraced homosexuality with the goal of tearing down society and starting all over again.

While Robert claimed to admire the Aquarian revolutionary in me, he secretly desired a Libran accommodation in which he eventually shared in what had been amassed. It was only natural that his tenets would prove more agreeable to naturally conservative reviewers and critics than my more subversive ones. It's equally comprehensible that his books would continue to win favor and be read by a younger generation of gay people who seek the same ends Robert wanted, to marry, to have families, to serve in the military, to be just like all the rest of the dreary straight world. At the moment that faction continues in the ascendant, under the preposterous sobriquet of "Post-Gay", but I (perhaps illusorily) believe that my way will ultimately be seen as the more successful one.

I could be fanciful and call these years of striving, Robert's "lost years." The truth is less glamorous and rather more interesting. Between the time Robert and Michael left Iowa and the publication of *Atlantis* was a mere three years. It was another seven years between the publication of *Atlantis* and Robert's novella, *The Others*. It would be another six years to the publication of his next book, *The Family of Max Desir*.

Meanwhile Michael went on to write and publish several books himself: in 1974, *There Are Giants in the Earth*, a book about sightings of mysterious man-ape creatures around the world; in 1977, *Hard Corps*, a study of the American leather S/M subculture; and in 1979, *After Midnight*, portraits of night people, folks who slept during the day and worked during the night, a book both well reviewed and commercially successful. In other words, Robert's partner seemed to have made (or had made for him) the right career decision: he was moving ahead full steam, with more non-fiction tomes in preparation: a book about beaches, another about lighthouses, a third concerning Alexander VI, known as the Borgia Pope, who presided over Counter Reformation Italy in its great Mannerist period.

Robert, meanwhile appeared to be dragging his feet, content to play spouse and mainstay. He seemed to have been working at *Max Desir* in one form or another several years before the Violet Quill began meeting. Another two and a half years would pass before it was ready in manuscript form. At the time, this was understandable, especially given Robert's stratospheric aspirations and his incredibly high standards.

Then something strange happened. No sooner had Bill Whitehead, senior editor at Dutton—then an independent company—accepted his first novel, then Robert began writing *The Blue Star*. That book was nearly finished by the time *Max Desir* was receiving its last reviews. Robert barely could wait for his first novel to come out in paperback the following year, before issuing the second in hardcover, in 1985, again through Dutton. He'd barely completed that book, when he was already laying out the outline for a third, *Second Son*.

He wrote that volume faster than any previous book and the only reason Robert's last novel had to wait till early 1988 to come out, was because Whitehead had sickened and died of AIDS. Robert's agent took the book to Crown Books—also then an independent company—otherwise it would have come out in the spring of 1986.

Suddenly Robert Ferro's work was everywhere. Putting into service his recent friendship with *Newsweek* book critic Walter Clemons (whom all of us knew was gaga over Robert), he managed to get Walter to write a cover piece for the influential national magazine on gay books and literature, with of course a special emphasis on his own work.

In other words, the *Commendatore* had reappeared in full regalia, and Robert arranged to call in every favor, cash in on each flirtation, play off every connection he had made in previous years, to ensure getting his books reviewed as widely as possible. Sales weren't at all bad, either: *Max Desir* in paperback especially sold well.

However—during those same blooming years for Robert, 1983 to 1988, Michael Grumley's writing career virtually dried up. Although he worked as energetically as ever on various projects and several of them seemed quite promising, none was ever completed as a book, none received a publication offer, or saw publication.

Stymied, Michael turned to fiction. First back to the Italian based novel he had titled *A World of Men*, and that I'd excerpted in *A True Likeness*, and when that book was deemed by their agent to contain material too similar to what was already in Robert's works, Michael moved to an autobiographical novel set in earlier years, in the Midwest, in Hollywood, and in New Orleans. He gave readings from this work in progress from 1983 on, and several friends, myself included, encouraged him, as it felt both authentic and distinctive.

What we couldn't help him with was the blatant fact that not too long ago he'd had a successful ongoing writing career and now suddenly he didn't; while Robert had not before had a writing career and now suddenly he did! Their friends naturally wondered what this might signify. Were we witnessing some species of psychological vampirism, similar to those depicted in several late Henry James novels where after being together so long, a couple involuntarily exchanged power, energy, even destiny? Or was it all less rarefied and far more haphazard than that?

These intangibles were soon swept away in the growing reality of first Robert and then Michael becoming symptomatic for HIV infection. As early as 1984, when Robert and Michael came to stay at my beach house at Fire Island Pines, I was sworn to secrecy about the already noticeable Kaposi sarcoma lesions on Robert's legs and arms. The duo only visited me during the week, when far fewer people were there, and even then they were careful who saw them out on the beach, spending most of their time on my private house decks.

The following year, Michael had a large skin tumor removed from his forehead, but assured us it was non-malignant. The next year was calmer and Robert's lesions had been lased off, seemingly with no lasting effects. But during the spring of 1986 in Rome, Michael began to suffer from severe headaches, which he attributed to the Chernobyl radiation leak. Europe was abandoned, and that summer and the following year, they rented a small lakefront house outside the village of Tully, in Orange-Athol country in north central Massachusetts, a place they'd happened upon due to the good offices of my longtime friend, Allen Young.

I visited Allen during the summer and so had a chance to see Robert and Michael in their new domicile. Both were writing—Robert completing *Second Son*, and Michael working toward a draft of *Life Drawing*. They were unusually antisocial, seeing no one locally but Allen—and then, he reported, quite rarely. The afternoon I spent with them was cut short by their need to nap. The dinner we made together at Allen's octagon house at nearby Butterworth Farm was marred by Robert being restless and criticizing everything. They left early.

I and my partners at Gay Presses of New York were anticipating reading Michael's finished book and putting it out the following year through the SeaHorse imprint. But when the manuscript arrived that autumn, it led to an abyss opening beneath my feet.

The manuscript was a jumble, both physically, and in terms of its structure and organization. Some pages were typed over others, others done with nearly invisible typewriter ribbon. Entire sections were missing or misplaced. Pagination was erratic. Characters kept changing names.

I persisted, I read the whole thing, then gave it to my partner, Larry Mitchell to read, without any prejudicial comment. His response a week later was "My god! We can't publish this mess!"

Getting Michael to even recognize the unserviceable condition of the manuscript proved impossible: my first, and only, exploratory phone call to him on the subject was met with by cries of betrayal, effusions of paranoia, and an adamant refusal to in any way amend the thing, followed by curses and imprecations. Thereafter, and until his death, Michael referred to me as "that former person" and refused to speak to me.

What had happened is in retrospect obvious: the HIV virus had proliferated, passed the brain-blood barrier, and had begun to damage Michael's mind: what is known as dementia. Ever loyal, Robert also cut me out of his life and tried to get the book published elsewhere. I heard from others that Robert began the difficult and long task of nursing Michael through several awful bouts of headache and pneumocystis. This went on for months. By early 1988, Michael was so ill, that Robert had to place him in a hospice that they would share, looking something like a hotel room, next to a Manhattan east side hospital.

As his partner declined to total invalidism, Robert began reaching out to friends. He and I became close again and remained so to the end. Michael was feverish and raving anytime I went to the hospital to visit. So I mostly visited Robert. We walked around the neighborhood, checked out antique stores, drank tea in little shops, re-arranged the furniture in the tiny elevator landing outside their new domicile.

Robert was clearly exhausted, much thinner, and his Kaposi's lesions had returned, this time internally as well. He spoke with barely controlled anger of what it was like to have the bad luck to become a medical patient: the numbing horror of being trundled about and anti-individualized which he compared to being a numbered prisoner at Auschwitz.

I urged him to write about it. But Robert astounded me by saying that he was now and forever done with writing: he'd recently completed an essay on gay literature to be delivered at the University of Michigan, and he'd laid his pen aside. He had done so much excellent writing in such a short time, I can't be blamed for disbelieving him. Thereafter we argued the decision. I couldn't help but think that besides depression Robert was in shock, and in terror.

I'd been involved in AIDS from the very beginning of its time in America. The first two infected men on the East Coast had been friends and former Fire Island Pines house mates of mine: Nick Rock and Rick Wellikopf. I was subsequently immersed one way or another with the progress of the disease and attempts to discover it's source, define it, and help solve it. Besides many, many friends and acquaintances, my straight younger brother—a weekend drug abuser—died of it in 1985. His younger wife, Donna, was also later diagnosed. As was my GPNy business partner, Terry Helbing, and my bisexual older brother, and finally my closest friend and life partner.

Meanwhile among Violet Quill members and colleagues, Chris Cox, George Whitmore, our one guest, Vito Russo, George Stambolian, and later Edmund White would all test positive for the virus. All of the people above but Edmund succumbed to it. Naturally, I kept expecting myself to become symptomatic and to test positive every day. Around me, loved one's illnesses doubled and trebled. Sometimes I would walk into a hospital ward to see one person and end up for hours, visiting a half dozen people I knew.

Like everyone around me I became expert in the disease, its manifestations, and because of my early connection with various AIDS organizations, I knew the newest treatments. Following a complex discussion of steroids as treatment for one series of symptoms—virtually a consultation—over a patient I'd visited, one hospital resident asked where I'd gotten my medical degree. "Here, and on the street," I replied.

But as deeply submerged in HIV as I'd been, Robert and Michael had been equally remote from it. They'd never even allowed a discussion of AIDS in their presence. I continue to wonder how much that ignorance and the concomitant ice-water bath of reality that must have followed contributed to Robert's utter demoralization over Michael—with natural reference to his own future.

Michael died in May of 1988. After his large memorial service, there was a gathering of friends held at the upper Fifth Avenue home of a friend: in fact the apartment that held the half-room sized aviary Robert had written about. There Robert cornered me and George Stambolian, who'd also been shown the Grumley manuscript, and he asked us what we thought had to be done to get Michael's last manuscript in publishable shape.

As he had already retyped it and physically cleaned it up, it was a mere matter of restructuring with bits and ends added and removed. Could Robert do it, he asked us. We thought yes: he knew as much about Michael's life as Michael himself. Thereafter Robert worked on *Life Drawing* non stop, with phone calls back and forth to me and George, checking on this and that aspect of the book.

He had a completed manuscript in mid July. Stambolian and I rapidly read it, approved it, and, upon Robert's insistence, swore to him our oath that we would see it into publication. (It was published in 1991 by Grove, Weidenfeld.)

A day later, Robert left his apartment and moved back to his father's home in New Jersey. By then, the Kaposi's had spread throughout his legs, his lungs, his stomach, and other internal organs.

We spoke every day by phone. As I'd been his gadfly from the onset of our friendship, I continued to try to goad Robert back to health, frightening him with scenarios in which I alone survived to tell the world about him: then I would paint the blackest possible picture.

Robert appreciated what I was trying to do, but it was too late. He died at his father's home, in his bedroom, awaiting a cup of soup, not ten weeks after Michael.

Δ

It has come to me anyway to write about Robert. I could say I've been circumspect here because I expect to meet him again in my next lifetime, as he so strongly believed, and I've had already had many tastes of his temper. But the truth is I cannot write anything but the truth. I loved Robert—we loved each other—in a way that only siblings ever do, and problematical as our relationship was, it was more than worth it: it was a privilege to have known him. So having to write this has meant having to relive that friendship, which I did again, with pleasure and sadness.

Having to read Robert's work again I'm pleased to declare that it holds up well, and the best of it—his three novels—richly and accurately convey his voice, his mind, and his life.

For years after he was gone, I've heard Robert's voice in my mind, prepping me, beginning with "Lou-Lou!" then going on to laugh or threaten or invite, and I now realize I've left out many anecdotes illustrating his sophistication, his vanity, his wit, his generosity. So I'll leave Robert Ferro with one moment I can never forget: it was on the top deck outside his bedroom at Gaywyck, before AIDS was even a shadow—and he turned to me and repeated Blanche DuBois' line, "Someday, I shall die—of an unwashed grape!" And Robert's smile after he said those words was amazingly enigmatic.

The Absolutely, Very Last Surrealist

Charles Henri Ford

The last SeaHorse Press author I became associated with was a legendary one, and our connection would take our publishing company back to the earliest decades of the twentieth century and Modernism. I'm talking about SeaHorse Press' re-publication of Charles Henri Ford and Parker Tyler's 1933 book, *The Young and Evil*. Gore Vidal had told me it was out of print for a long time and in need of being re-issued.

The truth was somewhat different: the book was never officially published in the U.S., but instead in Paris, by Maurice Girodias' infamous Olympia Press, and it was reprinted by Olympia Press again in 1960, at which time it slowly entered the U.S. via various sub rosa distributors. The co-authors in the Thirties were two cheeky young men, one of whom would go on to become a noted American film critic during a time when that was a great novelty. And in fact, Parker Tyler's books, *Sex in Films, A Pictorial History of Sex in Films*, and especially *Screening the Sexes: Homosexuality in the Movies*, were pioneering volumes, lodestones for all that was sexually ambiguous or erotically quirky in Hollywood.

Tyler's co-author was an even greater figure in the international art world. Charles Henri Ford was only fourteen and his sister Ruth Ford sixteen, when they wrote to Gertrude Stein and asked for some of her poems for their just-begun literary quarterly *Blue*. These two young Southerners of great precocity and beauty felt their talents were hidden under various bushels in the Mississippi of the Twenties and no sooner had Harriet Monroe, who published *Poetry* magazine in Paris, written to compliment them on their magazine's first issue and invited them to look her up next time they were on the *rive gauche*, then they entrained to New York, and soon were crossing the Atlantic on their way to France.

Once arrived, the young Fords' beauty and brilliance, along with their verve and intelligence, did the rest. They were invited everywhere by the Parisian intellectual set, photographed often, brought out to recite their own—more often Charles' poetry—and they became fixtures at the Gertrude Stein-Alice B. Toklas residence on the rue de Fleurus, at Harriet Monroe's salon, and in various other ateliers of *la vie bohème*. Ruth soon returned to New York where her acting talent landed her Broadway roles, leading eventually to starring roles, including premiering plays by Tennessee Williams. Her career only settled down a bit once she met and married the dashingly handsome film actor, Zachary Scott, in the Fifties and moved to Hollywood, where she rested on her laurels while her husband made terrible, popular, extremely profitable cowboy and pirate movies.

Her younger brother Charles, however. remained in Paris, where he soon attracted the attention of the surrealist painters and photographers then ruling the Parisian art world. Eugène Atget photographed the licentious youth exiting a famous Montmartre *pissoir*. In the photo, an advertisement picturing a devil's long, lascivious tongue extends across the foreground and appears about to enter young Charles' fly, which he's hurriedly buttoning. Being very handsome and blond and pale blue-eyed, Charles soon conquered men and women alike, including even the "Amazon" author, Djuna Barnes, who had just become famous for writing a much-hyped novel titled *Nightwood*. According to Ford, he moved in and began a sexual affair with Barnes around the same time that he was sleeping with most of the attractive bi and gay men of Montparnasse. While Barnes certainly helped him as a writer, both aesthetically and in terms of getting his work known, according to Charles, she was definitely the *lover* and he very often the busily fleeing *beloved*.

He threw Barnes over completely when he met a magnetic and muscular Polish-born painter then enjoying great popularity. I knew of Pavel Tchelitchew much later for his remarkable Museum of Modern Art painting *Hide and Seek*. But earlier he was considered one of the primo Paris *Surrealistes* of the Thirties along with Salvador Dali. And, according to Charles, the "absolutely impossible person that turned out to be Pavlik," ended up being the only person Charles Henri Ford admitted to having been in love with, and was the major emotional affair of his life.

I discovered this information from Ford himself, when I contacted him in the mid-Eighties. I'd mentioned his name and the novel once again to my business partner, Larry Mitchell, at dinner, and with typical modesty, Larry replied, "I think I know someone who might know how to contact Ford." Indeed he did know someone: Steven Watson was a scholar of the Americans in Paris period, and had written about it at some length in *Prepare for Saints: Gertrude Stein, Virgil Thomson, and the Mainstreaming of American Modernism*. I knew Watson better, however, as the author of the definitive study to date of the Harlem Renaissance. We met, we spoke, and it was Watson who told me the next time Charles happened to be in the U.S., and Watson gave me Ford's phone number at the Dakota apartments in Manhattan.

There, on a cold spring morning, I walked past the spot where John Lennon had been gunned down, got through the formidably uniformed concierge/doorman inside his black wrought iron "cage," and went to visit for the first time the legendary Charles Henri Ford and his partner, a somewhat younger man named Indra Tamang. The apartment was located directly under the rooftop eaves of the famous nineteenth-century Central Park West building, reachable only by a second elevator, obtainable on the next-to-top floor, next to those used for the rest of the apartments.

His flat proved to be two "artist's ateliers" combined: two Pre-World War II artist studios with various bright windows and dormers, with a small galley kitchen plunked within and an added-on bathroom. Oh, and many different storage spaces hidden under what was never clearly either empty or enclosed spaces. Light and cheerful, the studios consisted of a sitting-cooking-dining area and a separate double sleeping area with central open space for artwork. Several of the dormered nook-areas were big enough to also hold work tables or desks. It was all done in rather dark wood and somberly painted walls, littered with prints, paintings, and wall hangings, much of those Nepalese, Indian, or Tibetan. All the daybeds and chairs had heavy, much filigreed or Asian patterned materials thrown over them. The lamps and other fixtures were faded brass and very old bronze. It very much seemed a pre-Modern artist's studio, not unlike those in black-and-white photos I'd seen of Whistler's atelier or Matisse's studio.

When I first met them, Charles and Indra had just arrived from their home in Khania on the Greek island of Crete, had stopped off briefly in Paris, and told me they were only staying in the States a few weeks. I showed Charles several SeaHorse Press books, left him the Gay Presses of New York catalogues and our reviews, and told him Vidal had recommended his 1933 novel for reprint. I needed to know first: exactly how the rights situation of the book stood, and second if he were willing to let us reprint the book.

From what I'd been led to understand from Edmund White who had visited him in Crete, Ford had been ill, or was perhaps still ill. At eighty years old, he looked very distinguished, clearly still handsome, yet quite frail. Naturally, I was worried and I hoped to get at the least an understanding on paper between us.

Ford said he was interested in a reprint, and he declared that with Parker Tyler long dead without living heirs, that he, Charles, possessed full authority for handling all business regarding *The Young and Evil*. With that settled, I was assured that I wouldn't run into any rights problems.

But if I'd hoped to settle matters quickly, I was to be disappointed. Charles asked me to send him contracts at the Dakota and he would look at them. Meanwhile, I told him how much I could offer as an advance against royalties, at the same time apologizing that it was so little.

"Not really a problem," he assured me. "One reason I'm here in the States is to arrange the sale of my papers to the University of Kansas' Library Collection." He expected that to net him a great deal much more than what I could offer. Even so, another $3,000 wouldn't hurt his pockets, either. So I was optimistic.

Due to GPNy's scheduling, the actual publication of the book wouldn't happen for several more years, and since neither Charles nor I ended up being in a hurry about it, I soon got to know him—and Indra—better, which led not only to us using Tchelitchew's art, but also to an unexpected friendship between me and Charles—and to a lesser extent, of course, Indra.

Indra was a native of Nepal, and on their second return to Manhattan they quickly let me know that he and Charles had apparently made their most permanent home in Katmandu for many years, with bi-annual forays to Paris and Khania. It ended up that we knew several people in common. The West Coast poet James Broughton had spoken well of me—which rather surprised me to hear, as we'd met so briefly. Even more unexpectedly, the artist Paul Cadmus, whom I'd only met a few times, also had good things to say about me. It was clear from Charles' conversation that he pretty much still frequented "artistic circles," wherever he went, although most of them consisted of visual artists, and so beyond my usual range.

How Charles actually lived remained forever the purest speculation to me. With all those homes around the world, I naturally assumed he was quite well off. But a year after our first encounter, following what the newspapers said of East Asian political turmoil, Ford and Indra once again appeared in Manhattan, this time for a much longer period of time, with Ford reporting that they now considered themselves political exiles and definite *personae non grata*, because of something he wouldn't discuss, evidently having to do with either the Nepalese royal family or because the pair had harbored independence-seeking political revolutionaries in the capital.

Shortly after that, I heard from someone else that their Paris flat was up for sale. And a few months later, someone else mentioned that the house in Khania was sold.

What had been the source of Charles income, anyway? Tchelitchew's artwork? That's what Steven Watson and I surmised. And, we further surmised, either that the art had been all sold, or that by the Nineties the market for it had pretty much dried up. Once he was settled in New York, Ford did arrange a tasteful show in a chic European owned art gallery on Madison Avenue, a small Tchelitchew retrospective with only two demi-masterworks—at which copies of the reprint of *The Young and Evil* were also on sale.

But what soon became clear was that Charles Henri Ford was back in the U.S. pretty much for good, and that following two rather difficult years, including one of surgeries about which he would not speak, that Charles was at work again, at poetry, at his varied collages, and also on a volume of memoirs, to be titled *Water From a Bucket* (a title never adequately explicated), which he quickly assured me was already promised to a university press, lest I get any publishing hopes up.

I'm guessing that Charles, who was about as canny an operator in the art and literary worlds as anyone I've ever met, and more effetely ruthless by far than any mere Hollywood starlet or Broadway producer, was establishing a niche for himself back in New York.

Work on our book went fairly easily—we were photographing and reprinting the Girodias edition page for page. And we were adding Steven Watson's brand new introduction, a good piece of writing that would put the novel into full historical and aesthetic context. Charles would vet that essay in advance, naturally, and he would carefully look over the typeset pages of the finished book, before it went off to be printed and bound.

The only question we faced was how to visually present the novel. I'd shown Charles enough cover art of the books SeaHorse and GPNy had done to alert him that to me it was as important as to him, that in fact the cover art was really crucial to a book's success.

We were sitting in his Dakota flat one day, when the question came up once again, and Ford suddenly had a flash of insight—or of remembrance.

"You know, Fell-eese, when the book was first done, Pavlik painted a series of watercolors for it," Charles said.

I hadn't known this fact and I doubted that anyone but Charles did know it, now that Tchelitchew was dead.

"Pavlik tore apart a copy of Maurice's edition and sewed it back together, with these new pages added in, on which he painted the watercolors," Charles recalled.

My heart skipped a beat. Was there any chance that he actually had that copy handy?

In fact he had. It was in a steamer trunk that had just, at long last, come over from France, filled with things from the sold Paris flat. We got up, the three of us, went to the trunk, and opened it. While Indra and I held open the heavy old studded leather lid, the aged Charles half dove in and rummaged around and after a while emerged with the volume. We sat back down to tea as Ford leafed through it. He then handed it to me to look through.

"No one's ever seen it but Pavlik and myself," Ford said. "He was so enamored of me at the time," he added. "He begged me not to show it to anyone else. That must have been well over sixty-five years ago."

The drawing and watercolors were not only wonderful, they were totally period—the classical Picasso, Cocteau, Calder, Thirties neo-Classical period. They were also sexy and hot, including one rather impressionistically soft-hued aquarelle of two men sixty-nining.

The book was in amazingly good condition considering how old it was, but then it was a handmade tome, the pages taken from the original and all of it, including the artwork pages, stitched together within a handcrafted leather covers.

"Will any of them do as cover art?" Charles asked.

I thought the drawing with the sailor boy and Abraham Lincoln figure would do nicely, being saucy, period, and easy to reproduce in different sizes—and so good for smaller adverts I might place in periodicals. I said so, and he looked at it again and agreed it would be fun.

Then I asked if he thought we might use all the watercolors for the reprint, say inside the book, not spaced out amid the text as Tchelitchew had originally done, alas—that would be too difficult for the bindery, and too expensive to do—but maybe bound all together, as a portfolio.

To my amazement, Charles agreed, adding "But of course, I can't let the book out of here, it being such a memento."

No problem: I would send a professional photographer and together—since Charles was a professional photographer himself—they would shoot the artwork and we would work off the negatives.

When I ended up discussing this with Alvin Greenberg, our printer's rep, he was truly excited. And when I showed him the photo negatives, he was even more excited: although he'd worked with contemporary artists like Mapplethorpe and Stavrinos that I'd sent him, Pavel Tchelitchew was an acknowledged twentieth-century painter.

Of course they were wonderful drawings and watercolors, and they were beautiful, in Alvin's conservative, fairly straight-laced opinion, "High Art." He made it easy for us to present them as an open-out portfolio bound in at the end of the novel.

The publication of *The Young and Evil*, a "SeaHorse Book" from GPNy, ended up being one of the highlights of my publishing career, one of which I'm quite proud. I wish it had been more widely reviewed and written about at the time. It sold out only its first printing and thus just managed to break even financially. But Gay Men's Press in the UK bought the British rights and also put out an edition. So it was unquestionably worth the expense and effort.

As a result of how easily and of how well all that went, Charles and I became friends during the process and thereafter we remained close until I moved out of New York in 1995. I ended up interviewing him for *Chiron* magazine, a literary quarterly in tabloid form, and I discovered that he'd been born a few weeks before my mother. In certain ways, Charles felt that I was very much like the son he'd never sired, being similar to him in my easy-going ambition, my practicality, and my general optimism about life.

He would phone me up with questions about people, institutions, or foundations and he always knew I would tell him the unvarnished truth. Once he'd moved back for good to America, he realized that New York City was fairly unlivable during the summer. He'd heard me speak of Cape Cod where my partner and I spent a second summer in September and October each year, and so one March day, Charles organized an outing for the three of us, me, him, and Indra.

I would rent a car and drive us up to the Cape where he had a half dozen potential summer houses to look at. He paid for the car, gas, and even got us a free dinner and overnight stay at a friend's house near Falmouth. But although he liked the Cape, he wasn't crazy about Provincetown, and none of the houses we looked at would do for Charles's very specific, albeit to me mysterious and unspoken, requirements.

Two months later, he phoned to tell me he had found a summer house out in Montauk Point, not far from Edward Albee, and Peter Beard, whom he knew and liked and felt to be central to some sort of *sympatico* artistic-social set. But, he added, this had its own problem attached to it. The only real way to come and go between Manhattan and so far at the tip of Long Island would be to drive. He no longer did drive. And Indra didn't know how. Would I teach him?

I demurred, I recommended driving school. All to no avail. Charles insisted, then made me promise to teach Indra, and he rented us another car and said we would all drive out to the far tip of Long Island to do it there.

The next phone call I received before the date we were to go was a secret one, from Indra in another room while Charles napped, who told me that he knew how to drive already, that he'd obtained a learner's permit, taken courses and passed, but that Charles insisted that he learn "American rules" and simply would not hear of him driving around without my specific tutoring and aid. This somewhat calmed me about the upcoming trip.

So we embarked upon another long, overnight car trip, the three of us, dropping off Charles at Peter's while I found an empty road and put Indra through his paces. He was a little rusty, even with an automatic, but he picked it up quickly, and I soon had him driving through East Hampton and along the flowery, estate-dotted lanes of Amagansett until he began to feel comfortable. I even had him drive the four of us to dinner that night and back, with myself in the front seat, and, of course at Charles' insistence, loudly re-explaining things that Indra already very well knew. Sweet man, he played along perfectly.

Aside from Indra's driving and these after all rather fun—and paid for—trips, there was about Ford nothing that could be considered in any way odd or different. In later years, I would hear that he was very difficult to get along with, considering everyone competition, that he was demanding, that his ego was overbearing, that he treated everyone like servants. He was, one Parisian friend told me, *une monstre sacree*, (a sacred monster) whom one dealt with at one's peril, and at one's expense.

While interviewing Ford for that piece in *Chiron*, I realized that he'd already been interviewed and quoted so often over the years that it would be impossible for him or for me to really come up with anything spontaneous and fresh. I also recognized that Charles had so much made *himself* a work of art over the decades since he arrived in Paris in 1919, that it would be boorish of me to attempt to even pick at that wonderfully polished-to-a-gleam-over-many-years surface of his. Although I knew from what others had said that at times Charles could be mean, arrogant, and, above all, demanding, he'd never once been anything but kind to me—some of the real luck I've had in life is how very kind some really impossible personalities have proven to be around me. So, we had fun doing the interview, Charles going out of his way to turn it into really both a collaborative effort—i.e., my questions intrigued him—and a success: he came off as uniquely Charles Henri Ford.

He moved out to Montauk that summer and that pretty much ended our weekly contact, which never really picked up as closely again, But then, there was no real reason for it to do so—I was as much a realist, and busy, as he was. Although Charles and I spoke on the phone several times after I'd moved to L.A.—once about the subsidiary sale of the book in England, which took many years to pay the advance and never paid either of us any royalties—the last time I actually saw Charles was for a photo-shoot he was doing in which I became a subject.

He and Indra had rented a tiny midtown photo studio and he told me he was in the process of putting together a book of a new kind of portrait collage. Although he explained these to me, the only one I really came to understand was the one he did of me. He'd blown up to life-size a photo of a Roman or Greek statue's upper torso. He then placed this photo over my own torso, taping it around my bare back and lower torso. He then dressed my lower body in classical drapery, seated me in front of a scrim of classical background, placed a laurel wreath on my brow and photographed me that way.

I remember thinking as we did it, that it couldn't possibly come out any good. But Charles seemed pleased at the time and I never afterward asked about it.

If he hadn't liked it, he probably would have said, it was "an experiment that didn't quite work, like so many others." As an Aquarian, he was airily aesthetic-scientific that way. That was one of his sayings. As another, I appreciated it and understood it: We simply move on.

I was too busy during those years to really stop and think about how extraordinary it was that we would establish so instant and open and easy a communication and friendship. The truth is, I sort of expect people to behave rationally in that way, despite decades of experiencing them doing everything but.

Only when I was talking about Ford with Bob Lowe, my in-house twentieth-century cultural historian as it were, did I realize how rare a person and how truly significant this thin, frail, handsome blue-eyed man really was. Bob was afraid to meet him, he was so overawed. "Andre Breton just died," Bob told me one day. "Charles Henri Ford is now 'The Absolutely Very Last Surrealist Still Living.'" He said it like that, with capital letters, in quotation marks, as though it was the title of a chapter in a book.

At times, in the years since Ford's death, I've wondered what it was to like to live such a long and what must have been such a very *interesting* life. I have a feeling that someday someone will write that question about me too; and I know it's full of *longeurs*, hardly glamorous, and certainly not all it is cracked up to be: filled more with craft than with parties or fun or brilliant and passionate relationships. But even so, to have known Harriet Monroe and Toklas and Stein, to have known that climateric generation of writers that put America on the literary map, and then the European artists and poets who followed them? To have written poetry and made films? Isn't it like that song from *Follies*?—I've seen both the good and the bad times and I'm still here.

Then too, how would one go psychologically from being the most beautiful and desired boy and young man of one's time and place to being a frail eighty some odd years old? Does one make one's peace somewhere along the line? Does one look for younger versions of oneself? Or does one simply recognize that *no one* could possibly be that fabulous any more, and that someone on the ball and trying a bit, and a little more original than the others—like that Picano kid—will have to do, when one is *kaput*?

I should have asked. But then I guessed I'd be afraid of the answer.

Meanwhile, the saying I remember most and which most summed up Ford for me, and in a way that I try to use as my own, is what Charles said when I asked him at the end of that magazine interview, "In such a long, active life, filled with so many people, do you ever regret anything?"

"Regret," Charles came back to me grandly, "is *not* my milieu!"

The Saga of Terry

Terry Helbing

Let me say this up front. I never really cared for my business partner Terry Helbing.

My other partner, Larry Mitchell, was another story completely. Larry and I began, as I did with Helbing, as business partners and slowly, over the years, and mostly because of GPNy business, we became friends. I admired Larry's writing. I liked his friends and lovers. I found that he and I shared political, activist, and literary tastes. We'd talk on the phone for an hour and we always laughed a lot. It's a decade and a half after we stopped having any business to do together, and after I had left Manhattan for the West Coast, we still speak once in a while just to say hello, and to pick up our friendship all over again.

With Terry—for both Larry and me, Larry later admitted—Terry Helbing was... well, he was our business partner, and we dealt with him in a businesslike manner over the decade we knew each other. But he was distinctly less congenial, accessible, or similar to us in tastes.

For one thing, he lived and breathed theater. And while we were also interested in theater, it was never on the daily, or I could almost say hourly, scale that Terry lived theater. Most of the time that I knew him, he was a stage critic, and also usually engaged in one or another stage production, in one capacity or another. And in time I ended up being drawn into his theater obsession and having plays of mine produced by him.

His friends—most of them, I note, women, with the exception of the late playwright Terry Miller—later on confided in me that he was actually a completely different person than the one Larry and I knew for a decade: that he was fun, open, even vulnerable: definitely not the guy we knew.

Our Terry Helbing was brisk, efficient, an office manager, a careful editor, a perfectionist, a man with high and fairly rigid standards of quality and behavior. An intelligent and verbal man, I would later on discover he'd been precocious, a good student in high school and college, in fact the perfect teenager—i.e., leagues away from either Larry or I, who were pretty much rebellious screw-ups the first part of our lives.

Terry was in general pretty buttoned-down around us, and his wit, when it was infrequently revealed, wasn't of the whimsical or capricious kind, but rather of the barbed, brittle, and distinctly wounding sort. Only when speaking about things he cared for and loved—pop music, for example, which he knew inside-out from the Fifties on, and which he collected avidly—his attitude, demeanor, and tone of voice would soften, compared to how they were usually.

But not by a great deal, and he'd snap back to being Mr. Efficiency a moment later. In many ways he was what had been characterized in one of GPNy's published novels—Bob Herron's *Moritz!*—as a "Very Efficient Queen." Larry and I seldom experienced his worst side, but when others did if we were around, we rapidly got out of Terry's way. He could be caustically critical, astonishingly sharp-tongued, and he brooked little interference or opposition. Neither Larry nor I ever spoke politics around Terry; I think we were afraid we'd discover he was a Conservative Republican—after all, he was from the deep Midwest and his only living relative, an older sister, lived in Phoenix, Arizona, both politically retro bastions.

There were of course moments of congeniality, and as especially I got to know Terry better through our GPNy activities together over his kitchen table, such as doing publicity mailings for our new titles, or sending out GPNy catalogues to past customers, or the increasingly arduous (as we published more titles and seldom let them fall out of print) annual royalty accounting work, Terry began to slowly reveal more amiable—I almost wrote more human—aspects of his character and personality.

True, I came to enjoy some of his inconsistencies. For example he was a staunch vegetarian, although he never deigned to explain why, and I respected that. Yet, of all the people I ever knew, without any doubt Terry consumed the greatest amount of junk food, and the greatest *percentage* of it in his diet. All vegetarian, of course, predicating that potato chips, cheez doodles, and the like are all meatless, if artery-clogging, hypersaturated fat foodstuffs. I'd moved to a more vegetarian diet myself in that time and I tried to interest Terry in "real food." The most I managed to accomplish was to whet his interest in our local Chinese take-out place, and even there, he managed to consume those foods on the menu—noodles with peanut sauce, for example, or deep fried tofu—that contained the highest fat to food ratio. If he ever explained or rationalized his eating habits to me or anyone else, I can't recall. I watched in fascination, as he downed plastic packages of the most astonishing trash in the guise of food concocted by the most hypocritical, profit-crazed, American corporations.

Terry always made it clear that we were business partners, not friends. And that was okay with me, and it was in fact the way I expected our lives and relationship to remain. I assumed that Terry was this completely closed off guy and would always be a closed off guy.

I couldn't have been more wrong, nor more surprised by what happened.

It began some fourteen years after we became business partners: a Monday morning. That Saturday, Terry had left a phone message saying that he'd be bringing by some financial statements for GPNy that he had prepared, and that I'd been asking and asking for, because they were seriously overdue. He would come by Sunday afternoon, his phone message said.

Sunday came and went with no appearance by Terry, which was unusual as he was always on time. I left a phone message with him on Sunday evening and figured that I would see him Monday. By noon Monday he still hadn't phoned me and I had to go out for the afternoon. When I returned, there was still no message from him. I tried his phone again. *Nada.*

I tried his phone again on Tuesday morning. Still nothing. Tuesday afternoon, Alvin Greenberg, our printer's rep, phoned me and said he'd driven down to the city from Nanuet on Monday to have an appointment with Terry and give him prices on a new JH Press book they were planning to publish. Terry never showed, and never answered his phone. Alvin, who'd done business with Terry for several years, was amazed and understandably somewhat pissed off. I called Larry who agreed: I should take the prices over the phone from Alvin, and then go to Terry's place and find out what I could.

I climbed the five floors up to his little apartment and knocked and rang and knocked and rang and got no answer at all. I was going down the stairs wondering what to do next. Did I have his friend Rachel Green's phone number? Where was she? In Montreal, I thought. No? Well, did I know his friend Tish's last name? Would Jane Chambers' widow Beth, know anything? What phone numbers did I have? What did I know about this man and his connection, if anything, really? As I was musing, on the third-floor landing, an apartment door opened and an elderly woman looked out through the chained two inches of space.

"Are you looking for that fellow with the long blond hair?" she asked.

"Yes. We're business partners. Do you know where he is?"

"No. I don't know. But there were police here Sunday morning. Early Sunday morning."

"Police? What did you see? Was Terry hurt? Did you see him?"

"No. No. Nothing. Just police," and she closed the door and locked it.

Larry wasn't home. I spoke with my friend Donna who is an attorney and she spelled out the unspoken dark thoughts I was already trying not to clarify for myself: "Call the hospitals. Then call the city morgue."

I located Terry two hours later through St. Vincent's Hospital. Information there said he was in intensive care. Was I a relative? "His only living relative, an elder married sister, lives in Arizona," I told the social worker to whom I was secondarily connected. "I don't really know how to reach her, although one of his friends might. I'm his business partner," I explained. Then I added the magic words. "I've got his health insurance card." Fiduciary music to her ears. We made an appointment for the next morning.

Terry was all but a mummy, totally wrapped up, with broken ribs, fractured wrist, and his head bandaged except for three-quarters of his bruised looking face. He was also in a coma. I was completely stunned.

A young, small, slender, and very handsome dark-haired physician joined me outside the intensive care room. He was a neurosurgeon he said and he'd been the surgeon who'd operated on Terry late Sunday morning. He couldn't tell me what had happened to put Terry in his current condition. The police and ambulance drivers who'd been first on the scene had found Terry between the third to fourth floor, on the metal stairs of his building. He was sprawled out, upside down and bleeding profusely from the head. They speculated a few scenarios, robbery, attempted murder, the least sensational of them was that Terry had arrived home intoxicated late Friday night, and that he had slipped and somehow fallen. There had been alcohol on his breath and a high level of it in his blood-work, the surgeon said.

I was totally jolted by that statement. I remembered that Terry's parents had been alcoholics and he had regularly gone to meetings of children of alcoholics. One of the few personal conversations we'd had, he revealed how much he resented their drinking, how he believed it had ruined his childhood. I'd always assumed that, among with his various other prissy characteristics, which included vegetarianism, would also be a ban on drinking. Guess I'd been wrong.

As the surgeon spoke, I realized he was telling me that if Terry ever came out of the coma, that he would have trouble with his hearing, his voice would sound different, and he'd have blurred or doubled vision. "There was damage done in the five or six hours he must have lain there bleeding out before he was found. I could repair some things, but those particular optic and aural centers... Well, he'll definitely need a lot of rehabilitation."

I hadn't known brain surgery was so advanced in 1989 that the surgeon could tell me exactly how Terry would see and hear if he recovered... *If he came out of the coma!?*

Then came the biggest surprise of all.

"Of course, we had to take all the needed precautions, given his positive HIV status."

On top of everything, it turned out Terry also had AIDS. Another secret I was discovering.

I believe it was at that point that I asked if I could sit down.

Δ

Like my other partner in GPNy, Terry Helbing was a Midwesterner. Terry was born on May 21, 1951, in East Dubuque, Illinois. Like Larry and me, his family background was about as bourgeois as they come. Terry's father was a prosperous banker, and there was a previous child, Doris, almost two decades Terry's senior, who was seldom a factor in his life.

Unlike our families, however, Terry's had a peculiarly middle-class dysfunction, both his parents would become alcoholics, and once he was in New York, Terry would become a determining factor in organizing one of the first local chapters of friends and relatives of alcoholics, Al-Anon. Despite his railing on about his many problems with his parents when he was young, substance abuse would haunt his life, and end up proving to be the key to Terry's own undoing long after his parents were dead.

Unlike the rest of his family, theater was Terry's obsession from an early age up until his last days on earth. And so, oddly enough, was amateur bowling. As a twelve-year-old, Helbing was already a league bowler and champion in Illinois. Once he was settled in New York, Terry took up bowling once again, often taking long subway cum bus rides to the far-flung reaches of New York's outer boroughs and suburbs every weekend he was not on stage because that was where the bowling alleys and best players were. In 1987, Terry, Ken Hale, and Tim Contini, along with thirty-seven other bowling participants founded the Gotham Open Tournament, which became a significant link in the International Gay Bowling Organization. According to Web site content from that club, "Terry Helbing, along with Hale and Contini, was a crucial ingredient from the very beginning." The first Gotham Open Tournament was held at the Thirty-fourth Avenue Bowl in Long Island City (Queens) and was comprised of ten local teams; the first team winners were Terry Helbing, Dan Romer, Scott Sullivan, and Malcolm Navias. Their team name: Lies 'Em In Alley.

There were other advantages besides the merely recreational and social ones to bowling. Terry's regular bowling was immediately apparent in his usually excellent physical condition; he was tall, fit, but neither slender nor lightweight. And this was especially apparent in his arms and legs. Often, just as we would be entering some occasion—party, theatre, bar—Terry would roll up his sleeves so his muscled forearms showed, and he had dozens of very short-sleeved shirts that he wore out, even in the dead of winter, to showcase his biceps—which he sheepishly admitted facilitated sexual hookups.

Like Larry Mitchell, Terry had also left the Midwest for New England, going to Emerson College in downtown Boston, then as now one of the few four-year colleges specializing in communications and performing arts. When he arrived in New York several years after graduation, he intended a career as an actor, an aspiration he cherished and worked toward for the rest of his life. However, the way he ended up earning a living was at *The Drama Review*, under its second editor, Michael Kirby.

A little of the magazine's history is instructive, as it both parallels and reflects the huge upheaval going on in field of drama during this time, and that ended up making drama so important an art form. Begun as *The Carleton Drama Review* in 1955, it was taken over at Tulane University in New Orleans when prodigy Richard Schechner joined the graduate faculty. There it became the *Tulane Drama Review* and prospered tremendously by following Schechner's dictum that it "challenge prevailing ideas about theatre, what it is, how it should be presented, and the rituals and ideals behind it." When Schechner began to encounter increasing conservative political and community pressure against his ideas in New Orleans, he and the six other Tulane doctoral professors quit the school's graduate program *en masse* in protest and moved to New York University, in effect eliminating completely Tulane's theater department professorial staff and throwing the graduate department into disarray for years. They brought the magazine along with them to NYU and renamed it *The Drama Review*, thus retaining its well-known three letter logo. In New York, Schechner's talents were more appreciated. He quickly formed The Performance Group, which made its mark with his play, *Dionysius in 69*, which infamously "broke the fourth wall" by actively including the audience in the action, and sometimes even "kidnapping" people off the nearby streets to participate.

Schechner left *TDR* in 1969, and after a brief stint by Erika Munk, Michael Kirby took over as editor, gradually altering the magazine to make it less an organ of social and political rebellion and returning its focus to theater. Terry Helbing began as Kirby's managing editor in 1974, and eventually became associate editor, and he remained until 1986, when Schechner regained control.

While there, Helbing himself edited several special issues: one on Jewish Theater that was widely praised; another, path breaking issue titled "Sex and Performance" in 1981, which for the first time brought GLBT theater works into prominent context for the academic world of theatre. Despite no longer being at *TDR*, Schechner's influence on Helbing's view of theater was immediately apparent to anyone (including me) who worked with him on-stage. And it was indisputable in the name Terry chose for his long-running theatre column, "The Fourth Wall."

His influential *Drama Review* position would give Terry stature in his chosen field and prove to be an important launching post for him as a review and column writer, as an editor and publisher, and even to some extent as a theater producer—but if he ever wrote a play, or even a dramatic sketch, none of his friends or colleagues heard of or read it. Later on, it would be me, a fledgling playwright at the time, not the experienced dramalogue Terry, who would end up editing Harvey Fierstein's *Torch Song Trilogy* for publication.

Before working for *TDR*, Terry had already begun his acting career, even his gay theatre career, appearing in the 1973 Boston and New England touring company of Jonathan Ned Katz's gay pride play, *Coming Out!* When Terry moved to Manhattan he shared an apartment at Fourteenth Street and Fourth Avenue with two women—one, Rachel Greene, became a lifelong friend, helpmate, caretaker, and, eventually, his executor. Terry got more acting parts, including in the original TOSOS production of Doric Wilson's *The West Street Gang*, a play about the Stonewall Riots performed at the infamous sex club, the Mineshaft, in which Helbing played a policeman. That's where I first encountered Terry.

Helbing's acting career would go on to include starring roles in Terry Miller's *Pines '79*, which he also produced for the Glines. He also starred in *The Demolition of Harry Fay*, by Sidney Morris, and appeared in *Franny, the Queen of Provincetown*, an adaptation of John Preston's popular 1983 novel about an effeminate man's travails in a gay male clone community. In 1991, Terry's last on-stage performance was in *Cocktails at the Red Rooster*, a benefit for Joseph's Surgical, an AIDS organization. When the Meridian Theater re-produced it, Terry also appeared in Doric Wilson's *Street Theater*. And according to Doric, in his last two years of life, Terry worked hard and traveled much after his accident to regain his voice, eyesight, and motor skills, primarily because he was intent on reviving his acting career.

Helbing's competence, general coolness under duress, and growing experience also led to him taking on non-acting work in the gay theater scene:

first as general manager for the Sixth Anniversary Repertory for the Glines, but more importantly as a producer himself.

For many gay people who focus on a single art, Terry Helbing, like Larry Mitchell, me, and many other writers of the post-Stonewall era, worked in a variety of capacities and in many media. In many senses, we *had to*: there was so much to be done and so few people who were out, talented, and also willing to work. Edmund White drew a portrait of the sophisticated gay man of the Seventies who had a successful career, great personal life, good sex life, lots of community connections, and who also belonged to a gym, knew all the latest pop music, could cook gourmet meals, and knowledgably discuss soprano Montserrat Caballé's tessitura. It was funny but true and undeniably hard work, compared to today, when many younger gay men pride themselves if they can use the Internet and still have nice abs.

Terry co-founded the Gay Theatre Alliance, an organization dedicated to the growth of gay theatre, and he served as its president. He would soon collate and edit the *Gay Theatre Alliance Directory of Gay Plays*, which he would publish through JH Press in 1980, the first complete listing of GLBT theater works. Helbing co-founded the Meridian Gay Theatre Production Company in 1983 with writer Terry Miller, to produce plays and musicals with gay and lesbian themes. The Meridian became the only continuously operating gay theatre with a home base on the East Coast, as considerable a venue as Minneapolis' concurrent Out And About Theater, and San Francisco's Theater Rhinoceros. Helbing became Meridian's Artistic Director, and together, Helbing and Miller initiated a Playwrights and Directors Series which featured staged readings of new plays and also sponsored a national gay playwriting contest every year until 1987.

During the late Seventies and throughout the Eighties, GLBT theatre was a small, but extremely active and vital force, both in the GLBT world and in the theatre world. As I've mentioned before, gay plays ran the gamut from angry, social protest, to light hearted comedies, from psychological portraits of GLBT characters in crisis, to wildly campy rewritings of previous genres, stealing from Dumas-tragedies, Thirties movies, and Fifties television. Few shows that were put on failed to find audiences, and while these were not large audiences—a typical GLBT theater had sixty to ninety-nine seats—some plays, like Wilson's *Street-*

Theater, Jane Chambers' *My Blue Heaven*, and my own *Immortal* ran months at a stretch. Actors moved back and forth from Broadway to Off Broadway and into GLBT theatre, and from those into movies and television. Many straight actors of that era got their first breaks with substantial parts inside gay plays—Jean Smart and Brad Davis come to mind.

Helbing had already begun writing articles on theatre, books, video, and music for *The Advocate, Christopher Street, Soho Weekly News, Seven Days, Genre, Theaterweek*, and many other publications. If that wasn't enough to do, Terry began his weekly theatre column, "The Fourth Wall," in the *New York Native*, and became theatre editor of the paper. His column included reviews of shows, theatrical compact discs, insider news, and information about upcoming shows of all types.

And, as a sidelight, Terry still had time and a consuming interest in what was the largest private collection I've ever encountered of Sixties girl-group singers. His tiny apartment on Charles Street in Manhattan's West Village soon had several entire living room walls devoted to stacks of LPs of probably every R&B singer or assemblage of the era. Along, naturally enough, with several pink plastic and Naugahyde portable record players of that era, both useful and valuable—if campy (sporting poodle skirt motifs and florid, embroidered signatures by Pat Boone, Peggy Lee, and Diana Ross)—collectibles. The little free time Helbing had in his ridiculously busy career and his bowling club schedule was spent cataloguing and taping the Shirelles, the Chiffons, Martha and the Vandellas, Little Eva, the Angels, et al.

Their bluesey lovelorn complaints and bubbly enticements to dance formed the background music to our GPNy meetings at his flat, especially the annual royalty statement get-togethers that Terry and I had in his small kitchen, four floors above Greenwich Street, where we'd compile and discuss book sales, returns, and check amounts for not only Gay Presses of New York titles, but since it was easier for two to do it (and to get it right) than one, for our own individual presses too. There, on his faux-wood 1955 metal table, amidst his usual vast aggregate of soda, chips, Chinese and Indian restaurant takeout, we'd happily enumerate, chat, and slowly get to know each other better.

Terry had begun JH Press in 1981, only a few months before he, Larry, and I had our first lunch together to discuss beginning a new composite publishing company. A windfall inheritance from his unmarried paternal uncle, Joseph Helbing, after whom the press—JH—was named, facilitated the process. Terry's belief that his uncle was a closeted gay man did the rest. But it was mostly based on his experience as an actor, stage manager, director, and producer that he'd encountered so much excellent talent in GLBT theater that he felt it was time to do something about it, to in Terry's own words, "put his money where his mouth was." The Gay Theater Alliance and the Meridian Gay Theater would be two of the most important manifestations of his enthusiasm. *The Gay Theater Alliance Director of Plays*, one of the first books out of JH press, would be one of his most lasting contributions; along with his anthology for Heinemann, *Gay Plays Today* (1988), a compendium still used in many academic courses.

Among the most uniquely talented of those Terry had encountered when I first met him was his own personal favorite, writer Jane Chambers. Born in Columbia, South Carolina in 1937, Jane's life and career can stand as a sad if eventually triumphant paradigm of what it meant to be a woman—and especially a lesbian—playwright during the twentieth century. She entered Rollins College at seventeen, but found that she could only be part of the playwriting or directing courses there if there were empty slots after the men had already taken their places. Frustrated, she went to California's Pasadena Playhouse from 1956 to 1957, briefly to New York City, ending up in Poland Springs, Maine, the next year where she worked a decade in the fledgling field of local television, an area hungry for talent and unafraid of intelligent, competent women. Twelve years later, Jane finally got her degree from Goddard College, in Vermont, where she met Beth Allen, who would become her manager, and life partner. In 1971, Jane won the Connecticut Education TV Award for her play, *Christ in a Tree House*. The following year Jane secured an important Eugene O'Neill Fellowship and worked on new plays that were produced at the O' Neill Theatre Foundation in New Haven.

This led Chambers back to New York, although unfortunately not to the theatre, but instead to television where—tellingly—she went to work as a writer for a soap opera, *Search For Tomorrow*, winning A Writer's Guild of America award for her writing for the show in 1973. At the same time she helped organize the Womens InterArts Center, where she began a theater program.

Chambers was thirty-seven years old in 1974, when Playwrights Horizons produced, *A Late Snow*, her first Off-Broadway production and one of the first openly lesbian and gay-positive plays. Other dramatic doors remained slow to open. Only in 1980, did The Glines produce what has come to be known as Jane's signature work, *Last Summer At Blue Fish Cove*, with a superb cast, starring Jean Smart who would go on to major parts in film, television series, and on Broadway. The story of a group of women at a summer colony one of who discovers—and carefully reveals to the others—that she is dying of cancer, the play was a critical and financial success. It was followed at the Glines by her comedy, *My Blue Heaven*, in 1982, but also, and alas with terrible irony, by Chambers' own diagnosis of brain cancer. The last of her plays done in her lifetime was *The Quintessential Image* at the Women's Theater Conference in Minneapolis in 1982.

Jane Chambers died early in 1983, in Greenport, Long Island. A modest, cheerful, gracious and loving person, she is now considered one of the most important women playwrights in American theater. Critic Beth A. Kattelman writes: "Chambers was one of the first playwrights to create openly lesbian characters who were comfortable with their own homosexuality. She believed that this would help eliminate homophobia.

As Chambers told *The New York Times*, 'As we become more comfortable with ourselves, the rest of the world will become comfortable with us.' She opened the door for other playwrights who wished to write affirming plays about lesbians." Even so, in Jane's own lifetime she experienced only a few short years of dramatic accomplishment and acclaim.

Terry Helbing had grown close to Jane and Beth when they all worked together at the Glines, and they remained close right up to first Jane's and then Terry's end. Helbing made it a primary directive of JH Press that Jane Chambers' genius, so long kept down, denied, and then cheated by an early death, would flourish and become more widely known. From 1982 on, Terry published all of her gay-themed plays through his JH Press, as well as putting out her book of poetry: *Warrior At Rest* and her sci-fi novel, *Chasin' Jason*. He even reprinted her 1974 lesbian-themed gothic novel, *Burning*, previously published in a Jove mass market edition.

Helbing also worked along with Beth Allen as manager/agent of Chambers' plays, and in the decade after Jane's death, productions proliferated around the country. His own Meridian Gay Theater did several in excellent productions. Terry considered it a real coup, when, at last in 1987, he was able to gain publishing rights to what he considered Jane's best play, *Last Summer at Bluefish Cove*. He put out the usual Gay Play Script Series trade paperback but in addition, he published a signed, limited edition hardcover, with an introduction that Jane had written long before in preparation for the volume. Helbing's personal feelings found an echo in those around him. Chambers' books consistently proved to be the best selling of all JH Press titles. And when he put together his *Gay Plays Today* anthology, he included Chambers' *Eye of the Gull*.

Clearly those who had attended Chambers' plays helped the sales, but since GLBT theatre barely existed outside of a half dozen already named places, it must have been more mainstream play audiences as well as GLBT readers who helped raise the sales of her, and other gay playwrights' works during this period, possibly because there was so little gay literature being published at all.

Terry was close to other colleagues he published. Terry Miller, in whose *Pines 1969*, he acted in and published in 1982, was a lifelong friend. Helbing also enjoyed Arch Brown, whose comedy *Newsboy* he put out in 1983; Terry produced Robert Chesley's *Stray Dog Story: An Adventure in 10 Scenes* at Meridian and published it in 1984; and C.D. Arnold, whose *The Dinosaur Plays* were also published by JH Press in 1984. Named The JH Press Gay Play Script Series, this was going to be only one part of a much larger venture—the publication of all minority theatre of value. In addition, Doric Wilson confirmed in a recent conversation that Terry planned to put out a Black Play Script Series, and a Women's Play Script Series. When Francine Trevens took over JH Press' line following Helbing's death, she followed his wishes by expanding TNT's gay script series and by adding in many more women playwrights.

One of Doric Wilson's best known plays had initiated the original JH Press series: *Forever After*, subtitled *A Vivisection of Gay Male Love without Interruption* (1980) while *Street Theater*, subtitled *The 27th of June, 1969* (i.e., the eve of the Stonewall Riots) came out seven years later. Doric and Terry remained friends, associates, and at times quite vocal brawlers throughout Helbing's life.

Aside from Chambers, perhaps the most unusual of Helbing's working friendships was with playwright Sidney Morris. JH Press would include two of Morris' plays in its Gay Script Series, *If This Isn't Love* in 1982, and *The Demolition of Harry Fay* (which Terry had starred in earlier) in 1986. For those in literary academia who may be thinking that Morris' name sounds awfully familiar, it might well be. Morris was known as one of the foremost authorities on Medieval English verse, and he compiled several anthologies, still in print and used today, including *Carmina Latina*, an olio of bawdy texts in that dead language similar to those used by Carl Orff in his choral masterpiece, *Carmina Burana.*

The Terry Helbing Papers, fifteen feet of records and personal papers, from the 1960s through the 1990s (most 1970s-1980s), are now located at The National Archive of Lesbian, Gay, Bisexual, and Transgender History at New York City's LGBT Center.

Δ

A week after his accident, I visited Terry Helbing in the semi-intensive care, semi-regular hospital room he'd been delegated to. I'd been asked to come at this time. Terry was about as he had been the last time I'd seen him, with a few less bandages around his head and with more florid bruising apparent around his neck, chest, and arms, I supposed from the fall.

Statuesque Tish and petite Rachel, his two closest friends, were there, and shortly after I arrived three more friends did too, including a befuddled and very upset Terry Miller who'd only found about his friend's accident the previous day.

We soon exited his room which we'd overcrowded and Rachel called us to order in a nearby waiting room. Rachel was Terry's executor, both of his will and of his health care situation. This had been decided upon before—I'm guessing when he revealed his HIV status to her. She'd flown down from Canada, and was currently staying in Terry's apartment. She'd contacted his sister and husband and they were on their way from Phoenix. Rachel would remain in New York, and take over Terry's heath, his recovery, in short, his life. She was under no illusions about how difficult that would be, but she was committed to it. I was knocked out by her love and her selflessness. In retrospect, I still am.

Quickly enough it was decided that we six people would be Terry's support network. This was a concept gay men and their friends had invented over the past few years to deal with our friends and lovers dying of AIDS, which could often become a long, difficult, and indeed a quite harrowing affair, and always far too much for any one or even two people to do alone.

I felt distinctly out of place and even somewhat embarrassed to be among this group of close friends as they circled their wagons around their fallen comrade. Recall, I never really cared for my business partner. Still, I was there in the capacity of his business partner, holder of the health insurance policy, and Rachel would need me to take over and help her with JH Press, to which I readily agreed: Terry and I had talked enough about it that I assumed that was something I could do. Unable to escape the room without causing a stir, I listened and at last was persuaded to spend an hour or so one or two days a week, visiting Terry here in his room, either talking to his comatose form or reading aloud to him, both being fairly standard ways of actually reviving the comatose.

This "treatment" had somehow been determined to be the best way to have a coma patient snap out of a coma. Everyone—nurses, doctors, cleaning people, but especially Terry's friends—would incessantly talk to him or in some other way verbally engage his attention, for hours, every day. The schedule was made out and as I liked Rachel and felt very sorry for her and as I'd also gone out of my way to care like this for my younger brother six years before and then, somewhat differently, for Bob Lowe only a few years before this incident, I agreed to be part of it. It turned out to be an excellent decision with all kinds of odd benefits.

Because the method somehow worked: after ten weeks, Terry suddenly woke up. I was out of town for the event, and when I returned and met with Rachel and walked over to St. Vincent's with her, I didn't know what to expect. She'd warned me not to expect the Terry I had once known. Physically, Rachel said, he was the same Terry, if necessarily gaunter than before, and with shorter hair. So she prepared me.

It turned out to be completely insufficient preparation. When I visited, Terry stood up, and while his face and every feature were exactly as I recalled them, this was definitely not the Terry Helbing I knew but instead a new, and utterly different person looking out at me through those familiar gray-green eyes.

Rachel had explained to me Terry's "loss" as a result of head trauma. What she hadn't explained, and possibly didn't know how to explain, was that this person was a hundred and eighty degrees apart from the man I'd last seen on a street corner in the West Village several months earlier. This person was a child: innocent, trusting, smiling, eager, and a little unsteady on his feet. Furthermore, he was a child with AIDS, although he wasn't symptomatic yet. Rachel and I would take weeks trying to find a way to tell him about his illness. Now was not the right time.

First, he needed to be exercised, Rachel said, while she did something legal downstairs. A robe was put around his shoulders, over his pajamas, and unsteadily, Terry leaned close against me, and we ver-ry slow-ly walked down a hallway. He had nothing to say. It seemed he still couldn't talk well yet—the neurosurgeon had mentioned that—and in fact speech returned fast to Terry, although it would return with a completely different, and higher pitched, voice. But this six-foot child I was helping walk would touch me to slow down, touch me twice to stop so he could rest, and we'd sit, then he'd touch me to get up again and walk the long corridor and rest in another little waiting room.

I was more horrified by all this than I let on, and more than I could possibly utter at the time, and I'm still not sure I can express how deeply horrified I was. Like most people who live in and through the mind, what I most fear is losing my mind. Terry had in fact lost his mind because of an accident. He was an infant. He was a big, babbling infant. Objectively I could see why and how. It didn't make me a whit less horrified.

Rachel meanwhile had read entire books and medical tracts on head trauma and its many variegations and she was totally into Terry's pathology. I suppose because she first met Terry when he was younger, and so when he was still kind of innocent, the difference between a few months ago and now wasn't quite so unassimilable as it was for me. She spoke in great detail and with seemingly complete medical knowledge of his condition, of his prognosis and of his progress chart.

"What about his memory?" I asked. "What does he remember?"

"He remembers the people who love him," she replied.

Oy! That wasn't good.

"Is that because you are all around him all the time since he woke up," I asked.

"Difficult to say," she admitted. "But since we *are* all around him now, he does know he's loved and protected, and everyone from surgeon to social worker agrees that means he'll heal faster and better.

Her change of my word "you" to "we" was not lost on me.

Then Rachel added, "We've got plenty of women and we've got Terry Miller, but he still needs a strong, male figure too."

For better or worse and no matter how I felt about it, I was officially part of Terry Helbing's rehabilitation: Daddy.

I continued to visit Terry and to help him physically exercise. We walked faster and he more easily. I played ball with him, with a near weightless nerf ball, sometimes sitting, from lap to lap so he could improve his rather spotty hand-eye coordination.

He did begin to speak and he always knew who I was but his voice never changed back to that "seen-it-all, been-there-kid," cynical baritone I recalled. And it never seemed to lose that freshness and wonder I'd noticed from after his reawakening. Also his eyes remained big and innocent and trusting where before they'd been narrowed most of the time as though having to pre-filter light and life from entering his mental field of vision. Slowly, day by day, my horror at his condition began to dissipate, although my queasiness never quite did until Terry was back at home again.

Once or twice, Terry referred to "all my friends, who I love, and who've been so good to me," in his new six-year-old conversation mode with me during a particular exercise session, because by now he had progressed and was about six mentally, although maturing weekly. I said nothing back because how, after all, do you tell a six-year-old you never did actually love him?

Even so, it was clear: Terry had re-booted.

He was hospitalized for months, during which I was away traveling on a book tour weeks at a time, including to places like England and Japan. When I returned one time, he was out of the hospital and in his apartment again, living with Rachel.

When I visited, he was mentally progressing too—about in his new twelfth or thirteenth year: Still innocent, still sweet, even happier to see me. We went for walks around the Village and he'd tell me street names—he was reading now well, despite his vision problems, for that handsome young neurosurgeon had been absolutely right there too and Terry would undergo vision treatments the rest of his life—and Terry would ask me questions, some of which Rachel had foisted off, telling him to ask me, especially questioning about sex and relationships.

That's when the topic of AIDS came up again. Evidently Rachel had sat him down while I was gone and told him he had AIDS, at that time a more or less untreatable illness. Terry explained to me what Rachel had told him about the disease and we went in some detail, especially about some symptoms he might expect, some time in the future. He didn't quite believe it. He didn't quite understand how he had acquired the disease, and I knew too little in the way of details about his past to be able to tell him. I did try. He seemed generally disbelieving, and, because somehow, and I might be wrong on this, I never got the sense that after his accident Terry was ever again sexually active, at least not with anyone I ever heard of. (This has since been disproven by others of his acquaintance I've spoken with.)

By then, I'd been forced to move out of my wonderful duplex apartment on Eleventh Street where I'd been thirteen and a half years and I was now living further away from Terry on the north-westernmost edge of the West Village. I'd go get him on sunny afternoons and we would walk along the river front, which the city fathers in their infinite wisdom had finally allowed to totally decay to complete uselessness.

I began testing his memory a bit and it became clear that while he knew he had worked with me and with someone named Larry, that he only "remembered" that really because of what others—Tish, Rachel—had told him.

He seemed happy and proud of what he'd been told he and we had accomplished at GPNy but in an aloof, distant way, as though it were something that happened to someone he'd once known a long time ago. He was slowly and truly remembering his youth, the previous one, and his teen years, and even a little of his college years. And that's about as far as his memory extended.

What's intriguing is that little by little, Terry recovered his adult intelligence—he was able to go back to writing theatre reviews. But he never recovered all of it. His mathematical ability, of which he'd once been very proud, was pretty much gone, never to return. And his memory remained very limited, and quite distant from the present too.

I found this to be frustrating and continued to try to get back his memory to when we were first working together in GPNy. To no apparent avail.

There were several reasons for my trying. One was normal curiosity: how exactly did memory work? What could he actually recall?

Another was self-interest and company-interest, because, recall, Terry had been GPNy's financial officer. Aside from running JH Press which I now did completely, another job I had been forced to take over and now held besides Editor in Chief, was Chief Financial Officer. Let's also recall also that the night he ended up in a coma, Terry was supposed to have brought me and mailed to Larry three months worth of his accounting for the Gay Presses of New York: papers, by the way, that were *never found* upon his person, nor in his files in his apartment, nor anywhere.

Why should that be of any real importance, compared to the hell Terry had gone through?

Well, it wasn't really, except that after some weeks of going over what I could find in his flat of GPNy's accounts receivable and accounts payable and the company checkbook and Terry's previous months accounts, I still couldn't get any of them to fit together in any kind of coherent fashion. And, because somehow or other, although I couldn't ever figure out how, GPNy was missing money to the tune of, and I was never a mathematician, some *ten thousand dollars*! This was a considerable amount of money for a small press with modest profit margins and it might have opened up all kinds of abysses had Larry and I been other than who we were: i.e., less interested in money than in Terry's welfare. Sometimes I wondered if Terry had taken the money or used it somehow and was hiding the fact, got drunk and fell down, and thus unconsciously gotten himself out of the questions that would have arisen if we'd known the truth. Sorry, but I'm a novelist and can't help thinking like one.

Within a few months, Terry began showing symptoms of AIDS and despite the medicines of the day—mostly AZT—his illness followed the standard two-year progression we'd already become so achingly familiar with. This didn't keep him from continuing to want to be an actor. According to Doric Wilson, he was doing whatever he could to audition and in fact ended up playing in an off-off Broadway play by Sidney Morris.

Shortly after, I was once more visiting Terry in the hospital. One time, he clearly believed he was in a theater lobby during intermission, and I didn't correct him. Clearly the HIV virus had passed beyond the blood-brain barrier and was causing dementia. A few days later he phoned me, very upset. His good pal, Terry Miller, had told him that he was suffering mental lapses from the illness. It was more like degenerative vascular dementia, I knew. It took me a half hour to calm him down and tell him it wasn't really important. All that counted was that he feel better enough to go back home.

He did. And he remained home for a while. His job as theater critic for three or four journals meant he was going to the theater six nights a week. But now he was suffering from HIV fatigue and he'd grown afraid that between the drugs he'd zone out and fall asleep and miss something important. So he asked three friends to join him, one each night, to catch anything he might have missed, in effect, to back him up, the way that a disk or USB flash drive backs up files on a computer.

I agreed to be one of the three and for almost a year I saw theater one or two nights a week in Terry's company. Most of the hundred or so plays were indifferent, if well acted and well directed—simply not memorable. A few were standouts: for example, in two successive nights we saw productions of Jessica Lange and Alec Baldwin in *A Streetcar Named Desire*, and Peter Gallagher singing as Sky Masterson in *Guys and Dolls*.

Then Terry was hospitalized again. When I went to visit, just as I was saying hello, all the machines around him began going off, blinking and whistling. In seconds, a horde of young doctors and nurses had invaded the room and surrounded him, barking out orders and responses. When I last saw Terry, he was totally out of it, his body being handled by three of them.

The month of March had always been significant for GPNy and March of 1994 was no different. On March 8th of that year, Terry Helbing died.

Following the memorial service for him, Rachel Green informed me that I was one of his six heirs. A few minutes later, Francine Trevens approached me. She had worked with Terry at The Meridian Gay Theater, and in fact, had directed the production of my play, *One O'clock Jump* when it was paired with *Killer Bangs*. Francine already knew from Rachel that I had inherited JH Press from Terry. She didn't know what my plans for it were. If, however, I didn't want to continue to operate it, she was interested in obtaining rights for most of the plays already published. She and a friend were beginning a GLBT play production/publication company. She was especially anxious to obtain the right to Jane Chambers' and Doric Wilson's works.

It turned out that I'd inherited not only JH Press, but also a small sum of cash. I did sell Francine the plays and rights she wanted, for not much money, and in addition, the Doric Wilson play rights that SeaHorse owned. It had been three years since SeaHorse Press had put out a book. Most of our titles were down to under a hundred copies, in some cases down to a dozen copies. My other partner, Larry Mitchell, was now legally blind from macular degeneration. He had stopped writing. He'd even stopped talking about his Calamus Press putting out his friend Jeff Weiss' play trilogy, which he'd spoken of as an ongoing dream for a decade. It wasn't too difficult to see the writing on the wall.

Within days, I'd decided to close down SeaHorse Press as well. Coolly enough, I wrote official letters to any author who still had titles with SeaHorse Press ceding back their publication rights to them. I offered to sell them whatever copies were still in the warehouse, at a very deep discount. I then began a book tour of Germany for the twelfth anniversary of *The Lure* there, in a brand new translation. When I returned a month later, I would write the same letter to GPNy authors, giving rights back to them. I moved to Berlin, Germany for the summer of 1994.

My days as a publisher were clearly over. Among GPNy authors and friends so many were dead: Jane Chambers, Terry Helbing, Bob Chesley, Alan Bowne, Clark Henley, four members of the Violet Quill Club, David Martin, George Stravinos, George Stambolian, Robert Mapplethorpe, Terry Miller,

Greg Kolovakos, just among those I'd worked with at the presses, dozens more among my social group, and more were dying daily.

In the years to come, I did not look back, I did not think about it, I did not contemplate what it had been, nor what it could have become. Nor did I think about Terry Helbing's amazing life. Until now. Not once.

The Bike Race

Ricky Hersch

I'd be lying to say I recall when Ricky Hersch first appeared in my life. Undoubtedly he was in the background for some time, as I was in his periphery for years, as he was part of the large Taylor clan which seemed to fill every available room of the rambling house where my friend Gregory lived. Ricky and I met not cute but hostile. I remember it well because it was the occasion of one of Gregory's experiments—one designed weeks before to solve a problem on the extensive, mostly wild Taylor property: field mice.

The three-story rickety house was one of the first erected in that section of our suburb. My best friend Martin claimed it had been built in the eighteenth century when it was known as the Gossage Farm, but the original edifice must have been torn or burned down and replaced by a mid-nineteenth-century structure. It was painted an off-shade of green during those years (Russian Green, in fact, though no one knew that at the time) with pebbled gray slate on its scores of roofs and dormers. Built off the ground upon a fieldstone foundation only partly hidden by a cement coating, the house possessed a half-dozen porches and out buildings which during the Twenties and Thirties had been attached and appropriated as sewing rooms, laundries, pantries, and extra bedrooms as the Taylor family grew. The Hersch's had come to live there at the death of Ricky's father in the Korean War, after he'd sired a "baseball team" (my father's term) of kids. Ricky was the eighth, considered the baby.

This old house would have been a remarkable eyesore in our middle class neighborhood if it weren't situated rather far back from the street and if it hadn't been pretty well covered by a small stand of obscuring hickory trees—grown enormous by the time I was a child. Further hiding the ramshackle main house was a Concord grape arbor of some size and yield (and beauty when in full leaf and fruit, from August to October) attached to a trellised-over garage extension; and even more extraordinary, two dozen of the largest, hardiest, and most colorful azaleas and hydrangeas in the area (blue heads of flowers the size of a tricycle wheel)—the envy of my mother and other gardening hobbyists. Deeper within the acre of Taylor property other botanical splendors abutted scenes of utter dilapidation: a lilac tree that had drifted up into the telephone wires suspended enormous flotillas of perfumed purple blooms that shaded the Taylor's unsavory pet graveyard; the backyard compost heap, once declared a public menace, gave way to three comice pear saplings which almost curtseyed by October from the weight of their large and luscious yellow fruit.

Naturally in such a disorganized place field mice would set up nests, construct warrens, and thrive. There seemed to be a sufficient abundance of fruit, garden vegetables, and flowers for the Taylors, Herschs and the field mice to coexist peacefully together. Then there was Gregory's aged grandmother who hadn't stepped out of the house, or in fact beyond the backyard veranda, in five years since the day she had stepped directly onto the body of a particularly plump field mouse, which she had instantly killed and which had sent her spinning back into the house, screaming. Mr. Taylor and the older Taylor and Hersch boys had declared war on the helpless animals with varying results. Poisons and traps in an incredible variety of sizes and methods of mutilation were laid down monthly with little or no effectiveness. The field mouse population continued to thrive.

All this was nonsense to Gregory. He and his friends had nothing against the small gray-brown creatures. To us, their fugitive existence was simply another allure of the Taylor property as a play area. The yard was filled with children no matter the time of year—although it was most enticing in summer when it was most alive with toads, turtles, the numerous Taylor cats, and the Hersch puppies. It was also the coolest spot in the neighborhood because of all the shade trees. But, tolerant as Gregory was, he was foremost a scientist, so, for a period of six months those few field mice still alive in the traps were carefully killed, preserved, and dissected until he knew every capillary and nerve ending. Later on, once he discovered the properties of what he called "Greek Fire" —i.e., the diesel fuel kept in barrels behind the garage, used in the usually inoperable pickup Mr. Taylor owned, Gregory decided on a more elaborate enterprise: the mass extinction of the mice.

His plan had the elegance of a fine scientific experiment and the spectacle of a Cecil B. DeMille epic. He proposed digging tiny ditches connecting all the areas on the property where mice had been seen or their warren holes were suspected of being. These ditches were to be filled with Gregory's potential fire, and set alight. He enlisted our help in the scheme and we readily agreed. It was one of those long autumn weekends with nothing more inviting to hold our attention, and we all looked forward to seeing come true his vision of ringing the yards with a sizzling mouse-toasting fire that would last fifteen minutes and be otherwise unperilous. Gregory had verbally pictured the plan to us in images so sensational they dwarfed the Dresden firebomb photos his shell-shocked Uncle Joe from upstate New York had shown us.

It was a hazy afternoon promising a shower by sunset, when we were all ready. The small central ditch in front of us was filled with diesel fuel and the surrounding ditches were sprinkled with it. We'd already been given a test display, seen how the fire changed along a narrow slot of ground and gathered force until it intensified into a powerful beam of destruction that could enter a pinhole open in a mouse warren and explode it with a soft, fleshy burst of sound, scattering dirt, and decimated rodents. We were excited by the prospect of running alongside the ditches watching as one after another of the mouse communities—hated now because slated for death—exploded. Ricky Hersch biked into the yard right onto a ditch and rocked the front wheel, collapsing the carefully constructed earth battlement.

Gregory all but collapsed with the sudden frustration of his grand plan for extinction by his cousin's unthinking *deux ex machina*. Our other pals, Martin, James Kallas, myself, Billy and Andy Taylor, and even Cal Hersch, Ricky's older brother, jumped up from where we had hunkered down awaiting the conflagration and began shouting for Ricky to "get off there, stupid!" Which Ricky refused to do. When we ran up to him and attempted to explain what we were trying to accomplish, it was obvious from the sneer of his perfectly modeled lips, the disdain in his pale green eyes, and the toss of his long mahogany hair that he knew very well what was going on and why. And though he didn't give a damn about the mice—he scarcely gave a damn about his family, Gregory more than once had told me—it amused him to see his cousin's scheme so easily ruined.

"It won't work anyway," he said.

That meant to me that Ricky wanted to humiliate his cousins—and my good friend Gregory—yet again. Enraged, I pushed through the group, shoved Ricky off his bike, and commanded the others to rebuild the ditch so the experiment could continue.

I didn't see but I certainly felt the punch Ricky landed on my back when I turned to help them, a punch aimed at my kidney. I fell onto the ground, but managed to grab one of Ricky's legs, bringing him down too. Soon the field mouse holocaust was forgotten as he and I began to punch, wrestle, slug, and slap each other with the cold ferocity of grown-ups who've hated each other for decades. Feeble attempts by the other boys to stop us gave way to cheers and shouts. Soon, kids from nearby yards and streets ran to watch us knock each other down, get up again, then knock each other down again, moving clear around the property until we were at the front of the house. There, just under the third-story window we continued, until Ricky's mother, who'd been washing windows, broke us up by emptying a pail of soapy water on top of our heads.

Wet, groggy, black and blue, bleeding, surrounded by friends and protectors, I staggered to my feet to see Ricky do the same, ready to square off again, although it was clear that neither of us would be able to throw a punch if we tried. I hoarsely shouted, "And if I hear you're ever bothering Gregory again, I'll *annihilate* you!" By then Mrs. Hersch and two of Ricky's older sisters had come downstairs and were trying to hustle him into the house. Ricky was still able to stand his ground for another minute to yell back, "And I'll *decapitate* you if you try," before he was pulled up the back porch steps and inside.

Right then I knew I'd won our fight with a word—a word I'd heard in one of those by now forgotten Grade-B sci-fi films I'd recently seen—a word better than Ricky's word, more unusual, more appropriate, and possessing that magical sense that words still hold for children as they do for primitive tribesmen.

I remained at the Taylor's long enough that afternoon to watch Gregory's experiment succeed. Then James Kallas took me to his house, where his Aunt Damita (who didn't speak English) salved and bandaged the worst and most obvious of my wounds and bruises so that when I finally got home my mother could easily recognize that I was out of mortal danger, and so yell and threaten me with a week of staying in my room (which she soon forgot) with only half the passion she would have expended if I were truly hurt.

A week later, as the temporarily retightened quartet of pals walked home from school, I asked Gregory if his cousin had bothered him anymore. He said no. Then added, "But he wants to race you." Before I could say I would race him any time, Gregory added darkly, "through the underground road of the new shopping mall."

This was a real challenge and it was obvious that Ricky wanted revenge for my good word which had defeated him. Hillside Mall was a partly-finished edifice built on what had been a series of abandoned lots, which when completed—some said it would take another two years—would be the largest shopping mall on Long Island. The central core of buildings was almost a mile long and all deliveries were to be made through a road that ran beneath the mall, directly to scores of storage basements. The entire area was fenced off, forbidden. We'd bicycled around it dozens of times and knew there was only one weekend watchman. While he had a formidable reputation, he couldn't be all over the site at the same time.

We were most attracted by the long, sloping tunnels which dipped into darkness at each end of the mall. Junior Cook and his henchman, Mike Bayley, were the only kids we knew who'd ever biked into the tunnel and they reported that it was long, straight, dark as pitch, except for small ceiling-hung lights every few hundred feet. In their recitations, long after the experience, awe and a sense of danger overcome by the slimmest margin was apparent. If fourteen-year-old toughs felt that way, you can imagine how we would feel. And that was to be the location of the bike race between me and Ricky Hersch! Naturally, I told Gregory I'd take up his cousin's dare, and my friends began to discuss what kind of flowers to place on my grave. But I didn't set a date for the meeting and almost a month went by before Ricky did, which built my confidence. It could only mean one thing: Ricky was as afraid of the race and location as I was.

Δ

Children are the best anticipators because of their impatience, their unsteady grasp of time—it's "entirely" psychological, subjective; and clocks are the biggest liars—their construction of futures and emendations of those futures all conspire to aid them. Watching a child anticipate, we feel certain he'll be disappointed with the banal activity when it arrives. Hasn't that happened to us innumerable times? Or has it? Children need an actual acknowledged catastrophe to be disappointed in a plan or project they've invested so much in. Amazed, we observe them sincerely delighted in seeing for the fifth time a full-length cartoon they know half the dialogue and all of the action too. They clearly haven't forgotten it, yet it has become in some way new, unexpected, unparalleled in their experience. Some Zen Buddhists believe that if we could all honestly recapture this enchantment with what life offers as though it were always new, we would not become children but wise men: we'd live forever, balanced on the ingenuous edge of security and the unprecedented.

Greatly as I and my friends had anticipated the bicycle duel with Ricky Hersch at the unfinished Hillside Mall, detailed as were our various, ever-altering scenarios for what would occur there, none of us were actually prepared for its eventuality. This might explain our surprise—and my own momentary consternation—when Gregory met us in the school yard after lunch the Monday after my parents' "discussion" of my reading and told us that Ricky wanted to speak to me. At first I was certain he was going to back out. But when the four of us went to the deepest recess of the paved school playground where Ricky's cohorts from Six-Three hung out, I knew he wouldn't be able to back out if he wanted to. Nor, surrounded by my own friends, could I. We locked onto each other aloofly; the other eight or nine boys kept their distance but remained well within listening range.

Ricky opened up by saying, "I see you're all healed up."

I countered offhandedly, "There wasn't much to heal up."

His green-gray eyes narrowed a bit as he inspected my face. "No? Well there'll be plenty after Saturday."

"I'll race you anytime. Any place."

"Under the Hillside Mall, "he quickly said. "Saturday at four in the afternoon."

"That's fine," I countered, watching for a reaction.

None was forthcoming, but his pretty face did seem to soften a bit, and for the first time I noticed how dark and straight his eyebrows were, except over his left eye where the fine hair was devilishly raised in a tiny mischievous caret.

"Good," he said. "I'll meet you there."

The other boys quickly gathered as Ricky and I stepped apart. They too agreed to meet at the entrance to the mall on Saturday. All of us would be needed on bikes, they thought, to keep track of the watchman and to distract him from the race if necessary. One of each friend would have to be stationed at the tunnel entrance to make sure we set off together, two more at the exit to declare the winner.

My only concession to the race that week was a complete overhaul of my bicycle. I wanted nothing to fail me. I inspected the French racing tires to forestall any rips in the thick outer brushed-silk grooves, the slender rubber tubes within. I reset the sprocket gears and tested them at different settings until I found a combination that would start off slowly in first gear, sail into a strong cruising second, then give me a lightning jump in third for the last lap of the race. I cleaned and polished the gears until they shone. I tightened and polished every connecting bolt on the bike. I stripped off the front basket, the front lamp, even the tiny tool kit. I experimented with the seat and handlebars until I'd achieved as angled-in a relationship between them as my body could fit. Aerodynamics meant speed and I intended to be riding almost horizontal—just like the prize winning French bicyclists. I removed the fenders—mudguards, my mother called them; at the speed I expected to be traveling others, not I, would have to watch out for splashes. A month before, I had installed a small handbrake attached to a black wheel drum that cost twenty-five dollars of my allowance money, and found that it, rather than the old foot brake, gave better control in sharp turns. Fearing that in my excitement I might instinctively hit the foot brakes without meaning to, I disconnected them.

To test out this almost-new speed vehicle, I took a long ride out to a huge concrete paved parking lot connected to a shopping mall in Manhasset, similar to the one where we would be racing, and ran the bike through its paces, turning myself at the same time as I tested its abilities in u-turns and sudden descents. It required some getting used to. Right after the race I would have to change some of the alterations back: a hair-trigger response was the last thing I wanted when dawdling around the neighborhood. But it felt marvelous; for the first time I understood how a machine and a man could be a single integrated unit bent on one aim—winning. By the time I was done, it was dark and I had to ride home without a horn or headlight, through side streets, extra alert to any unexpected traffic. That night after dinner and television, I quietly went down to the garage to check if the machine had sustained any damage during the difficult test. None.

Martin, James Kallas, and Gregory arrived at my house at three the next afternoon. We fooled around for a half hour, then got on our bikes without a word and rode to the mall. Ricky's friends were already there. One had been there on and off all day and had been chased off by the watchman earlier. He described the man as a "linebacker, a real bear." No one had seen the watchman since they'd arrived although they biked around the place twice. One boy was still out in case the watchman made a last-minute appearance.

Ricky showed up wearing an overlarge, old leather jacket that I recognized as his father's, the dead G.I. I guessed it was supposed to be his lucky charm. Its cracked brown shine set off his pale skin, his dark straight, hair, the tiny commas of red high on each cheekbone. I thought I'd never seen a handsomer boy. For a minute I wished we didn't have to be opponents but could be friends. Knowing that could not be, I made another wish, that Ricky Hersch would never grow old: would always remain as he was that afternoon.

We shook hands, then Martin and one of Ricky's friends rode over to the exit. The scout approached to say that all was clear—no sign of the watchman. We all rode to the entryway, peered into the dark unknown at the end of the open ramp, all of us hesitating with one excuse or another, half-on, half-off our bikes, pedaling idly around in small circles, talking. When Gregory spotted a gray Chevy coming our way, both Ricky and I said: "The watchman!" "Let's do it!"

"Now!" I answered.

The car closed in fast. We heard someone shouting, "Hey, you kids!" out the window. But we were ready. On the mark... *Go!* We swept down the incline into the tunnel as we heard our friends yelling and speeding off above.

If ever for a split second I believed in any concept of Hell, it had to have resembled that almost soundless, incredibly fast race under the uncompleted mall. We both hit a light bump at the bottom and as our bikes easily jumped over it. I could make out what seemed an endless nothingness dimly lighted by yellow ceiling lamps within chrome casings placed so far apart that long stretches of darkness lay between. Streaks of puddles from the last rain suddenly splattered under our bike tires, the carcasses of rats and cats and who knows what other animals lay alongside them, sometimes right in the oil-slicked water. With each flicker of the distorting vague lamplight, I was able to make out our shadows: the side walls we sped past sketched with damp mold chalked with the names of prospective businesses they would become cellars for. A few concrete loading platforms. A parked truck facing us (we flashed around either side). Walking, we might have seen more, been able to read the names of the stores, clearly identify and thus negate the sinister ambiguities of these features. But I had popped into second gear as we'd landed and I could hear the madly regular pedaling of Ricky's feet as we raced along the rugged concrete road, swaying slightly every now and again as a sudden gust of fetid air struck us from God alone knew what quirk of ventilation or atmosphere. I was already half-nauseated with the close dampness, half-blinded by the ever-changing light, short of breath from exertion, unsure most of the time exactly where Ricky was (I thought just behind me). After he switched into his cruising mode, all that told me I wasn't alone in the unexpectedly eerie long tunnel was the sudden unsyncopated ghost of a splash as he followed through each puddle.

I knew I was ahead: my bicycle had been primed to win and my legs were pedaling so fast the gears spun out twice—but I coasted, lifting my feet off a second until they caught again. I was so in rhythm with the bike they always caught exactly right before the bike could slow down. I thought I heard voices ahead, wondered if it were another distortion—like the light, the air, the wind currents—inside the tunnel. Then I thought I saw a steady growing glimmering ahead. I prepared myself to shift into third gear for the ascent, glad to be getting out of the place. I sped into a new kind of light that I knew had to be from the outside. When I looked behind I could barely make out Ricky. I felt a bump beneath the tires just like the one we had hit landing, and I was about to go up, out of the tunnel. I'd won!

Looming in front of, above me, was a huge bulk of shadow. At first I thought it was far off, another parked truck perhaps, and I prepared to get around it. Then it seemed to turn, turn around and become a recognizable figure—the dreaded watchman. He must have seen us ride down and drove to this opening to catch us.

My bike shot up into his large, swearing face, and he threw his arms out and began to zigzag so I couldn't get past. I aimed for the space between the far side wall, and he threw out one paw and tried to grab the handlebar. I was going too fast for him to hold on, but he exerted enough thrust to add a new vector to my direction and to send the bike into a sharp swerve, directly into the wall. I saw the bike lean over, begin to fall beneath me. I couldn't stop, it was going so fast, so out of control. I didn't even have time to put out a foot to somehow brake myself—the normal reaction in such a situation. I gripped the hand-brake and it squealed like a dying animal as the wheels slid on the pavement. The bike and I impacted the wall straight on. With my left arm raised to cover my face, I flew right over it, hearing the metallic clangor of the bike on the other side. Astonished, spinning over the wall, hitting the pavement, I actually saw stars— blue, yellow, red stars against a black satin scrim—just like characters in comic books when Superman or Batman socked them. I heard yelling; the watchman was furious. Everything fell away—sight, hearing, touch.

Only for a second. I opened one eye, couldn't open the other, and saw the huge man above me, both hands on Ricky's shoulders. Ricky stared down at me, horrified, I thought—this is the end, I'm a goner and closed my eyes. Everything in my body felt broken. I blacked out again.

I could hear Ricky's voice very close to my face: he must have knelt down. He sounded frightened. "I think he's still alive. I'm not sure. You look."

"He'd *better* be alive." The watchman sounded frightened too.

"Look!" Ricky said.

"No." The voice backed away. "What in the hell were you kids doing down there in the first place? You're not supposed to be here, damn you!"

"I saw you grab him," Ricky said, with amazing sang-froid. "I was right behind. I saw you grab him. If he's dead, it's all your fault. I'll testify in court."

"*What?* You weren't supposed to be down there."

"If he's dead," Ricky repeated, "you're going to be in real trouble. You deliberately grabbed him. You killed him."

I felt hair brush my lips: Ricky's hair from its silky length as he leaned over to listen for my heartbeat. He must have found it, because he suddenly whispered. "Can you get up? If you can move, jerk your right leg."

I didn't know whether I could get up or not. I knew I didn't want to be dead, so I jerked my right leg.

"He's alive! His leg moved!" Ricky said excitedly. "You'd better call an ambulance. Quick! If he dies because there isn't medical help, you'll really pay for it!"

The watchman must have come closer, because Ricky said: "No! Don't move him! Don't touch him! You might make it worse. I take First Aid in school. You aren't supposed to move an accident victim. His guts might fall out or his neck and back could be broken."

"Jesus!" the watchman said. "Stay here with him. There's a phone in an empty store I use as an office. Don't move him. You goddamn kids. All I need now is a lawsuit. Or to lose my job because you little bastards had to come here and race your..."

His mumbling became more distant, was finally gone.

"Can you get up?" Ricky asked. "If you can, you better do it right now."

I opened my eyes, saw gray sky, attempted to move. Ricky helped me to my feet. "Anything broken?" he asked.

I wasn't sure. I nodded "no" though my left leg was killing me.

"Quick," he said. "We've got to get out of her before he gets back or we're really in Dutch."

He pulled my bicycle up from where it had crashed, and placed it more or less under me. "Understand?" he asked me.

I nodded again, wobblingly gripped the slightly askew handlebar—my poor bike!—lifted myself onto the seat and almost fell off. Ricky held the handlebars and urged me to try again. I did. The bike wobbled badly on the right side. He saw it, and gave me his bike, then took mine.

"Come on! Let's go!" he whispered. We pedaled across the shortest distance of open paved parking lot into some trees separating the mall from the next street. "Come on!" he insisted. Painful as it was for me, distressed as I was by the condition of my bicycle—the handbrake completely gone, the seat awry, the front wheel spokes bent—I had to laugh seeing him ride it like a clown in the most distant ring of the circus. It kept pulling to one side, and he had to constantly lean the other way. It couldn't have been easy, but he did it and kept looking back to urge me on.

We got through the trees and I followed his shortcut through someone's backyard onto a single lane macadam road through a section of one story cottages I'd never seen before. Then over an unused railroad track half hidden in tall grass, through empty lots onto another single lane street I wasn't familiar with.

Only when we'd gotten onto our side of the Cross Island Expressway did I feel safe enough to give into the chills and trembling that had begun to take hold of my body. We rode along the service road. I swerved onto one of the endless lawns that fronted the expressway, almost crashing into a tree. I fell off the bike clutching myself: I'd never felt so cold in my life.

"What's wrong?" Ricky asked. I rolled on the ground, shivering. He got off my bike and dragged me through a stand of trees into what looked like a secluded dale. I couldn't speak through the chattering of my teeth. "Holy cow!" he said, looking at me. "You must be in shock!" He ran out, came back with the two bikes, then dropped beside me, whipped off his father's leather army jacket, and placed it over me. That helped warm me, but I still shivered. He thought a minute, then decided he had to do more. He carefully lay down next to me on the grass, making certain to fit himself alongside my entire body. I clutched at him from under the jacket and shivered until I thought my teeth and bones would break apart and fly out of my body in all directions.

The shivering stopped. I felt warm. I opened my eyes, and turned to thank him. No words came out. But Ricky seemed relieved and he moved all over me, touching my arms and legs, checking for broken or fractured bones, he said. Under the jacket his hands roved, across my ribcage, my back, up my neck. Everything worked, he said, matter-of-factly. I was just "shook up by the fall. Got up too quickly."

When I was able to speak, I said. "I didn't want to race you."

He seemed surprised. "Why not? You won! You're the best bike racer in the county. Everyone knows it."

"I didn't win. I fell."

"You didn't fall. He knocked you down. That big fuck!" The last spoken in real anger. "Of course you won the race. You were the first one out of the tunnel. If I were first, he would have grabbed me and knocked me down instead."

His logic was too impeccable to deny. I began to shiver again and he came under the big jacket with me again and huddled close. "Don't talk. We're just going to stay here until you feel better. Okay?"

We remained there almost an hour until I was filled with looking at the concern on his face, filled with the texture of his long dark hair—every strand tinted an identical black walnut—feeling its soft texture across my face when he leaned close, filled with his boysmell and boybreath and the strength and security of his arms, all within the slightly nutty-scented, hot sheepskin ambiance of his father's bomber jacket, until I was no longer trembling and beads of perspiration had broken out on his forehead.

Unwillingly I told him I felt okay, honest. Completely relieved, Ricky threw off the jacket and once again tested me for breaks or fractures or sprains. We discovered some lollapalooza bruises, one gash half the length of my left leg, another on my left forearm, a bump on the side of my head: none seemed serious. Ricky acted like a doctor in a movie, making me stand up, bend over to touch hands to toes (I couldn't, got dizzy). He asked if I could ride. I thought I could, sore as I felt. So he banged around the front of my bike with a bolt-tightener from his tool kit until the spokes were more or less straight, the wheel less bent, the seat re-angled. We got on the bikes and slowly rode back home.

A block away from the Taylor house, we saw almost a dozen bikes parked around the huge front yard hickory tree. Ricky motioned me to stop. I wondered why.

"Back there you said that you didn't want to race me?" he asked. "Why not?"

I shrugged. "I don't know." I looked into his startlingly colored eyes. "I guess I didn't want to see you have to lose."

He blushed and seeing that, I did too: we both realized the admission I'd just made.

"What a jerk! When we tell them what happened to us, no one will even bother to ask who won."

I could already see him calculating how to tell our story most dramatically. We would ride into the Taylor yard and I would all but collapse. Our two groups of friends would jump up and ask what happened, where had we been so long? We would collaborate on a fantastic story, beginning with the truth (which was interesting enough) but really elaborating on what we'd seen or thought we'd seen speeding through the tunnel. I'd let Ricky take over and relate how I'd been stopped by the brutal, stupid watchman and how Ricky had outwitted him and gotten us away.

"You're right, I guess," I said. "But don't tell them how I couldn't ride anymore and fell down and how you had to put your father's jacket over me and all. Or I'll tell who won the race."

"You do and I'll tell them not only how you needed to be held like a big baby but that you kissed me."

"I didn't! That's a lie!"

"No. But you wanted to. It's the same thing."

"I didn't. And it's *not* the same thing."

My feelings exposed, I felt trapped, aware that I was blushing, angry that he had read my thoughts so easily, so correctly.

"What's the difference?" Ricky said airily.

It was later that night, after dinner, as we sat in the living room watching television, in the midst of my family for once oddly all there, that I wondered how long Ricky and I would keep those secrets. A week or so later, in math class, I let myself imagine what it would have been like if I had kissed Ricky, and let myself be kissed back.

I was determined to find out.

My Second-Childhood Friend

James

James was my childhood friend, I don't mean that I knew him for decades or that we played together back in the Fifties in Arizona where he grew up. I met James only last year, a little more than a year ago in fact. It was an all-day writing/publishing seminar in Manhattan hosted by the Publishing Triangle and I was a panelist. Afterward, as I helped fold up chairs and put them away, I said hello to an acquaintance. James was with him and introduced himself to me in that most startlingly forthright way of his. He asked me, "Are you seeing anyone?"

It took me half a minute to figure out that I had been asked out on a date. I fudged a little, and then said I didn't date. James said that was okay, he didn't mean that kind of a date anyway. It was said so refreshingly, with two big innocent blue eyes, that he got my phone number.

He phoned a few days later. It took only one dinner at a local restaurant for me to discover that James hadn't been lying. This wasn't any ordinary date and James wasn't an ordinary person. Although he said he was attracted to me, he also told me that he was HIV-positive and indeed symptomatic, and although he played it down, I already knew from experience what that meant: a fine romance, with no kisses.

That first evening, James made his pitch: what he wanted in me, his new friend, he declared, was not a lover, not a boyfriend, not even a sex-buddy: what he wanted was someone to go out with occasionally, to talk with about books and writing, current events, nature, and science. James had recently developed a foot infection and he couldn't get around all that well until it slowly healed. So he was bicycling. He wanted me to get a bike and to bicycle with him. He promised to teach me how to play chess, which, oddly enough, I'd never learned. He promised me we'd see interesting new places and have fun. Just what a ten-year-old boy would say to another ten-year-old boy.

And so it was. I got a bike from a friend who'd had an accident with it and whose father had fixed it—not very well. I dragged the bike home on the subway and together, James and I fixed it in my living room. Then, pleased with our labor, we went bike riding.

It had been *years* since I'd biked in Manhattan, but James knew all the short cuts, all the untrafficked routes, all the choice little off-ways and by-streets. He showed me lower Manhattan by day—and even more interestingly—by night. One of us would hear of a fireworks display or of an unusual nineteenth-century clipper ship berthed at the South Sea Seaport, or a jazz concert at Battery Park or a Dominican Republic gala at some East River parklet, and we'd jump on our bikes and take off. But he never did teach me chess.

Sometimes another friend of his would join us on our bike jaunts, and several times James and I found ourselves bicycling right into the middle of hot spots: the Democratic National Convention where we'd snuck behind police lines to get a better look; Chinatown and Little Italy on the night of the Fourth of July, with people tossing wrapped ten-pack sticks of firecrackers under our bicycle wheels as we tried to speed away before they exploded.

More often, we found ourselves exploring areas we barely knew or had never heard of—an amazing residential suburb hidden deep in Harlem, a tiny craftspersons' colony behind the smokestacks of industrial Brooklyn. James would call me up at ten o'clock or even later on a summer night and tell me he wanted to go bike riding. And, as with any childhood friend, I would hesitate only a minute, then sacrifice my television program, movie or book to rush down the elevator to meet him.

When I arrived, he'd already be in the lobby, sitting on the stone bench opposite the doorman, his lame foot sticking out, looking pensive. But he'd stand up and greet me with his leprechaun smile. "This is what I thought we'd do tonight," he would begin breathlessly as though already in the middle of doing it. Or "I've been thinking about this article I read today in the *Times* science section," and we would be off.

For me, the last few years have been a sort of second childhood anyway. Not because suddenly I'm roller skating and bike riding and playing backgammon, cards, checkers—all childhood activities. But because with the death of my last close friends and especially with the death of my companion of sixteen years, I've found myself suddenly at sea, unsure where I'm going and why, where I've been, and what it could possibly signify. Confused as to what I'm still doing on this planet when so many I loved are gone. Loss unmoors us. Twelve years of constant, devastating loss have snapped my guide lines, cut my guy wires. I exist now in a child's world again: fearful, uncomprehending, not knowing what to do, or where to turn next.

James was fascinated by this aspect of my life. For him, it was only with the arrival of his positive—and fatal—HIV test results, rather late in his illness, that his own childhood really ended. It was only then that James found himself a journal-writer, a poet, a bookmaking craftsman, a computer aficionado—a grown up.

James' views of gay life were by no means entirely positive when I first met him. Because of his background and especially his ultraconservative mother who raised him alone, James had fought his homosexuality much of his life. He'd been married and had a son. He'd divorced, entered destructive relationships with men involving drugs. While I had existed for decades within a large, sophisticated, creative, and beneficent gay environment—an environment now obliterated by death—James seemed to barely touch gay life. And when he did, he found it exotic and after all not very consequential. Now, it thrilled him to suddenly make new friends, like myself and several others in his various Gay Men's Health Crisis meeting groups, with whom he could be fully himself: gay friends with whom he could talk and argue and discuss and discover and grow.

Once he came to know me better, James also found himself a task: to reconcile me back to life. Although I was physically healthy, I'd lived with constant death for so long and so closely, that I'd really grown sick of living. With everyone I'd ever loved dead, I was repulsed by life. I was disgusted by the teeming throngs of the unheeding who happened to be alive. By contrast, and although he was often sick and in pain, James, loved life. Not with the desperate grasp of the ill, but with the sane curiosity of the healthy. He simply wanted *more* of it.

We would bike ride late at night downtown though the immense, empty, echoing, lighted-at-midnight buildings of Wall Street and the Financial Center, then back home up the Lower East Side past the Clinton Street Housing Project. We would stop for hot onion Bialys just made that minute at Yonah Shimmel's Knishe Bakery and, as we chewed our fresh-made bread from astride our ten-speeds, James would wonder aloud about the life of every family in those immense projects, every person behind those scores of windows and tiny balconies.

Being diametrically opposed at the very basis of our two existences and beliefs, we argued, of course. We would bicycle a while, then he would tire and we would stop for a rest at that circular park in the heart of Stuyvesant Town, or at the little blue-lighted, wooded over-harbor area at the end of Battery Park City on the Hudson River, with Miss Liberty in direct full view, the lights of the Verrazano Bridge dancing in the distance, or that miles-long bike path that runs along the East River, where we'd stop to face a spectacular view of the Williamsburg and Brooklyn Bridges, the huge Domino Sugar sign and plant behind them. Once in these perfect settings, we would attack each other's most cherished beliefs.

James couldn't understand my intense misery, my sense of loss of the world I'd lived in so long. When, as he would point out gesturing around us, there was still *so much* to have.

What was the difference how much there was around us, I would argue back, when I didn't want any of it, while what I did want I could never *again have*.

I was being foolish, sentimental, and wasteful, James would counter. He had clearly never loved anyone as deeply as I had, nor had he ever had friends and lovers as worthwhile as mine had been to me, I would say to him, or he would easily realize the immensity of the loss entailed.

James consistently used his optimism and his cheerfulness to cudgel me into thinking his way. I, however, used my bitterness and cynicism and, in our arguments, I even used his health condition against him, cruelly, as a stiletto.

All this, James would say embracing the world, and yet stupid Felice wouldn't even reach for it. All this, I would respond, and it would all be taken out of his reach so soon!

Then we would agree to disagree. We would get on our bikes and ride again, and all the frightful things we'd said to each other would be forgotten. We'd point out details as we rode past them, signs, people out late, just like childhood pals who fought hard, got dirty, then got up, brushed themselves off and were pals again. We would arrive at his building or at mine and hug and shake hands and make a tentative date for our next outing. James never managed to eliminate my depression. I never managed to dent his optimism, or in any real way affect his belief in the future.

Even during his one, mercifully short, final stay in the hospital, James would always find something new to learn and discover. When he could do so, he'd be upstairs in the library at Sloan-Kettering Hospital and whenever I would visit him there, I'd be told to bring only serious magazines with me: *Natural History, Discovery, Scientific American, The Atlantic*. As James' body weakened, it seemed, paradoxically, that his mind sharpened, his spirits rose, his cheerfulness grew, his mind lifted free to range farther and farther.

Once or twice, when I visited, James even said he hoped to get well enough soon so we could go bike riding again. He thought it would be a really good summer for bike riding.

So far, it has been.

I bicycle around the lower tip of Manhattan to the Staten Island Ferry, and across the Brooklyn Bridge to Cobble Hill, and of course down to the Hudson River parks almost every day now. But I bring my Walkman or a book with me these days. And now if I do miss James, I find that I'm seldom alone. For while it's still unclear whether or not James succeeded in reconciling me to life, it is clear what he gave me—himself, and those parts of the city I'd not seen or had forgotten: gifts of inestimable value.

James kept me distracted and interested and intrigued and sometimes irritated every moment that we were together. He did so selfishly, and yet selflessly, as a child would.

James was my childhood friend.

Nightly Visitor

Bob Lowe

The little building squatted upon the forlorn far West Village triangle like an unhappy afterthought. One of three aged, two-story constructions, it seemed to hug the narrowest end of an imperfectly rectangular city block, holding on for dear life. Of course, by then, it had seen grander days.

In the earlier part of the twentieth century, an elevated subway crossing Manhattan at Fourteenth Street had arrived at a conclusion right here, upon a giant turntable where railway cars were twirled around and then propelled back uptown again on their shuttling way. The raised steel structure that girdled the cobblestone plaza had competed with horse-drawn carts and carriages, with early autos, and pedestrians for which of them could make the most noise, stench, and mess below. Sited only two short blocks from the Hudson River, where Atlantic liners of the prestigious White and Cunard lines docked, and where ferry services from Hackensack and Tarrytown had their terminus, the triangle had once been a large marketplace, a bustling center of life and commerce. Even after the Elevated was torn down and the cruise liners moved to more northerly docks, and the ferries no longer disembarked passengers nearby, the triangle remained a nexus of business: a fresh produce market by day, surrounded on three sides by permanent meat market structures.

By night, the cobblestone triangle was another kind of focal point. During the Twenties, speakeasies and dives, beer-gardens, and ethnic eateries had jostled knock-kneed next to Federal era townhouses with their sober facades, graceful railings, and wrought iron-grilled windows. On that edge of the Little

West Thirteenth Street, night spots had prospered for years, before attaining a slow decline. But as the ninth decade of the century opened, the last of them—El Alcazar—a Spanish restaurant with adobe outer camouflage and Arabic style signage, was barred shut, the last to go. At around the same time, the fresh produce market relocated up to Hunts Point in the Bronx. True, a few blocks further west, around the old Gansevoort Street customs house where Melville had scrivened out proseless penultimate decades, warehouses continued to be used, and the four block long meat market repulsed the rare astray pedestrian with its never totally washed sidewalks, where gobbets of fat and flesh reeked in the gutter. By then the rough cobblestone piazza itself had fallen into desuetude. People still lived in the area, mostly on side streets, in rent controlled warrens within the previous century's tenements, but there weren't many tenants during the Sixties and Seventies: the area was out of the way, abandoned, too far from the center of anything commercial, cultural, or cool.

A few attempts at reviving the triangle and maybe even having it renamed had abortively begun, and a male model of some note along with his girl friend had taken over a building across the street from the old row of bars and the El Alcazar, two of a handful of pioneers intent on reviving the area. Few followed them to that particular city-edge, and even that thrust at gentrification failed when the model was awakened one night by a burglar, fought him off, and was killed with a twelve inch screwdriver. Even though the burglar also expired of his wounds, that was all people needed to hear: Once more the triangle seemed to sigh then once again go silent.

So I was surprised when I heard that Michael Fesco had taken over the little corner property there and was planning to open a bar. Once a Broadway musical gipsy dancer turned entrepreneur, Fesco had already done fairly well commercially. The Gay Seventies' ultimate private club, Flamingo, next to which all other discos—Studio 54, Paradise Garage, 12 West—were always compared and always found to fall short, had been Fesco's venue, until it (or he) somehow fell foul of the N.Y.P.D. and was closed. As the Eighties began, he'd already opened another club in Chelsea, around the corner from the roller-skating disco, which was hanging on nicely, especially with its Sunday afternoon parties, featuring one cutish, wild, hetero bartender who took his break by dancing along the full length of the twenty-eight foot long arc of concrete bartop. (He'd soon leave New York for a spot at a TV series called *Moonlighting*, and stardom.) Now Fesco had this new place, which was to be a "casual, neighborhood bar, with an upstairs darkroom, where local guys could come in, have a few beers, talk, and get off," all a few blocks from home.

Or so said Racey Peters, the manager of the bar. Racey came from the South as was apparent just looking at him. He was tall, deliberate moving and circumspect in his speech, with unwashed dank black hair that fell off his head like plastic sheeting: a look he encouraged by applying various automobile engine additives as pomades. Racey possessed the hard, flat body of someone born to grate himself down on a chain gang, and a face that some might find handsome, but which others called generic Mississippi White Cracker, with an added perpetual bad-attitude scowl. To experience Racey at his most amused was to ascertain a lip curled a quarter inch with half of a single exposed canine tooth.

I'd met him maybe a year before in the Glory Hole, up West Street, where after satisfying myself in the usual manner, I'd peeked in curiously to a double booth on my way out where Racey happened to be carrying on with another rough-looking guy, and I had paid for my prying by being pulled into the booth, and into a scene of passion with more than the usual percentage of raunch. After about fifteen minutes of being stripped and manhandled by the pair, I managed to get away—albeit with most of my orifices invaded by a melange of mouths and limbs—more or less intact.

A month or so later, I'd come across Racey and his band on-stage, at one of those fly-by-night Punk Rock lounges that seemed to mushroom overnight throughout the city in those days, this one hosted by gigunda drag-impresario Dean Johnston and called The Pubic Hair Club For Men. Along with his instrumental trio who more or less played, Racey grabbed at his substantial boner, while screeching and howling out his "current hit song," *Fuck You—And Your Mother Too!* Following this performance, I'd been astounded to be accosted by him at the bar in a surprisingly familiar manner as he verbally played me up to the guy I was trying to bag as a quote, "hot little fucker," which indeed did help me bed the guy later that night.

But I'd never have gotten into Fesco's new neighborhood bar if only Racey Peters was involved. No, instead it was Bob Lowe who'd been talked into working there two nights a week, and Bob was at that time the person closest to me. I never got a clear understanding of exactly *how* he ended up there. True, Bob had been head bartender at the Cock Ring, a little place at the foot of Christopher Street at the Hudson River's edge that had taken the gay community by storm in the late Seventies. On weekends, crowds would be lined up, vying to get into the bar and its boudoir-sized dance floor. And it was through this contact that Bob—and I too—had entered the after-midnight, after hours bar and club scene which had helped me write my novel, *The Lure*, so authentically.

But Bob's only connection with Fesco since then had been as a "living statue" on a plinth wearing a black leather outfit during one of Flamingo's notorious Black Parties. Of course, his two years' earnings at the Cock Ring paid all of Bob's first year and part of the second at the New York School of Law, when he matriculated there. Now he was in his second year, living nearby, in a small flat on Horatio Street, in a building the local police (who knew its denizens well) called "Love American Style," after the current TV program. And although he never gave details, I guessed that Fesco, who was no fool, thought Bob would bring the trade into his place too. Meanwhile, Bob said, until it hit he could study his law books whenever the place was empty, and still make a few dollars.

That studying ended up being a great deal: the new bar was empty most of the time. Bob had begun working there mid-September, while I was still living out at Fire Island Pines. It would be another month before I actually got a look at the place, even though it was only six or seven small West Village blocks from where I lived. By then, I'd received lengthy phone calls from Bob from the bar, telling me about Racey's antics, as well as Michael's own attempts to get the place going, which included stripping all the upstairs walls of plaster, leaving bare brick, not really that necessary in a room that's supposed to be pitch dark. In fact the first time I stepped foot in it, I overheard the place referred to as "Fesco's Folly."

That occasion was a party for someone or other, a kind of Sunday afternoon pre-beer bust. The piece de resistance of that fairly ho-hum affair was a pair of Racey's denims, draped over one of the bathroom *pissoirs* in such a way that using it you *had* to urinate on them. He explained to someone who asked when he would know the denims were "ready" by saying, "I guess, when they dry out and can stand up on their own." He of course planned to wear them during his band's next gig. Although he gave no sign of recognizing me, Racey followed me upstairs to the newly wall-stripped "back room" when I wandered up there to see if there was any "action?" There wasn't. At least not until Racey arrived, with his squid-sucker like mouth and his octopus-like arms, at which point it was all I could do to keep my pants on and in one piece, before making my escape.

The combo of Racey and Fesco somehow suggested to me that this new place would—like most of Fesco's places—become a hit. But it didn't and somehow that was all right with Bob, and even with Racey, for the next two months that it lingered on after opening. For Racey, of course, it was a hangout for him to have sex with pretty much whomever he wanted. While for Bob it was a way to get paid while studying law with the unusual distraction of a customer or two. That's the way it was explained to me and that's the way I took it. Soon enough Fesco would get wise and staunch the money flow, but until then why rock the boat?

So I guess I was surprised when I began getting phone calls from Bob, from the bar, at around the same time every night, just before midnight. He'd been there since ten p.m. I knew and would remain until one or two in the morning. But all of a sudden, he was phoning me, often for a second or third time that day, very much wanting to talk, but saying very little. He needed to talk to someone, I began to feel. He wouldn't let me go to sleep *until* we'd spoken. Outside the bar, whenever he and I were together and I mentioned this new habit of his, he explained it by saying, "Well, no one comes in. So I get lonely there." Or even, "The bar gives me the creeps."

It was one of the oddities of our already odd relationship that we sometimes had sexual affairs with others which we might mention to each in passing, but which were usually unimportant, and which didn't in any way bother us or alter our commitment to each other. It was partly a function of the era we lived in. It was also how we'd begun our relationship and so how we'd decided to stay "together." Sometime in the beginning of his first year of law school,

Bob had begun seeing a designer/decorator named Reggie. I, meanwhile, had begun dating two guys: one blond—Randy, one dark-haired—Neal. As a result of these extracurricular activities, Bob and I seldom checked each other's schedules very closely. Even so, I'd gone so far as to begin to worry about Bob. Partly because whenever we did see each other, he wasn't looking his usual absolutely beautiful self, but instead a little—haggard? a mite—gray? I couldn't put my finger on it. He knew I didn't like going to the new bar because Racey would invariably try to get my pants off me, and I wasn't that interested in Racey—and definitely not in front of Bob.

Then one night, at midnight, Bob called, as usual from the bar, and this time he sounded quite different. I was brushing my teeth, preparatory to going to bed, and was fatigued from an over-occupied day. But I sensed something going on in his voice and didn't like it. I asked if he wanted me to come there, that night, right away. And he said, "No. It already happened." While I mulled those enigmatic words over, he added, "But I'd like it if you came tomorrow night, around this same time. Say, quarter to twelve?"

It turned out the following night I was going uptown to dinner at the Upper West Side apartment of recent acquaintances, the Ferro-Grumleys. Based on what our mutual friend had told me of these events, I knew I'd get out around eleven p.m. Add a subway ride and I'd arrive at the Little West Thirteenth Street triangle around eleven-thirty, eleven-forty. So I told Bob I would see him there the next night—and exactly when.

That following day turned out to be yet another busy one—I was about to launch a new SeaHorse Press book, always a lot of work and worry for me—then I had dinner, at which Robert and Michael had several new people for me to meet, the reed-thin but achingly handsome Colin Streeter, for some reason or other dressed in a gardener's uniform; novelist Julia Markus; and their especial pal, writer, and recently a successful jazz singer, Suzanne McCorkle. The evening was fairly fabulous, people-wise, even if food-wise it was merely pasta with ricotta and a salad since the F-G's were in yet another financial slump—the women had brought dessert and I'd brought wine. So I really had to tear myself to get downtown by midnight.

I recall that I was full of high spirits from the evening's events, slightly buzzed if not high from the wine, and that I didn't even mind the longish walk to the bar from the Eighth Avenue subway line at Fourteenth Street, through a mostly deserted area. Bridge-and-tunnel guidos cruising syphilitic hookers and only slightly more upscale trannies were pretty much the cream of this area's sparse population in those days, although today Armani and Barney have chic emporia there. The cobblestone triangle upon which Fesco's bar stood provided the only light for blocks around that night, and it was as moribund as I previously recalled it.

When I got there, Bob was at the very front of the bar, nearest the street side windows, perched on a stool, with a text-book and a notebook open. The place was otherwise empty, although a disco mix by Roy Thode played loudly. I'd figured Bob sat where he did for the light or because it was closest to the street and any possible street life. I would soon discover the true reason.

He offered me an apéritif, but I was interested in sobering up before heading home to sleep so I took a tonic water with lot of ice instead. We chatted, I about my day, and the people at the F-G's dinner party, he about his day at law school. We'd reached a point where we had nothing further to say, and we were about to lapse into silence, when Bob suddenly turned and faced the rear wall of the place. It was a long rectangle of a building, with the bar on the south side, the east side half wall, half windows, a corner doorway, and the north side again half wall, half windows for almost one entire length—except for the last five feet or so which enclosed what once had been a hat check room. Another door opened to the street right there, but that was kept locked most of the time. And near that back door and checkroom a wooden stairway rose straight up to the second floor and the dark room. I knew all that, as I'd been there a half dozen times.

Even so I was surprised when Bob turned to that back wall and stairway, ignoring me as I spoke about someone or other. I turned too and this is what I saw: At five minutes to midnight a mass of ash-gray smoke descended the stairway as though tumbling over itself. It stopped at the foot of the stairs and formed itself into a figure. I don't to this day understand how I could tell, but I could definitely tell who the figure was and even how the figure was dressed. It was an African-American man about forty years old, with a wide, almost cat-like face and a somewhat squashed-in broad nose. He was dressed in an overlarge jacket with a sort of checker-board pattern, which looked vaguely yellow green, and he wore darker, almost chocolate-colored trousers of some fine material, well pressed. The shoes were newish and two-toned: white and oxblood. He wore a light brown pork pie hat, askew on his close cut head, with a single feather sticking out of the band. He was holding what looked like an empty wine bottle. The clothing was Bebop era, no later than 1941.

A second after he had consolidated at the foot of the stairs, he somehow became both the ash-colored smoke and a solid figure again as he flowed forward, directly into the doorway of the hat check room. Then he was gone.

I looked at Bob, who looked at me rather queasily but didn't say a word. Neither did I. I got up and walked to the back of the place, looked up the stairs, inspected the steps and floor, and examined the hat check room. Nothing. Not a thing.

"What is it?" I asked.

"What did you see?" Bob asked.

I told him what you just read.

"You're pretty observant. Anything else?"

"Yes, he looked stoned, not on liquor but as though he'd been shooting heroin."

"That's what Racey said. He comes every night. At five minutes to midnight."

"He doesn't know he's dead," I said. "He shot up on bad stuff, OD'd, I'm guessing somewhere upstairs, at eleven fifty-five p.m. and every night he comes downstairs, looks around, and goes into the hat check room."

"Racey thinks he leaves here every night," Bob said.

"But you don't?"

"I'm *here* every night," patting his spot, as far away from the apparition as he could get and still stay in the building. "That's why I *stay* here. But what if one night he decided to come for a drink?" he fretted.

"He's already got a bottle," I said hoping to calm him.

It only partly worked. "What if he does?" Bob repeated.

"He won't. He doesn't know he's dead. He'll repeat this action every night. But I doubt that he'll do anything new. They usually don't," I added.

I remained another hour. No one came in, and at one-thirty that morning Bob closed up the register. I walked him home which was on my way home.

In his building foyer, Bob said. "I can't stay there anymore. I'm just too... you know?"

"Creeped out. I know. Well, don't stay. Can't you find a temporary law-clerking job through school?"

"It'll be real work, instead of studying like this all night," he argued. "But I can't stay there."

"Does Fesco know?" I asked.

"We're not sure he believes us. You saw? Right?"

"I saw. I'll tell him if you want."

"Don't bother," Bob said. We kissed good night and he went up to sleep.

To all of our surprise, Fesco abruptly closed the bar the very next week, and paid Bob and Racey for another week after that. After a month or so, Bob began clerking, a job he got via school, for two women lawyers, one of them British who had been married and divorced from the film director Joseph Losey. After he'd graduated with honors, Bob would take her place in the firm and become junior partner; he'd remain working there happily the remainder of his far too short life. As for Racey, I would see him now and again over the years, usually at some raunchy new bar or club opening, and usually manage to get away before he spotted me. Then I heard he'd returned South where he'd made something of a go out of singing and playing rockabilly.

We never referred to that evening again, Bob and I, the rest of our years together. Except once, only once, when I needed potent ammunition against the specious words of his vile mother. The place was Cabrini Hospital in Manhattan where we'd brought Bob several weeks before with severe pneumocystis pneumonia, and where he'd remained, in and out of intensive care, as first one then another vital part of his body began going completely haywire before shutting down. In the fourth week of this abomination, it became clear to me that he was probably not to going to ever get out of this place. I had plenty of time to be with him in the hospital, but usually his mother—we uncordially, mutually, detested each other—was around, refusing to leave his side. One day as I entered, I heard her bullshitting him that he was getting better and would be back in New England soon, recovering. I'd just that moment spoken to his doctor who'd told me that Bob's body was going into an organ by organ shutdown. He said he'd told Bob the same thing an hour earlier. I was angry at her for lying to him. Instead of filling his mind with nonsense, she should be preparing him to cross over. This was now my unwelcome, difficult, obligation.

Once Bob and I were alone, I held his hand and told him what his doctor had told me, and what I knew he knew too about his lack of a future. He told me he was afraid, very afraid, and that's why he let his mother prattle on. I asked him not to run from what was happening, but to attempt to embrace it, difficult as that seemed. But he kept arguing with me. Finally, I asked him to remember the little bar where he worked on the Little West Thirteenth Street triangle, so many years before, and what we'd seen there, what he'd shown me. Was that what he wanted, I asked Bob, to be so utterly unconscious in life that he didn't even know he was dead? To be so fearful and blank that he would keep doing the same stupid action over and over again for eternity? I begged him to reconsider.

Bob stopped arguing. He went silent and a few minutes later he began coughing, then needed ice in his mouth, then the pillows plumped, and there were another dozen distractions, before the she-wolf stalked in again and our private moment was over. But I knew from the way he looked at me in those next few moments that I'd gotten through to him with that memory, and that he'd remembered and been horrified all over again by that nightly visitor and worse, by the possibility of turning into one himself.

So I was relieved, if appalled, when two days later, I discovered that Bob's consciousness had already left his body. He'd had what they called a "massive cardiac event" and the witch woman (even Bob referred to her as Fafner, Wagner's dragon in his Ring cycle) had forced the hospital staff to attempt to resuscitate him. This, despite the fact that the letters DNR, "Do Not Resuscitate," were all over him and the room, from outside the doorway to the chart hanging at the foot of the bed, to the tag around his neck. Of course, once she realized too late the ghastliness she had precipitated—if only to go against his and my wishes, since I was his health executor—the dragon took off, sidling back to whatever infected aperture she'd crawled out of. But while I was deeply disheartened, having to daily care for a machine-breathing body without any mind inside it—shaving it, washing it, etc.—day after day until I had nightmares about it, still and all I judged this was a better situation than if it had been the opposite: body ravaged, mind still active. Wasn't it?

Naturally enough, once his body too was gone, as must happen, I'd wished I'd kept my mouth shut. I wished that I still had contact of some sort, *any* sort with Bob. I even, yes, I even wished that he could have become my own personal nightly visitor.

Secret Ceremony

Grandpa Ralph

When I woke up it was still dark, yet I knew that it was Grandpa who was waking me and at the same time making sure I'd be quiet. It was still cool out, despite the late summer August date, and I hesitated getting out of the warm, high, double-mattress bed. But Grandpa ungently pulled my light blanket off me and whispered close to my ear:

"Get dressed now. Don't make a sound. Don't wake your mother. Meet me down the stairs."

In all of my ten years of knowing him, I'd never heard a tone of voice like that before. So, I did what he said. This wasn't going to be anything ordinary if it were to be kept secret even from my mother.

Before I even reached the steep stairway down I bumped into my older brother. He seemed a lot less awake than me. Even so, if he were involved in this too it was suddenly a lot less interesting.

"Cm'on," we heard Grandpa urge from the foot of the stairs. With him down there was Uncle Rudy, our mother's youngest brother. He and his young family lived in the lower floor of what had once been a huge country farm house, since divided into two—the upper floor—seven rooms of various size, surrounding a central room with kitchen and stove—for Grandpa alone, although all of us had been staying with him in rural Rhode Island for almost a month that summer.

"Where's Tommy?" I asked.

They both hushed me and hustled me and my brother out of the hallway onto the porch and down the stone steps. Enough time, however, to feel the icy morning dew on my face, and to see every star in the heaven facing me.

"He's still sleeping," Uncle Rudy said. "He's too small."

For what? My curiosity was up again.

Upstairs, after pulling on my jeans and big shoes, I'd checked my watch and it said 4:09 a.m. A good watch too, worth almost twenty dollars. What were we doing going out at 4:09 a.m.?

Grandpa led us around the stand of six tall English beeches that framed and shaded the house, around the side lawn toward the chicken coop that was now a combination garage and tool shed. Behind us, the vegetable garden lay breathing in darkness, only the giant sunflowers each twice the size of my head were visible in the thin glints of yellow light thrown by Uncle Rudy's torch. Looming above their one-and-a-half-times-a-tall-man's-height was the unseen bulk of the Indian graveyard that separated Grandpa's property from our father's mother's land, a far smaller and less handsome farm.

My brother and I remained outside the shed, while the men went in. He was still extremely sleepy, but I was totally awake, completely alert as I watched the crossing beams of the two torch lights inside the shed. I heard Uncle Rudy bump something and swear for a minute in that nasal speech all of our New England relatives possessed and which I thought was so cool I imitated it back in New York during the rest of the year. Then a little bulb was turned on.

From out of nowhere came the ghostly high-pitched wail, freezing me to the spot. Equally sudden, Uncle Rudy dashed out of the shed, muttering, "Son of a gun! Son of a gun!"

He vanished toward the noise and I realized two things at once: the wailing was a sound that could only be made by Sarah-Jane, the smelly, cantankerous, eat-everything goat Grandpa kept tethered back among the corn flowers not far from the garbage piles, and, I'd been hearing that same wailing from Sarah-Jane in my dreams tonight for some time before Grandpa had awakened me.

"You boys come in here," Grandpa commanded. I'd never heard him command anyone but his dog, Silk, before. When we got into the shed, he was barely visible from the chest up, so we couldn't see his face. But his torso was illuminated and in its light we saw in his hands the dull blue metal glimmer and shined woodstock gleam of two rifles.

"Take these," he again commanded and handed us each a rifle. "Do you know how to use 'em?" he asked. My brother began to mumble something. I thought we were being asked to go shoot someone and immediately, and truthfully said, "No, sir!"

"Well you sure made enough noise playing with guns to know how," he concluded. "This here is the trigger. This here is the release. You just release it and point it and pull the trigger. You can do that," he said with so much conviction I didn't think to question him or deny it. Instead we took the guns. Mine seemed awfully long and heavy until I held it down by my side where it oddly felt lighter, probably because it was better balanced carried that way.

"These aren't loaded, are they?" my brother asked.

"Hell, yeah, they're loaded!" I'd never heard my Grandpa curse before. Now I was sure he'd been taken over by some creature from another planet who was forcing him to do terrible things—and all of us along with him.

Just then Uncle Rudy burst through the shed door. "She's okay. Just scared. Saw us out here and thought she could gain some sympathy."

He went to the wall, pulled down two rifles, and as we watched, he cracked them open in the middle and began filling their revolving cartridges with bullets, handing one after the other to Grandpa and even to me until our arms were full. Then he put away his box of bullets in his upper corduroy jacket pocket, and took two rifles.

I now had about a million questions to ask. But Grandpa had already shut off the garage light and was shooing us out, back along the path we'd come and down the little stone staircase onto State Street.

"You boys stay quiet," Grandpa hushed me before I could even formulate how to ask question number one. "And listen."

"Listen for what?" I asked: question number two.

"Don't worry. You'll know what," Uncle Rudy answered.

At the end of the property, where Atwood Avenue began, a group of shadowy figures—men and boys from their voices—were waiting for us Among their hushed tones I could make out the voice of my Uncle Georgie as well as across the street neighbors, Clay MacInerty, Jess Rocco, and Lester Hawks, and with them each of their boys. As we got closer, I noticed that each of them also carried at least one rifle, including my age-mate and playmate for the past two summers, Donnie Hawks.

I immediately fell in alongside Donnie, whispering, "What's up?"

To my surprise, Donnie was crying. "They got Trixie," he bawled.

Trixie was his dog, part collie, part Beagle, and all stupid. One of his few failings as a boy and friend was how much Donnie doted on this mutt, which to my knowledge hadn't any good qualities, except the cunning of begging successfully for table scraps, although Donnie always insisted that Trixie was as faithful as Lassie in the TV movies series, and so worth a dozen better purer-bred animals.

"Hush up, you boys!" Clay MacInerty said in a hard voice.

The pack of us crossed Atwood Avenue, totally empty and devoid of traffic at this hour of the morning. We began walking alongside and in its double lanes, headed in the direction of Knightsville. I knew that because I could make out the red and green warning lights atop the giant radio tower that sat upon, dominating Conanicut Hill.

We kept together, me trying to stay up with the others as much because I was afraid to lose them in the dark as for any other reason. My brother also kept up, but he was in the middle of the pack, and he'd pretty much fallen back asleep and was sleepwalking as he had done so often—and sometimes done spectacularly—in the past. I tried to close my mind to what was happening and at the same time to keep it open because I knew that whatever this was that was happening, it wasn't really Grandpa invaded by aliens—unless they'd gotten all these other folks too—but it was utterly unlike anything I'd experienced or been part of in my young life, unlike anything my mother or sister or younger brother or younger cousins or my Aunt Anna sleeping at home would be part of. I was trying to keep Donnie's continuing muffled sobs out of my ears, at the same time I was listening for what I didn't know. Instead of something marvelous or horrible however, I merely began to pick up bits and snatches of half phrases of conversation among the older men.

They'd been seen at the Diebst's place only a half hour ago.

They'd been bothering Lang's Alsatian bitch on and off all night until she'd broken her chain and run off. Lang didn't know where to.

They'd gotten inside Morelli's pullet house just after the family had gone to bed and had either killed or drawn out a half dozen hens and left his Rhody cock lying dead. Those remaining wouldn't lay for a month now. And that was with Morelli diving out of bed and shooting into the chicken fencing from his bedroom window to scare them off.

Trixie had run off with them.

At last I suspected I knew what they were talking about, what we were doing headed along this empty road at now 4:28 a.m. in total darkness, and what we were listening for. Little as I generally paid attention to adult's talk, especially in the summertime when my own pleasures were all that ever concerned me, I'd heard enough in the past week about a gang of dogs that had grown feral and come up from Johnston in the past week, hiding by day but running—and wreaking havoc—by night.

As I realized this, the pack of hunters stopped short. A half dozen voices turned toward a sound from afar that I'd already been hearing without making it part of my consciousness for the past few moments. Now clearly and unmistakably the yipping and yapping and barking and rabble rousing of a pack of dogs gone wild.

Uncle Rudy led us off the highway and into Farmer Brown's big cabbage and kale fields. Earlier this summer he'd grown green and yellow wax beans in adjoining plots and I'd broken my back all one day picking them, earning a lousy quarter dollar a bushel-full. But that was late July, this was late August, and the kale and cabbage growing there now wouldn't be ready to be picked for another few weeks.

Our group was now moving a lot faster. I could hear the pack of dogs also moving, sidewise to us, and so—suddenly—did the men leading swerve us horizontally through the kale patch whispering, "C'mon you boys, don't be slowpokes." Even my stumbling brother had to wake up.

I'd begun to panic. After all there were something like ten of us, including myself who couldn't shoot and my brother who was sleepwalking and Donnie Hawks who was still crying and obviously too upset to use any kind of rifle, and we were at what looked to be the gates of the local Methodist cemetery, about to face off in the dark with a pack of wild animals that sounded to be close to fifty and were rumored to have stolen and completely eaten a two-year-old child down on Dyer Road.

I simply didn't have the luxury to panic. Didn't have much time to do anything but try to keep up with the men, and hold my rifle correctly, so it wouldn't hit the ground and go off accidentally. In fact, the faster I ran to catch up, the faster the men ran, until I thought for sure they'd leave me behind—the last thing in the world I wanted now that I knew what terror we were going to face and how the pack of dogs we appeared to be getting closer to might suddenly outflank us and appear at our end.

We all collapsed into another outside the graveyard gates. The men had lost the sound of the dogs, or the dogs had caught our scent in the night wind and had cannily gone quiet to elude us.

Once again we trudged, past the old stonework and wrought iron fence, until we'd reached a depression of almost clear ground.

It seemed we were just about to reconnoiter, when I caught a hint of a yip awfully close, coming out of that copse of woods to the right. So did Donnie Hawks. Thinking it was Trixie, he dropped his rifle and all but headed off to follow. My Grandpa caught him and threw him back at me. That one yip I'd heard turned into two and three and within a matter of seconds, scores, and the woods around us was now filled with the sound of dogs barking and yipping and howling and making every damn noise they could think of to make.

I don't know how much on purpose it was, how planned out, or simply how instinctive, but the men formed a circle in those few moments, backs to each other, leaving just enough room for us younger ones to get through. I heard the sound of rifle locks being released around me, and then from Uncle Rudy and someone else too, "Jesus, there must a hundred of them!" before the dogs attacked our circle and the firing began.

I fell onto one knee between Grandpa and Uncle Rudy where I was certain I'd be safe, lifted the rifle to my shoulders, smelled the oiled metal, and in all that turmoil, I pointed, released the lock, aimed at a mass of what I was certain was wild dog flesh and pulled the trigger. The report sent me back onto my ass, but I got back up and saw my brother and Donnie Hawks—still crying—both standing and shooting, so I stood back up and did the same.

One gigantic black fiend seemed to know what to do; it would jump at all of us smaller kids. But when it tried it with me, two bullets rang out: Grandpa's and mine, and I don't know whose bullet or if both were needed to kill it. The men began to throw down their first rifles and were working on the second, and I was about to use my last bullet, and the noise of the dogs and the noise of the dozen guns and the dust being kicked up and the men swearing and the cries of wounded animals and the sudden stench of gunshot and dog shit was all too much for me. Yet when my Uncle Rudy dropped on one knee to reload his two guns, I thrust my cracked open one at him and I shouted "Me too!" He smiled up at me and filled it and snapped it closed before filling his own, dropping a box of cartridges on the ground for me to get later on, and I turned around and aimed and shot and aimed and shot again in the slowly growing by now blue not black light, seeing a shot animal—some sort of mangy chow—twist in agony and fall to the ground.

I loaded up myself twice more from the ground and saw at least one other animal definitely fall to my shot.

Then it was over. Not the noise, nor the stench. Those grew. And the sound of the wounded dogs was pitiful. About thirty or more lay around us writhing on the ground or chasing themselves to get at the bullet in their side or back. But the others had scattered or were barking at us from so far away we could no longer see them in the growing light. The men broke rank and went around putting the wounded animals out of their misery while Grandpa and the rest of us stood with nothing to do.

I found myself holding onto my Grandpa's pants and wanting to cry at all the carnage we'd just done that was only now being revealed to me. Off in the distance we could hear occasional noises, and Jess Rocco came by to tell us to gird ourselves and reload for another possible attack.

It never came. The single shots putting dogs to death continued for another five minutes then we were all headed out of the gully and up the path past the graveyard again—one or two men following and turning around to play guard in case the pack did come back. The leaders had been killed however—especially a giant wolfhound, and the big black mixed breed dog I'd seen and shot at, alongside Grandpa.

I kept holding onto him, and I was trembling, all the fright I'd held back, coming at me with full force all at once, until he stopped and handed my brother his rifles and sent him on, and bent down to me, creaking his eighty-nine years-old body to hold me close and to harshly whisper, "You sure as hell know how to use a rifle! Why did you lie to me?" So all I could do was look up at him, admire his astounding grace and presence of mind to so change around a long burst of tears into stilled pride, and I helped him stand up again, him leaning upon the barrel of my rifle as Donnie Hawks and his Dad came by, dragging a sackful of what could only be dead dog.

"Trixie," Donnie said, without a tear. "Stupid damn dog!" He kicked at the sack, then took off again, dragging it up the hill while his Dad held his shoulder hard.

It was just about light, the sun still behind some low clouds, when we got back to State Street and the hunting gang broke up, and still the sun hid while we put away the guns in the shed and crept into the house and up the stairs and kept really quiet and got undressed and went to our bedrooms. Grandpa was coming to bed besides me, hushing me. And I was thinking I'd ask him something about what happened out there tonight, about what we'd done and why he'd taken me along, so I lay there thinking about all my questions while I heard him go to the bathroom. But I must have fallen asleep before he got back, because it was almost nine-thirty in the morning before my mother came and shook me awake.

My older brother, oddly enough, was brightly awake, eating his cereal and happy that he'd gotten a prize in his bowl even though it was only another Dick Tracy wrist radio that couldn't work as good as the cheapest Walkie-Talkies you buy at the Five & Dime. But I was still sleepy enough for my mother to comment on it twice.

"Couldn't you sleep last night?" she asked.

I mumbled a reply through my cereal-filled mouth. She asked, "That was you I heard last night?" she said sharply, "About four?"

How could I deny it. I looked at Grandpa, sitting at the table reading the morning papers, his empty pipe hanging off his lower lip.

"I'm asking you a question, young man!" she now said so peremptorily all I could was admit that yes, I had been up around four. "I knew you shouldn't have eaten all those apples," she now said. "No more fruit unless you ask me first."

I felt four years old. Ashamed. My brother and sister giggled at this humiliation, even my little brother, too young to know what was going on, let out a laugh.

"Don't ride the boy so, Sister," my Grandpa said, oh so casually. "He's almost grown. He's going to have to find out for himself what makes him sick and what doesn't."

"Not while I'm still around," my mother said, in her bossiest tone of voice, and threw me a look as though to say, I should just try it. But she abandoned the table following that, and took the baby with her, followed by my brother and sister. I also got up to leave, but my Grandpa reached over a hand and stopped me.

He kept reading the paper, and I just sat watching him for the longest time. Until finally I thought I'd burst, when he put down the paper and taking off his fragile, gold, half-lens specs, said, "You had a question?"

I still had a million questions, but all I could think of was poor Donnie Hawks.

"Why did Trixie run off too? She was just a dumb yard dog."

He laughed a short harrumph. "They say," he spoke slowly, as usual, "Every dog has its day. Guess Trixie wanted to have hers."

Even though it killed her? I wanted to ask. But I'd had my question, gotten my answer, so instead, I said. "Poor Donnie."

Grandpa went back to his paper and I went outside to play and I didn't grow up for a long time. But when I did grow up, I found myself forced to recognize the fact, and to recognize it somehow because of that night in semi-rural Rhode Island.

But the one time—this was years later, and we were driving up in that state, visiting again as adults—that I brought up the incident with my older brother, he looked at me oddly and said, "That never happened. That never happened," he insisted. "That was a dream I had."

Road Test Number Three

Philip Picano

The messages on the answering machine told the story I'd missed that weekend: my aunt had been taken ill. Her condition was critical. She had died. The funeral was in a few days. My father couldn't drive all the way. His doctor said it was too soon after he'd spent weeks in the hospital for a heart condition. Taking a train, even a plane, was unthinkable. I'd have to drive him.

Now if you had asked me how I felt about a four-hour drive to Rhode Island with my father as the only other passenger, I'd probably place it midway on a scale between dining on broken glass and having bamboo shoots hammered under my fingernails. But it was lovely spring weather and I had nothing to write under deadline, so I told my father I'd call my cousins to see when we should arrive for the funeral, then I'd call and rent a car.

"Don't rent a car," my father said. "We'll take my car."

My dad's car: a twelve-year-old Pontiac mid-sized sedan. "Formerly owned," because he refused to pay what a new car cost, despite the fact that during my childhood, when he was less well off, he always bought new cars directly out of the dealer's showroom and scorned anyone who didn't. A "formerly-owned" car that my dad had bought very inexpensively and that he'd only driven locally, in Central Queens, maybe once a month as far as into Manhattan. No trip longer than that.

The last time we had been in a car together, also a long trip to Rhode Island for this same aunt's birthday, had been in my dad's '79 Ford station wagon, another formerly owned vehicle, this one not a sickly maroon but a lively deep green color surrounding plastic fake wood, and only slightly less than half the size of your usual Caribbean cruise ship. The one time I had parked this vehicle for him I'd needed a compass and sextant as well as a strong memory of all of Euclid's basic laws. Only eighty years old for that trip and in considerably better health, my father had driven and I had "navigated."

Which had gone like this: Me: "Here's your turn coming up, Dad. Here it comes! This is the turn!... Okay, *that* was your turn!"

Later, I'd declared to anyone who'd listen that the next long trip we'd take, I'd do the driving myself.

Now I would be. At the time I was still a resident of Manhattan to whom driving is a profession practiced by people with incomprehensible accents, no geographical skills, and a compulsion to revenge themselves on the world for the fact that someone of a differing political persuasion bombed the hell out of their natal picturesque village, forcing them to move to the outlying slums in the Bronx or Brooklyn.

However, very un-Manhattanite-like, I'd been driving a great deal by the time this trip arose. Up and down California's Pacific Highway One, all around San Francisco and Los Angeles, back and forth to Cape Cod, up to Vermont to visit friends who lived in the country. I loved to drive. Hell, I even drove down to South Jersey for a wedding with a woman friend, that's how much I enjoyed it.

This had not always been so.

In fact, it was something of a major sea-change for me. Until only a few years before, when I obtained my driver's license for the second time in my life, it had been—are you ready?—twenty-five years since I'd last driven. And I'd only gotten my new license again because my companion developed cytomegalovirus "floaters'" in his eyes late in his HIV infection, and as an attorney with business all over the state, he needed to try cases in person at various out-of-city county courthouses. If he couldn't drive, I who had no fixed work hours, could certainly drive him. However altruistic a reason, this never did work out as planned: he died before I got my license.

Why had I not driven for such a long time? When anyone asked, I usually hemmed and hawed a bit, then explained about those five traffic accidents I'd been involved in less than ten months of a particular *annus horribilus* in the Sixties. The bad run had begun with an especially spectacular accident outside Rome in which myself and two women friends (one of whom was driving) wedged into the front seat of a Triumph TR-3 had ended up not only completely off the *AutoStrada del Sole*—indeed forty feet off the road—but more impressively, some twelve feet off the ground, in fact, caught between the bifurcated trunk of a large chestnut tree.

My bad car luck had continued with more accidents: in a taxi in Rome, in a friend's car in Paris, in a double-decker bus in London. It had concluded with what could have been the most serious of all, a motorcycle spill outside Newell, Georgia, when I happened upon an oil slick in the southern lane of Route 301 while going sixty miles per hour. The bike and I had fallen to the road and slid for so long, so far, I remember having time to wonder if I would actually cross the nearby Florida State line.

Luckily, my "leathers" had taken most of the brunt of that: they ended up completely worn through on one leg and one torso side, i.e., ruined, and so while I had not broken, fractured, or sprained anything, I had done considerable damage to my pride and my self-confidence. Eagerly, I had taken up the generous hospitality of one of the families sitting upon one of the dozen verandahs I'd noisily slid past, staying the night and enjoying a home cooked dinner and a peach pancake breakfast.

So, although I'd been driving in only two of the five accidents, I had seen The Writing On the Wall.

For a closer look at said script, all I really had to do was to glance at the palm of my right hand. When I was nineteen, an otherwise irritatingly nebulous, ginger-haired psychic-for-hire in a Brighton tea salon had tapped that very palm, at what she'd pointed out as my "suddenly interrupted life line" and had concluded, "Interesting life, Ducks! If you should manage to survive this bit of porridge!"

More even than the accidents and the interrupted life line, there was other unfortunate history connected with my driving—history also involving my father.

He had taught me how to drive as a teenager. Or, to be precise, he had chauffeured me around the vast empty parking lots at Green Acres Shopping Center on Long Island a few winter Sunday afternoons, and after long lectures on defensive driving—"You're a soldier parachuted behind foreign lines! Everyone's your enemy"—he had allowed me to get behind the wheel of his gorgeous ice-blue Bonneville sedan for three minutes at a time, to nudge his car at about six miles an hour as he shouted "No! No! No!" or "Not so fast!" or "Wrong way!" This occurred until we were both too nervous to go on and I called a stop to the mutual torture.

To give a little background to these non-events, consider the following: I was hardly a tyro behind the wheel at that time. I'd been racing my go-cart around this very parking lot for several years, scores of times. Not a car, you say: a go-cart is just a chassis with two lawnmower engines! Okay, but in high school Driver Education, I'd put in six hours maneuvering that old shell of a Fairlane sedan mounted to the shop floor exactly for such training purposes. As well as manhandling a real—even older—actually mobile, pale green '53 Ford Deluxe coupe around the neighborhood, accompanied by a gym teacher in the passenger seat who spent most of his time struggling with a crossword puzzle and who, when he did remember I was at the wheel, would occasionally toss me a clear cut instruction he couldn't help but undercut with some appended ambiguity, such as "Turn left, deep into the white line." Deep into the what? And how deep?

Nevertheless I did manage to pass the school's Driver Education class and so it fell upon my father's shoulders to take me for my first driving license road test shortly after my sixteenth birthday. A glowering and dour Saturday morning, filled with gloomy predictions from him about how inattentive and dreamy I was—and therefore how much of a danger to every other human being not merely on that stretch of road I'd be driving, but also a quarter mile on either side. Unawake as I was that early morning, still I couldn't help but be depressed.

The man giving me the road test was nattily dressed—tweeds, vest, ascot, Panama hat—a stout, fortyish, African-American man with a wonderful goatee. He doubtless heard my father's final instructions, and doubtless also possessed an irritating father, because he 1) didn't give me anything particularly difficult to do during the road test, 2) seemed pleased both with himself and with my driving, 3) allowed my confidence to rise, 4) was nice enough to explain to me how one trimmed a beard to get that kind of goatee when I finally got up the nerve to ask him, and 5) best of all, he passed me with high marks.

This turn of events signally failed to cheer up my father. We drove away from the DMV test area in as somber and speechless a gloom as though during the road test I'd mowed down an entire Cub Scout troop and not bothered to stop to count the bodies.

Or rather he did. I clutched at the temporary driver's license I held in my hot little hands, the paper that spelled out "Freedom," spelled out "Grown-up" spelled out, "You Can Do It!"

My dad remained in the garage with a visiting friend while I went to tell my mother the good news. When I returned with her invitation for coffee and cake I arrived at the ajar garage door in time to hear my father's friend say, "Well, you were wrong! He passed." My father grunted some very grudging assent. His friend replied, "So? How does he drive?" I waited. Finally my father muttered "Like a Newport debutante!"

Now to a sixteen-year-old boy, this statement impugned not only his driving ability, but also his seriousness, his future, his manhood itself. It was devastating. And I'd never forgotten it.

Decades later, I had to admit, my father had pinned my driving style to a tee. I drive fast, casually, playing loud music and singing along. My single finger on the steering wheel tapping the rhythm, my hair in the breeze of the open windows, I glide across four-lane freeways at eighty miles an hour. I'm alert, I'm careful, I seldom get tickets, I seldom have accidents. But you tell me it takes six and a half hours from L.A. to San Francisco? Sorry, I do it in five and a half with a half hour for lunch and two other stops to pee. When friends visiting my Cape Cod rental had to make a train, trust me, with me at the wheel, they might leave their stomachs somewhere near Wellfleet, but they always made their train in Hyannis!

Perhaps one reason for this total non-change in my driving skills was the circumstances surrounding Road Test Number Two. This experience began blandly enough and progressed fairly well, before threatening to become total disaster. I should start at the beginning.

By the time I applied for my second New York State drivers license, much in the intervening years had altered: including how unwelcome new drivers were to the state, and especially the city of New York. While it is not as expensive, nor as difficult to obtain a driver's license in the Big Apple as it is in say, Bonn or Tokyo or Singapore, where it can cost a thousand dollars and take up to a year, believe me the difficulty level is up there among the top five.

Little did I suspect this unspoken official attitude when one sunny afternoon while I was in Chinatown doing wok specialty grocery shopping, I walked down a different street than I usually did to my subway stop and found myself in front of a large, dreary, gothic building called The Tombs, a famous criminal court house and jail. Oddly enough, right next door in a similarly designed building was the Department of Motor Vehicles. Laden down with a shopping bag from Kee Woo Superette as I was, I nonetheless decided to look in and confirm for myself exactly how long I would have to wait on their notoriously long and glacier-slow moving lines to pick up an application for a learner's permit.

I was so astounded by how empty the lobby was, that I went up to the window and innocently asked. A woman with tons of falsely black curls and huge rhinestone framed glasses handed me an application, some other papers, and wrapped it all around a DMV booklet on driving. "Too bad you don't have proof of age," she consoled me, "Or you could take the written test right now."

It turned out I had my passport with me, and so I did have proof. I then filled out the application and other forms and she pointed me to the door where the written tests were given. Again, miracle of miracles, I noticed only a few people waiting to take the test. Even so, I thought I shouldn't tempt Fate *quite* so far: I ought to at least *look* at the DMV booklet, no? So I took it outside, across to a brick retaining wall fronting the big State Supreme Court House at Foley Square. There, while gobbling scallion pancakes and a persimmon I'd just bought off Chinatown street vendors, I skimmed the booklet, stopping at pages with charts and figures to be memorized and at those areas of the driving laws I wasn't sure of. About an hour later I took and passed the written test.

That was the easy part. What I only discovered once I'd been handed my Learner's Permit was that I now had to take ten hours of accredited driving lessons. And it would be another month minimum before I could take the road test.

"More like three months," the Hispanic clerk assured me. And when he saw I lived in Manhattan, he added a new caveat, "No road tests there. You'll have to go to Brooklyn. They're already booked five months." When I asked if I couldn't take the road test some other place, he said, "Sure! Queens, six months, Bronx, seven months. But wait, Staten Island is only three months!"

So, not having a clue what I was letting myself in for, but knowing it would be the fastest, I signed up for a road test in Staten Island in three months. Then I went to driving school.

I'd seen driving students in their bright red Corsairs and Escorts with big "Student Driver" signs on top all over the West Village. Especially along Greenwich Street, where they would attempt parallel parking, so I had the name of a local driving school.

The young woman with the intense Brooklyn accent who signed me up told me I'd need eight hours on the road, and two hours in class, with DMV mandated films to watch on alcohol consumption and road safety tips. The cost for four two-hour lessons would be a hundred and thirty dollars. They expected me to know everything in the booklet. The instructor would tell me what I specifically required to pass the road test.

I showed up the next day check in hand for my first lesson, and met a sad-eyed, not unattractive guy in his early thirties who behaved and dressed like an out of work actor, which it turned out he was. We took an elevator down to a basement garage, and he tossed me the keys, saying, "You know how to drive, right? You just need a refresher?"

"Right," I said, taking the keys and opening the driver's side door and getting in. I put the key in the ignition, then looked at everything on the dashboard, doing anything I could to put off the moment of starting up the car. Tried out various levers, as he said, "That's smart, familiarizing yourself with the car. That's high beams, wipers, parking lights. Why not just back out of the space and drive onto the street?"

I guess it *is* like swimming, because while I was far more nervous than he had any idea of, I did as he asked, backed out, slowly drove up the ramp and out onto West Fifteenth Street. Following his directions, I turned left, went to the corner, stopped, and waited. There, right in front of incredibly stupid me, was not the empty roads of the far West Village which I'd pictured myself driving on for this first lesson, but instead the very different 4:30 p.m. Seventh Avenue traffic jam in full swing.

I should have panicked. I actually was planning to panic. But after all, I knew these streets. I'd had an apartment here for twenty-five years, I biked here daily. It really was familiar, so although the traffic was thick and slow, and turbaned cab drivers sideswiped in front of me by about an inch and a half, I found it fairly easy going. And while I'd never planned on driving much in New York City traffic, the truth was I would need to know how bad it was, if only for coming and going off the East and West Side Drives on those real, long trips out of town that I intended to take.

The instructor had me turn off before traffic for the tunnel got too heavy, then he got me onto some less trafficked streets: in fact the very ones I was utterly familiar with from walking and biking. "Pull over to the curb."

I did as instructed. "Did I screw up something?"

"No you're doing fine. In fact if you can be this unruffled in heavy city traffic you'll do fine. You obviously know how to drive pretty well. What I'll do from now on is concentrate on drilling you on what the road testers are looking for. They have certain things they're after, you have to know."

I was surprised, I suppose. I mean aside from some slow driving in my companion's Celica coupe along an unused lane of the Sunrise Highway coming home from Fire Island Pines several months before, I'd not been behind the wheel in a quarter century!

Howard's low key approach—we were on first name basis by the end of the first lesson—and his dry sense of humor, increased my confidence. By the second lesson, he was telling me stories about some of his students. Most were people who'd never driven before and had to learn fast because they'd gotten company transfers out of Manhattan to places where they would need to commute. The most frequent repeaters were women, Howard said. Mostly because it had been knocked into their heads over the years that women were poor drivers. In his opinion, Hispanics made the best mechanics and Asian women the worst drivers.

Then there were those women who failed their tests again and again and came back to school again and again—asking for Howard. "With one, on the fifth time," Howard said, "I joked 'We've got to stop meeting like this.' And she replied, 'Yes. My husband is getting jealous.'" It turned out she had the hots for me." Did he for her? Did he ever? I asked. Howard shrugged, "I take 'em on a case by case basis."

And at a later lesson, when he knew I was an author and had free time, Howard suggested that when I got my license that I also take up being a driving instructor for extra income. He explained what additional instruction and reading was needed to become accredited to teach driving and added, "You'll meet lots of women." "Yeah, maybe, "I replied, "But I'm gay." Only momentarily startled, he said, "Well, you'll meet lots of guys too!" Had he ever...? I had to ask, to which Howard replied, "I'm not saying yes, and I'm not saying no, but like I said before, I take 'em on a case by case basis." We laughed. But as he wasn't my type nor I his, and that's as far as it went.

Because the road test was still a month away, I held off my final driving instruction lesson 'til a few days beforehand. By then, my life partner had suddenly sickened, been hospitalized and in a matter of five weeks he'd died and I no longer had the use of his car.

I could have stopped right there, I mean after all, the very reason I originally had for getting another driver's license no longer existed. I was still in a state of shock, a morass of fuzzy non-feeling, shot through with thoughts of suicide, but something inside me said, "Go ahead. Do this. It'll be useful." For what? Driving into a stone abutment at ninety miles an hour? Well, given my state of mind, that actually would be useful, wouldn't it? Why eliminate such an obvious solution?

In typical Catch 22 form, a driver's license was needed to rent a car for the road test to get a driver's license; but my friend Joseph Arsenault agreed to rent a car for me to use in the road test and, as he'd actually recently resided in Staten Island, he agreed to sleep over my house and drive me to the road test. We thus arrived at the day before my noon appointment somewhere in the depths of Richmond County, with me driving because—get this—he was nervous on city roads.

We picked up the car late, uptown, and had dinner in a place he knew near Columbia University. Arriving at my place quite late, Joseph parked in front of my building. I thought he was too close to a fire hydrant and said so. He said he'd pay for any ticket he got. And so to bed.

Next morning after breakfast I go to get the newspaper. No rental car in front of the house. I instantly understood. The car had not only been ticketed, it had been towed. A phone call confirmed this. It was now ten o'clock a.m. In the next hour and a half I had to take a hundred and eighty dollars out of my ATM machine, get the car out of DMV storage, and drive to my road test. Believe me none of this was as fast or simple as it sounds and it didn't help that Joseph was broke and more than contrite. All I wanted was action. At 11:30 a.m. I finally had the car keys in my hand. We were at Thirtieth Street at the West Side Highway.

Now Joseph wavered. He'd not driven on a highway in a long time and was nervous about it. So I got in and drove, down Manhattan through the Battery Tunnel, along the Belt Parkway, across the Verrazano Bridge, through Staten Island. Still upset, Joseph wavered again, but since I had the day before looked up the spot on a map, I located it easily. It was a stretch of road behind a four-block long mall in the midst of suburbs. It was eleven fifty-one as I parked in back of another car. In seconds some ten other cars pulled up behind me. Essentially in the middle of nowhere, we sat and waited.

A statuesque young woman in tailored suit with a clipboard suddenly appeared. She was the road tester and took the first car. When I approached, she said, "Someone will be here for you. We were just on a coffee break."

A few minutes later, a slender, very handsome black-haired fellow in a gray suit showed up and gestured me to pull up to the line the previous car had just vacated. He also had the clipboard, and told Joseph to get out of the car. He got into the driver's seat, buckled up, looked at me with a scowl and said, "Roll down the window. You're using hand signals."

Up close, he looked to be maybe twenty-six, Southern-Italian American, and even handsomer than before: I mean movie star handsome, with luxuriously lashed eyes of ice-blue. I must have mooned at him a bit, because he immediately asked, "What are we waiting for?" Confirming, if further confirmation was needed, that he was in a Substantially Bad Mood.

Thus began Road Test Number Two. It went downhill from that point in every way. I guess he wanted me to feel the brunt of his anger by making me use hand signals for everything including turns and thus screw up my concentration so I'd fail the test, but while I found them inconvenient, that was about all, at least compared to the true distraction of sitting next to such a complete stud—*Hello gorgeous!* That and not the hand signals, that and not having the rental car towed and having to pay so much money to get it back and almost be late for the test, might have screwed up my concentration. As it turned out, much more to distract me would shortly come my way.

I drove away from the mall and following his detailed instructions turned left into the residential street. That turned out to be the penultimate direction of his I'd be able to achieve, despite the fact that his road test had only just begun.

At the next corner, as I waited at the stop sign he instructed me to turn left deep into the lane and go two blocks. I had my hand out the window and was awaiting traffic to thin out, when two cars from opposite directions decided to turn without signaling each other or me. Not ten feet away and in perfect profile to us, they slowly but surely mashed into each other's front ends. Ker-rassh!

I immediately changed my hand signal, and backed up the car. I parked at the side of the road. I shut off the engine and got out.

"What are you doing?" Gorgeous asked.

"It's a accident. According to the DMV booklet, I have to see if anyone is hurt and report immediately. There's a phone."

I checked to make sure that no one was dangerously hurt—the two women drivers were merely stunned—and phoned it in. We then waited, for police cars and an ambulance to wail into view.

At which point, I returned to the rental car where my road tester was waiting. Clearly I couldn't go directly ahead. The intersection was blocked by crashed cars, and now by cop cars.

"Okay, back up," he said, nonplussed. "This is as good a place as any to do a three point turn. Use that driveway."

I began to do as he'd instructed but just then two children decided to pull their wagon into the driveway, and so I had to use the next driveway for the three pointer to go back the way I'd come. At the following stop sign, he said, "Now, as before, I want you turn left, and deep into the lane."

But when the light was in my favor and I could move, it turned out that two women with baby strollers had already stepped out onto the street, and were blocking the lane. I gestured for them to cross the street, but they were chatting and didn't see me. I blew the horn and gestured. They remained where they were.

I turned to Gorgeous. "I can't do what you want."

"Turn right," he sighed. However, halfway down the length of that street turned out to be blocked by an oil truck delivering fuel that had just nicked a light pole and was stopped to inspect damage. He was going nowhere soon.

"Now what?" I asked Gorgeous.

"Another three point turn," he groaned. Not bothering to name a driveway, and thus letting me choose.

I did and went back the other way, turning out of the still congested intersection, I drove up the first street that looked passable.

By now, even I could tell Gorgeous was helplessly lost, his original road test pattern and probably two more patterns were totally broken. As I drove, he kept looking out the window and it was all we could to find our way out of those similar looking residential streets filled with one obstruction to his directions after another—in one case a large St. Bernard dog was sleeping in the middle of the road which I had to go around—until we could find our way out and back to the mall.

Finally I did spot the test site. "There!" I shouted, "Up ahead!"

Gorgeous was clearly relieved and frazzled. He made me back up the street I'd just driven through a bit so that I could parallel park, behind what looked like a carpet cleaner's van.

I did so, just as I'd been drilled to do it by Howard, in the requisite three smooth steps, and I stopped.

"Why aren't you pulling up?" Gorgeous demanded to know. "You have to pull up behind the van. Pull up, pull up!" he shouted. Just as the van driver in front of me, that I—but not he—had noticed inside the van's cab, threw the van into reverse and suddenly backed up directly into us, stopping an inch from the rental car's bumper.

The road tester swore, leapt out of the car and ran to the van driver's window, shouting.

Mr. Carpet Cleaner had seen his error and he pulled away, squealing tires. He didn't even hesitate at the stop sign but charged past it and around the corner.

When he was back in my rental car, Gorgeous instructed, "Pull up now!"

I did so and thus completed my parallel parking stint. I also managed to *not say* what I wanted to so badly, i.e., that I had noticed what the road tester had missed: the van driver at the wheel of a running vehicle not paying attention to anything around him, which was why I hadn't pulled up into the space.

"Okay! Okay! Let's get out of here!" Gorgeous moaned. "Back behind the line of cars waiting."

I pulled up alongside the mall where Joseph was leaning against a light pole reading my copy of the *Times*.

"Okay! Shut it off," Gorgeous said. He wrote something on one page and on the top page scrawled a giant letter, then threw something in my lap. "Fill it out yourself."

I'd been waiting for him to tell me whether I'd passed or failed. Which he clearly wasn't about to do. So I looked at the paper, and noticed it was an official Temporary Drivers License. "In the future don't drive so fast." Gorgeous concluded, and pulled himself wearily out of the car. Without looking at me, or any of the other cars waiting for him, he strode across the mall parking lot and directly into what looked like a saloon, I supposed for a couple of stiff doubles.

"What happened?" Joseph asked.

"You won't believe it," I said, laughing. Then I showed him. "I passed. God, what a heartthrob he was! Every time I had to turn around to do some maneuver I couldn't help but stop and look once more at that gorgeous face!"

So, you now understand why, my father had to be desperate to be traveling with me. I mean desperate.

The day of our trip I sat in the driver's seat of his twelve-year-old formerly owned mid-sized Pontiac and noticed some obvious discrepancies: "Where's the handbrake?" My father didn't know. He'd never used it. And the speedometer! It only read up to eighty-five miles per hour. "Fuel-injected," he explained, "Saves gas. Work it up to cruising speed."

I'd driven dozens of rental cars after getting my second license, which meant that in no time I was relaxed behind the wheel of this car too. As I drove along

the West Side Highway out of Manhattan, we began to talk cars. My father told
me about his own very first car, a 1932 Pontiac, a sporty ragtop with a rumble
seat and white walls, bought for six-hundred dollars. He'd driven with a friend
on a new road to Montreal and slept overnight in Lake George. "Whenever we
would come to another car," he said, "We'd stop, get out, and shake hands."

"You're kidding? There were so few cars then?"

"You bet. And, people with cars then were a better type of person."

The first half of our trip to Providence my father and I made good time.
I was bothered a bit by the fact that the car had no "pick up" for passing.
Not that I zip in and out of traffic. But I'm also not crazy about being unable
to escape a sixteen wheeler with a nodding off driver. So I chose to take the
Hutchinson and Merritt Parkways, where no trucks are allowed, and only
switched back onto Interstate Ninety-five when I had to.

Once we had arrived in Rhode Island, my father took advantage of having
a chauffeur. The funeral wreaths had to be purchased from a particular florist
in Cranston. And where precisely was that bakery in Silver Lake that sold wine
biscuits unobtainable in Queens, promised to his friends back in New York?

My father's directions were memory-guided and so very tight: I had to
be alert for sudden turns, at a second's notice, and very often into streets that
looked more like alleyways.

On the third day of our visit, my father said, "You're not bad for a new
driver... New compared to driving sixty years like me," he explained.

"When I was learning you thought I'd be a terrible driver! And
dangerous!"

"Never," he protested. "Wasn't that your younger brother?"

"No. Me. You said I was too dreamy."

"Mmmmmmm," was all he replied.

Following the funeral, I began to notice even less pleasant oddities about
this formerly owned car. It began stalling after traffic lights. Well, not exactly
stalling. The ignition remained on, and something was spinning, it just
wouldn't go forward very far or at all fast. The second time this happened, I
mentioned it to my father, who replied, "Must be the spark plugs."

He promised to look at them, and indeed, once we'd returned to where we
were staying, he actually opened the car hood and peered inside and fooled

around. The next day, while I was driving, the same oddity happened again. It only seemed to happen in stop and go traffic, but even so, it was so odd, it began to worry me. My father took over the wheel. He was clearly befuddled; but he didn't think it was anything serious. If it were a rental car, I would have had it replaced. If it were my car, I would have driven to a garage. But it was his car. His decision.

The next morning we were to drive back to New York. He once again looked under the hood and fooled around with something. The car began well enough. It was really only an hour later at the Connecticut state line that I realized the car was losing power. It would not go over sixty miles an hour, no matter what I did. So I told my dad, moved into the slow lane, and worried more.

An hour later, outside of Madison, Connecticut the car's speed dropped to around fifty, and even in the slow lane I was being consistently passed. That was when I noticed white smoke in the rear view mirror. At first, I thought it might be from another vehicle. But as cars passing us began honking their horns and pointing to the back of the car, I realized the white smoke was coming from the formerly owned twelve-year-old mid-sized Pontiac.

"Hey Dad!" I shook him awake and pointed out the smoke.

He seemed baffled by its appearance.

"Shouldn't we pull off the highway?" I suggested. "Isn't this a sign of something really bad?"

"Nawwww! That's black smoke. White smoke isn't that bad. Although I wonder what could be causing that?"

I tried arguing the point, but we got nowhere. Then a sign for food ahead showed, and he suggested we stop for a bite and "rest" the car. Okay by me.

I needed a cup of coffee anyway. Because while he was clearly unconcerned; I now was thinking of alternative methods of getting home. This object was clearly not going to get me there.

A half hour later, rested and refreshed, I took over the wheel again. At first all was okay. No white smoke. By five miles later on the highway it was going not faster than forty miles an hour. Then thirty miles an hour. My father took over the wheel of the car. Then I began hearing strange sounds from within the hood. Clanks and clunks, Hisses and swisses. More clanks and clunks. I pictured the entire engine breaking loose.

Just beyond New Haven on an exit for Orange, there was one final, very loud clank, almost but not quite an explosion, and the car died. The term "engine seizure" danced through my mind. I'd never experienced one before, but this clearly was such an event—much akin to a fatal coronary infarction in a person.

I managed to direct my totally astounded father halfway up the ramp off the Interstate. There the car stopped utterly. When I got out to take a look, black smoke was coming out of the exhaust, and fat globs of smoking hot black oil were dripping from beneath the engine onto the tarmac. Even a cursory touch of the hood showed it to be hot. I managed to get it open enough to convince myself there wasn't any fire. I'd pictured the engine resembling some Cubistic jumble of loose gaskets and detached cylinders, but at a glance I couldn't see anything obviously wrong.

Some fifteen minutes were required for my father to get over his amazement and anger. I tried pushing the car, got it a bit up the ramp and had to be content. I told my fuming dad to stay by the dead vehicle while I went for a phone.

Some ten minutes later I returned, no phone in sight. By then, I'd noticed a car stopped at the Pontiac and someone talking to my father. He waved to me, got in the guy's car, and they stopped where I was walking back. A Good Samaritan was taking my dad to a local service center. I'd wait at the car.

I did so, on the exit way grass, reading the daily paper. My dad and the kind stranger reappeared some fifteen minutes later. Someone would come to look at the car. We both sat on the grass. About an hour later, someone with a white tow truck arrived, looked inside the engine and said, it had to be towed. This young man was convinced from what I'd told him that indeed the engine had seized up. They'd have to put in "on blocks" to see for sure.

Back at the garage we waited another hour for someone to look at the car. He decreed the engine a wreck. My father could leave it and junk it, or he could have it towed. That would cost maybe two hundred dollars. Even before the kind stranger had appeared, I'd suggested to my dad that we take out the jack and remove the license and just abandon the vehicle where it was. Being out of state, it wouldn't be that easy to trace. I'd already done this with my older brother coming and going to Providence fifteen years before, when his old Falcon had severe carburetor trouble. We'd been picked up by a Methodist minister who driven us right to my door.

But my dad wouldn't hear of abandoning it, nor of junking the car. He'd ride with them while they towed it back to Queens, even if it took all night. I loaned him the fifty dollars in my wallet and he stayed at the garage, awaiting the tow. I had to be back in the city for an evening appointment, and got the younger guy at the garage to drive me to the local Amtrak station. I arrived home about seven at night. My dad—and the formerly owned twelve-year old mid-sized Pontiac—arrived at one a.m.

He had the engine replaced at the dive where he had bought the car and he continued to drive it, albeit a lot more gingerly, for the next few months. Until one frozen winter afternoon when, as he was driving it up his own street, one wheel hit an ice patch, and the car suddenly accelerated from twenty to seventy miles an hour, smashing directly into a light pole. My father was shaken but unhurt. And wise enough to take this second hint from Fate. He sold the car for scrap to the nearest garage and bought a pale blue 1990 Buick Regal coupe. Formerly owned, but in pretty fine condition. I know, I've driven it.

Just a while ago, in fact. I was on a book tour that took me back to New York and I went out to Queens to have lunch with my dad. He's older now, and in even more fragile physical condition. The car looked good and he wanted to drive out to Mineola to pick up something for a friend, then treat me in a good Italian restaurant he knew of on the North Shore. As we were approaching the car, he tossed me the keys. "You drive."

I did. And it was plush and smooth, comfy, nice, a bit softly slung compared to the rougher edges and road feel of my own sporty little coupe. But it was a pleasant summer afternoon drive and even though my dad did get a bit lost looking for the restaurant, we eventually found it and we had a great lunch.

As I was driving him home I reminded my dad of our previous long drive together. "After that trip," I said, "I was sure you'd never want to drive with me again."

"That stupid car!" he moaned. And then, "No. None of that was your fault. You're a fine driver." He assured me: a vote of confidence years after I no longer needed nor wanted one—which didn't mean I didn't value it. "No, you're a good driver," he said. "Alert. Sure... You can drive me anytime, anywhere."

The Taystee Bread Man

A Boyhood Idol

I don't know about you, but in my life people seem to fall into two basic types: either they are unprecedented or they are variations on someone I've already known.

Naturally, when I was a child, everyone I met was unprecedented, as were most of the people I encountered in my teens. As I've gotten older, surviving where other supposedly hardier types have fallen from accident, war, and disease, I've noticed certain almost archetypal figures return again and again under different names years later.

One such figure I call the Central European Over-cultured Gentleman. Another is the Seductive Young Blond Beauty, who can be of either gender. A definite third is The Taystee Bread Man. If I were ever to arrive at completely believing in the Buddhist doctrines of reincarnation and "working out one's karma" from past lives, this return of certain very evident "types" of people in my life would constitute considerable substantiation.

Only a month after going to work for *Art Direction* magazine at the age of twenty-two, while listening to Diana, Mary, and Flo singing "That Boy" in my Jane Street studio apartment one night, I suddenly realized that although I knew him only to speak to, and thus not very well, that Ron Mallory—the magazine's advertising salesman—seemed to possess more than a slight physical resemblance to and might indeed be considered to be not much more than a variation upon someone I'd known as a child: my first love, in fact, although I was unaware of it at the time—The Taystee Bread Man.

That's what I called him. I never knew his real name.

Before my father's business expanded and became specialized in wholesale produce selling bulk only to airlines, hospitals, and smaller food stores, it was a small supermarket in Richmond Hill, a long, singled-storied edifice abutting the service road of the newly constructed Van Wyck Expressway. Outside and in, wooden stands held fresh produce. Indoors was a grocery store and small delicatessen. From the age of eight on, during the summer and on Saturday afternoons all year 'round, my older brother and I worked for my father.

Ostensibly this was to teach us how to be good bourgeois as well as to prepare us for the day in which Picano's would become Picano & Sons—a day that in my case never arrived. The bulk of our work consisted of trivial odd jobs that none of the clerks wanted to do, and chief among these was the repacking into their proper wooden flats of empty soda bottles that had been returned for deposit all week, which would then be picked up by trucks delivering fresh bottles of Coca-Cola, White Rock, Yoo Hoo, Nehi, and other local sodas.

It wasn't hard work, and our other jobs—stacking empty crates, sweeping up—were equally easy. We were usually done in a few hours and could hang around the store, or go out to the nearby park and play. A side benefit was that we got to drink all the soda and eat all the snacks we wanted.

In the back of the store, just past a huge old wooden refrigerator (I recall its applied aluminum exterior was in that stylized art deco style and in retrospect guess it to be from the mid-Thirties and that it had dozens of beveled glass windows on four tiers) a small office had been set up with most of the required trappings: desk, telephone, easy chair, filing cabinet. Here my father napped after lunch, and here I would hide out if I'd had another fight with my older brother or simply stay in to be out of the sun on hotter days, reading my newest comic book, or playing with my latest toy purchased at Krantzler's Candy Store at the end of the block.

Others used the office, including a few of the deliverymen. They would get a soda and a sandwich made up front, then come back to the office to eat and read the newspaper. I never discovered who got selected for this honor—probably the most easy going and most likable of the multitude of canned goods, soda, bread, and pastry men who delivered all morning and half the afternoon. But one of them was the man who delivered Taystee Bread, a company that had begun an enormously popular TV and print-ad campaign and was thus very successful.

My Taystee Bread Man first arrived while I was reading the Classic Comic version of *The Man in the Iron Mask* in the office and he said I should remain in the easy chair, he'd sit on the ottoman: a Naugahyde seat removed from someone's van. I'd been raised well, however, and immediately got up and gave him the better chair. As he ate his lunch and scanned the sports pages of *The Daily Mirror*, I looked him over above the pages of my comic book.

The Taystee Bread Man was tall and broad-shouldered, wide-bodied yet slender, and he looked lithe and yet strong in the two-piece, dark green uniform with its accents of carmine at pockets and sleeves, which all the company's deliveryman wore. He had what in memory I'd have to call an ugly-pretty face: not immediately handsome, not model-perfect, but once you really looked at it, devastatingly sexy: skin a bit rough yet not really scarred from acne, large warm hazel-brown eyes, a generous mouth with a lower lip fuller than the top, strong ruler-straight nose. His hair was sunny, light brown, iron-straight and full: unlike my own curly hair, his grew out and down from the middle of his head, like a living cap, and it must have been a cinch to cut. At the time he couldn't have been more than twenty-three or twenty-four and he wore a wedding ring.

Unlike most adults who made a point of ignoring me, the first time the TBM came into the back office, sat down, and checked the local team's stats in the paper, he asked what I was reading. Even better, he listened to what I said, he looked at what I considered the more spectacular drawings in the comic, and he even admitted he'd not read the book it was based on. With the democracy of childhood, I said he could borrow the comic, and after I'd insisted, he did borrow it, promising to return and to bring other comics.

Again, unlike most adults, who never remembered, never mind kept their promises to children, the next Saturday the TBM was back with the comic as well as two other Classic Comics: *The Deerslayer* and *Twenty Thousand Leagues Under the Sea*. We talked about *The Man in the Iron Mask*, discussing the characters and their motivations. He was patient and interested and when I asked him about the Verne comic he'd brought me, he really opened up. He told me that he'd been in the Navy and knew all about the ocean and being a sailor.

The following Saturday, the TBM showed me some of his Navy mementos and brought me more Classics Comics. I'd anticipated his arrival as I would a friend. And why not? He never condescended to me, never lied to me, never made a promise he didn't keep.

It was summertime—when the clerks at my father's store would sit outside in the fresh air under long awnings and my father would drive home for longer naps—when I began to see the TBM more often. Not every day. He delivered bread and other baked goods to us on Tuesday, Thursday, and Saturday. He began to let me sit on his lap and he would casually put his arm around me as we read through a comic together. One time he fell asleep with me like that. I don't know if he was ever sexually aroused; sometimes I did wriggle around on his lap until I found a comfortable spot, and he never seemed to mind or told me to stop squirming.

Recalling it, I'm surprised to find myself thinking that either he was completely naive and had no idea what he was doing, which was possible, or if he did know, that he must have been a terrifically cool customer, He never touched me where he shouldn't have, but he would scoop me into his lap in an instant and keep me there while he ate his lunch and read his paper, right until it was time for him to leave. I'm certain that had he done anything in the least bit sexual I would have gone along without any hesitation, and not for those reasons the so-called child-abuse experts give—out of innocent trust and caring. No! I would have done it because the TBM *excited* me; whenever I was with him I was in a constant state of mental and probably also physical *arousal*.

Our friendship lasted throughout summer and into early fall, when our meetings were curtailed to Saturday only by my return to school. My father saw us sitting together several times and I think he felt a bit guilty that he seldom held me in his lap like that or found the time to share my interests. He was probably a little proud of me too, of the fact that I was bright and interesting enough at nine years old for another adult to take such an interest in me. Whatever he thought, my father never said a word about it. And when I've asked him recently, he claimed not to remember the TBM at all.

One Saturday before Hallowe'en there was a new deliveryman on the Taystee Bread van. I asked week after week for my TBM, but the new one didn't like children, and he never told me why my friend had left the company.

I was very upset that first day, for several more weeks more I was disappointed; eventually I forgot about him. Several years later, when I was a relatively grown-up twelve-year-old, the TBM's replacement's replacement told me that he'd known my friend, and that my Taystee Bread Man had suddenly quit his job, left his wife—they had no children—and *re-enlisted in the Navy*.

That's all there was to it. Only in later years did I wonder why exactly, my TBM had left his marriage and his life.

Had our relationship alerted him to his own homosexuality, something he'd perhaps been only somewhat aware of before he met me? Did he go back into the Navy because in those days, that was one of the few places in the U.S. where you could be homosexual without causing too much of a stir?

I like to think so. I like to think that long before I even knew what it was, that I was being a gay activist. And he was my first client.

As for Ron Mallory, he was my TBM friend with a mustache and with green rather than hazel eyes. He was more unkempt too, less sociable and less easy-going, *and* he probably had a drinking problem.

Of course I'd never sat in his lap. But don't worry. I planned to. And having already broken one man's heart by the age of nine, I was certain I could do it again.

The Real 'Devil'

Diana Vreeland

My friend picked me up at the airport and since it was still early evening, we joined other friends I'd met through her. During dinner I mentioned that I'd seen for the second time on the plane ride coming back, the film, *The Devil Wears Prada*, and marveled at how well it held up on a second viewing.

The two women insisted that the book and the film were based on Anna Wintour, the current and long-time editor of *Vogue* magazine. They cited reviews and promised to send me proof.

But when I spoke with other people who'd been in Manhattan in the 1960's through 1980's, they assured me that I had been correct: the model for the "Devil" that Meryl Streep played to perfection in the film, was only *secondarily* Wintour. Streep had modeled herself and her behavior on the real "Devil," the editor of *Harper's Bazaar* and then *Vogue* for a total of fifty years, a woman whose death was on the front page of every newspaper in the world, the totally despotic arbiter of fashion in America for most of the twentieth century.

Her name was Diana Vreeland, and a few years after her death, the Metropolitan Museum in New York City did an exhibit on her influence on fashion. It was Vreeland who ruled the roost—Wintour, the latecomer.

I still haven't told those friends about the day that I interviewed Vreeland, and what an utter sweetheart she was to me, that afternoon in 1966, and afterward too.

Δ

On my return home from living in Rome and London, I began looking for a job. I'd been a social worker before I'd left, and although where I'd worked they'd bent over backwards to get me back, offering me a free graduate course in Social Work if I worked for them for two years, I had had enough with helping people. I wanted to become an artist—or at the very least, since jobs as an artist were rare, an art director.

So those were the listings I looked up in *The New York Times* classified employment ads. There weren't a lot that Sunday morning, but there were enough, and the next day I showered and dressed, put on a jacket and tie, and sallied forth. I was expecting nothing the first day, and yet, I was young, and so I guess I was expecting everything that first day too.

The third interview of the morning was in the same building where the *New Yorker* magazine was located and seemed promising. It was less than a block from a subway station, in midtown Manhattan.

The offices of *Art Direction* magazine, like the operation itself, were small and if not exactly chic then at least not like most of the offices I'd been to the previous weeks looking for work. Those had been downtown and had been either grungy or ultra sleek. This office had a little bit of character: mostly in the form of magazine covers on the wall that were interesting to look at.

I had phoned ahead and after a few minutes of waiting in a lobby, I was called into the main office by the assistant editor, a brisk young woman, nice looking, a little zaftig, well dressed, and utterly dismissive.

She took me through a small warren of office cubicles to an office with a full series of windows at a corner. I was introduced to the editor in chief, a man named Ralph, who half stood to meet me, revealing instantly that he used a cane, and was crippled in one leg—I guessed either from the Korean War or polio.

Ralph was of Irish extraction, with a nice, not handsome face, penetrating blue green eyes, and curly, slightly graying chestnut hair. His face was mobile and expressive and his voice was sweet if low—he might have sung high baritone. This very favorable impression was of course partly true and, I would later discover, partly job interview fabrication.

He looked over my resume, as I sat staring out the windows at all the other Manhattan offices around us with people bustling about, speaking on phones, or conversing face to face. It all seemed so grown up.

"There's a *year* missing between your last job and today?" he pointed out, not unkindly.

"I was in Europe."

"For a year? What are you, rich?"

"No, my motorcycle was destroyed in Genoa by another driver and I had to stay in Italy to collect the monthly insurance payments."

"You drive a motorcycle?"

"I used to!"

He looked at me and I could see him mentally shaking his head—a motorcyclist, loafing abroad.

"So you just lived in Rome. No work?"

"Well, I did work but I didn't put it down on the resume because I didn't think it was relevant."

His pencil was poised over my fairly empty resume.

"I worked as a voice-over performer at *Cinecittà* for several months," I said. "And then—" I tried swallowing my words, "As a sort of assistant screenwriter."

He looked up, his eyes shining at me. "You wrote movies in Rome?"

"Terrible movies. Spaghetti westerns. Sword and sandals epics. Bad sci-fi. Terrible horror. I mostly just tried to keep the scripts internally consistent for the writer/director I worked for."

I'd meant to quash any ideas of glamour, but he asked the name of the director.

I told him, and he whistled, "I know that name. He won the Golden Bear in Berlin."

"He's totally gone for the money since then," I said.

I did not tell Ralph that the guy had been my lover—and that all that money had more or less kept me in clothing, jewelry, and motor-scooters for over half a year.

"The movies were awful." I repeated.

"Scott Fitzgerald wrote movies. William Faulkner wrote movies."

"I'll bet they didn't write *Vampire-Women from Alpha Centauri?*"

For a moment I was afraid he'd seen the movie and liked it.

"So…" he concluded with a little hum in his voice. "You're a writer."

"No. No." I tried to quickly disabuse him. "I'm an *artist*. "

"We've got an opening for a writer. You could start tomorrow."

"I applied for the job of assistant art director." I tapped the resume. "See! 'B.A. in Art.'"

"*Co-major* in Art," he corrected me, "Co-major in English and World Literature. You received Departmental Honors in *that* Department, it says here. Or isn't that true?"

"It's true," I admitted.

"And you what, wrote for your school newspaper? Magazine?"

"Never! No! Neither! I keep telling you. I was an artist. In high school I painted sets for our shows. In college I painted, sculpted, and did collages in the studio there. I'm an *artist*."

"Why are you fighting being a writer?" he asked me. And when I didn't answer, he added, looking away from me, "My dream is to leave this job and become a full-time writer and write a novel. I would give anything to write a movie. Even a terrible one!"

"I like to draw, to paint," I said simply enough.

He rumbled about a bit and I thought: this interview is so over.

"Look I understand if you…" I began.

"The assistant art director's job is filled," he said. "They should have taken the ad out of the Sunday paper."

"Thanks for talking to me. Nice meeting you." I began to get up.

"Wait!" he grabbed me by the wrist and pulled me down again.

"Look! This guy was hired only on Friday," Ralph said quickly. "He's really raw. I don't know how he'll work out. So maybe that job can be yours. Meanwhile, since you have all this writing experience, and are apparently flexible and can learn new things easily as proven by your work in Rome, we really need a writer here, fast. The gal in my News Department just got a job at a big advertising firm and she's leaving at the end of the week. Why not come in, take over her desk, and let's see what happens?"

He then named the weekly pay, which—while not much—was higher than the other job.

I needed money badly, so I hesitated.

"She'll train you. It's not a hard job to do," he went on. "And when that other position opens up, you're right here on the spot to fill it. In the meanwhile you can do art at home. On the weekends. You don't have to stop doing that."

"Let's say I say yes..." I began.

"Say yes, and I'll get you a week's paid vacation in the first year. Remember, as a journalist, you'll be talking on the phone with art directors from the biggest ad agencies in town, all the time here. Your possibilities are endless."

When I continued to hesitate, thinking it through, Ralph stood up, "Jane! Come meet Mr. Picano. Felice is it? Jane, come meet your replacement, Felice."

That's how I began that job.

∆

I hope you paid attention to the above scene, because it illustrates the old, philosophical chestnut-question of Free Will versus Destiny—in this case in the life of Felice Picano. Keep this in mind at all times: Felice Picano didn't want to be a writer. He wanted to be a *visual artist*. Yes, he could write well. He could also paint, sculpt, and do other visual art very well. For that matter, at age twenty-two, he could sing well, dance well, play the clarinet well, and probably swing on a trapeze pretty well. But in retrospect, this was the *first step* in which Fate stepped in to quash Felice's life wish and chosen career and to impose Its own choice upon him for Its own obscure reasons. Throughout the next twelve years, Destiny would go through a progressive series of all kinds of extreme and sometimes quite tasteless deceptions and ruses, some similar, others quite dissimilar to the above, but all of them inexorably leading in the same direction: so that Felice Picano in fact *did* become a writer and *not* an artist. As Destiny, recall, not Felice, wished.

∆

What I had really wanted when I went out job hunting in so dilatory a fashion was to hang out for a bit longer: I'd only been home from London a week. But here was a job open, and I either had to let it go, or take it immediately.

Felice Picano

This was not calculated to make me a happy trooper at *Art Direction*, where I began work the next morning at nine a.m.

As for the person I was replacing: Jane was raven-haired, slender, short-tempered, expert, and annoyed by me and by having to train me when she clearly preferred just taking off. Against that, was the very substantial benefit that she was busy getting prepared for her new job, which meant she was out of the office a great deal—hours at a time, sometimes returning with shopping bags of clothing—increasingly so as the week went on.

She gave me reams of ad agency-generated publicity pages that she had gone through and checked off to become tiny little news stories. I was to turn all this cleverly done verbiage into a single small paragraph.

I thought I'd done a good job with the first batch, but she sneered and cut those down to even smaller paragraphs, eliminating all but the facts. In a week, I had learned how to do that pretty well.

She threw around names of art directors and agencies, magazine editors and photographers and designers at such speed I couldn't copy them all down. She made me feel like I didn't know a thing. The truth was: I really didn't know a thing in this area.

I did meet the new assistant art director I hoped to replace, a fat-boy, nerdy, African-American guy whom I liked on the instant. The man he was working for, Franz, a thin, overeducated, dyspeptic, Austrian émigré who appeared to be have become so jaded that he was probably last aesthetically excited by the *Jugendstil* movement, was as annoying and annoyed as Jane. I wondered how such a small office, consisting of at last count only seven people, would have so many people I didn't like. Besides the art staff, there were three of us in Editorial, the two salesmen, the publisher and his secretary: a middle aged woman who was superficially nice but whom I heard on the phone with her friend "Ceil" dishing all of us when she thought no one was listening. I'd met Ralph's assistant editor: Lynda was in the cubicle in front of mine, with a bit of a window view, but she was frosty, acting as though I'd not make their high standards and be gone very soon, so why should she even bother getting to know me?

After Jane left, I was handed her materials directly. At first Ralph marked out those pieces he thought important, but I also began getting mail myself—

directly to the "News Editor"—and soon I was going through these and if anything struck me, I'd mark it and leave it on Ralph's desk. Most of the time, he agreed with the mark up: "Small story—1 par."—meaning one paragraph long.

There were also several outsiders who had their own regularly read columns in the magazine, and they were treated like minor stars whenever they came into the office. They'd meet with the publisher; often Ralph went out to lunch with them, and Lynda, the assistant editor, would rush out to talk to them, and return all flushed as though they had quickie sex in a closet.

Jane had left three months of "feature stories," since all three of us were supposed to write them in addition to our regular work. Ralph mentioned this after about two months, and he told me that it was now up to me to get some ideas and to generate features of my own. *Yecch!*

To my disgust, Austen, the assistant A.D., was *not* fired, although he evidently screwed up regularly, and Franz complained of him on a constant basis to whomever would listen—usually the publisher's secretary and Lynda.

Since Austen and I had lunch once a week, I once brought this up and he good naturedly replied: "I'm a minority!" as he gulped down his foot-long sandwich. "Don… the publisher …and Ralph, felt they had to hire someone who was a minority. And now that I'm here, it'll be hard to get rid of me."

I was kind of glad, as I liked him. But there went my art director's spot. And indeed Austen remained there, even after Franz retired. He even became something of an ally to me, although it always seemed to me he wasn't really fitted for the job, which was so technical, and he always seemed swamped with work.

As for all those wonderful art director contacts that Ralph had pitched at me to get me potential ad agency art jobs: *forget it!* I mostly spoke with assistants and when I did get to meet the head A.D. he was usually so busy pitching some new ad campaign for my news section, I could barely get a word in.

On top of that, these guys were always a decade or so older than me. As I looked about sixteen at the time, I would walk into the (usually) upscale midtown Manhattan restaurant where we were meeting for lunch and eighty percent of time I was asked 1) if I were lost, 2) if I were meeting my father, or—3) I would be carded. At the really fancy ones, the *maitre d'* would finger my tie, checking that it was silk, and not one of the dreaded alternatives.

The A.D.'s I met there too were surprised by my youth. By this time, I knew some of the argot, the lingo, the "Ad-Chat," most of the names, and even which agencies had which big accounts, and after five or ten minutes, they would relax around me.

As for getting a word in edgewise, first let's talk about these (mostly) men and their so-called lunches. If you've seen the HBO drama *Mad Men*, you will have some idea of how they looked,—buttoned-down and clean cut to the max—how they dressed—sharp and expensively (J. Press, Brooks Brothers, and the really upscale ones at Dunhill), as well as how they thought and spoke—misogynistic, homophobic, racist—and those were the ones I deemed likable.

I, however, wore my curly hair longish, and lived not in a suburb or the Upper East Side but in the West Village, and to all of them I dressed, acted, and must have seemed utterly "downtown," i.e., they considered me a stoned hippie—despite my rep tie and Irish wool sports coat. This wasn't so bad, because as they often pointed out, I wasn't in the ad biz, they were: I was an (always said as though it were in quotes) "artist." I guess I must have fulfilled their visual idea of a bohemian. Especially when they found out that by the age of twenty-two, I'd already lived in Europe a year.

After about the fourth of these lunch meetings, I learned that my co-diners—unless they were of Jewish or Italian backgrounds—seldom actually ordered lunch and if I wanted to eat something, I'd better stop a waiter myself and order it. Three martinis comprised the usual noonday collation. Not to mention other goodies. Once, at a meeting at a very large ad agency, I was shown into the executive men's room: all black marble. When I went to wash my hands, I spotted the tell tale trickle of blood that is made after you've withdrawn a hypodermic needle. Diabetes, maybe? But knowing how highly-stressed out these guys were, and how easy it was to get, I immediately assumed the DOC (Drug of Choice) to be Methedrine.

My first feature story assignment from Ralph was a doozey: Video-tape had just come in—go on laugh: but this was in media-primitive 1966!—

and Ralph wanted me to write up a big story on how it could be used in commercials instead of film.

I almost quit right then. I did audibly groan, especially when he told me he wanted me to get all the technical data comparing video-tape to old-time Kinescope, used for recording old live TV shows and commercials. I sulked around so much the rest of that day, that Ralph approached me at closing time, five p.m. and said if I did a good job with that feature, that he'd let me choose the topic of my next one.

My reply: "Austen says he *can't* be fired and he's not going anywhere."

To which Ralph muttered, "*Everyone* can be fired."

Δ

The video-tape story was about as horrible a first-time feature story writing experience as I feared it would be. I revised it four times. Ralph clearly didn't understand the concept of electro-magnetic tape-recording even long after techno-stupid I did understand it. He kept sending my article back for details and explanations. I began arranging lunchtime job interviews.

Finally the article came out and it was hailed as brilliant, innovative, first rate, way ahead of the pack. Throw in here any similar clichés and you've got it. Ralph went out of his way to tell me all this.

My reply: "If, like Cezanne, I can paint one apple really well, I'll be happy."

"Have you thought about the feature you want to do?" he asked.

I lied and said no.

In fact, I wanted to write about Andy Warhol's film, *Chelsea Girls*. It had been playing at a midnight theatre on lower Sixth Avenue for about five months and it had taken my set by storm. Besides the plotlessness of it, the disconnectedness of it, and the dual screens throughout much of it, in effect showing two movies at once, it was a distillation and summation of all that Warhol and Paul Morrissey—his camera man—had been doing up until then: with the wonderful surprise that Factory hangers on like Viva, Bridget Berlin, and especially my friend, Ondine, could really come across and deliver on the screen.

A week later Ralph asked me again and this time I suggested the film as a feature piece and told him why. I insisted that *this* was something that was truly "brilliant, innovative, first rate, way ahead of the pack."

He clearly had no idea what I was talking about, and said he would think about it. I was to call the Factory or the distributor for images. Those arrived, he thought about it another week and then said, "Tell you what. It's not a feature. What about a news story about the split screen?"

By now I knew how conservative he was, and said, "Even Lynda thinks it's important!" His assistant editor was as conservative as he was.

"Write up a small story and put it into her 'What's Hot?' section."

This would mean she would get credit but at least the story would appear in the first two or three editorial pages of the magazine. I took the compromise.

The next week I came up with a feature about how rock and roll had changed LP record covers—mostly because of the San Francisco style "hallucinogenic" stylization.

Again I had to write it up as a "What's Hot" story, although now I could sign it with my byline.

The following month a trio of ad execs who'd left cushy spots to open their own company, Wells Rich Greene, sent me over Mary Wells' designs for Braniff Airlines that would revolutionize airline advertising and make the fortunes for the small Brazilian carrier and the new agency. Wells Rich Greene had designed everything—including the outsides of the planes and the stewards and pilot's uniforms.

And so another "What's Hot" story for me, this one taking the entire first page of the section.

Without wanting to, or even really knowing how, I became the go-to-guy at the magazine for those hot new A.D.s opening their own "boutique" shops. Soon, I was getting as much mail addressed to "What's Hot" as Lynda. She, nicely enough, didn't complain.

By this time I'd met Bob Herron, and we'd become lovers, and I was now living amidst an exciting, fun, close knit group of pre-Stonewallers in a group that I later would call The Jane Street Girls. Three, four or more of us socialized daily, hung out all almost every night, watched (the original) *Star Trek* together, traded books, records, and even tricks, and we were inseparable on weekends. I'd also met a group of stoners living in a commune on West Twelfth Street, headed by an older man, Jan Rosenberry, who was at the time V.P. in charge of advertising at Bristol-Meyers. Clearly, any interest I might have had in art, art direction, or indeed work at all was now reduced to the absolute minimum. All I was interested in was the pay—and my upcoming paid vacation. I wasn't even looking for other jobs, feeling I could handle this one by more or less dialing it in, as long as Ralph made no demands on me.

It was into this situation that one day he dropped onto my desk a two-page publicity puff piece from *Harper's Bazaar* about it being the staid, old-fashion magazine's hundredth anniversary. Ralph had written on top, "Make this into a feature about the artists and photogs they worked with."

Now if I knew little about technology, I knew even less about fashion. I barely knew that fashion existed. And what I knew was really only a result of the junior high school I'd gone to, where I quickly discovered the guys were far more sophisticated at thirteen than I was at twelve and dressed in really neat chinos— with belts at the back above the butt: accenting that part of the body, and they wore shirts in the new colors of that time, the mid-Fifties, colors like hot pink, charcoal, slate grey, and sky blue. Since then, there had been one more exciting fashion development, hippies and rock musicians. We imitated the Beatles, the Rolling Stones, the Who, and Jefferson Airplane closely in our casual and weekend wear with close-fitting military style second-hand jackets, bell bottoms, big loud paisley scarves, and color-saturated, tie-dyed and frilled shirts.

Let me add that what I knew about *Harper's Bazaar* could be fitted into a thimble.

I told Ralph that. He said, "Learn. Go to a library."

New York's cathedral-like Forty-second Street Public Library was four blocks away, and I did go there for two full afternoons, and looked at hundreds of issues and copied down dozens of names and dates and it was all pretty much a jumble. I'd had enough Art History classes to recognize that the old issues I was leafing through had distinctive styles—*La Belle Epoque* was Art Nouveau, Post World War One was Art Deco and *Moderne*, then came World War Two and Post-War and those designers so famous even I knew their names: Chanel, Dior, Balenciaga, et al.

Still, I dithered. I didn't feel I knew enough. Ralph would ask every two days: "How's that feature coming along?" And I'd answer, "I need more material. I need more time."

Finally he sat me down one afternoon and demanded that I write the feature story.

I told him point-blank, "I feel really uncomfortable with this material. This is more Lynda's thing."

"Lynda's got plenty of features." He seemed to ponder, then he said, "Tell you what, why don't you go talk to someone who will be able to put it all into context with you. Call her and interview her. She was the person in charge of *Harper's Bazaar* for years."

He gave me her name, and that afternoon I called and asked to speak to Diana Vreeland. The woman said, "She's now at *Vogue*." Embarrassed, I called *Vogue* and I got an underling, identified myself, and said, I was doing a feature story on the century of artists and photographers in fashion and wanted to speak with Miss Vreeland.

"She actually called back?!" Lynda was astounded later that afternoon. Ralph was out of the office.

"Well, her assistant did," I admitted. "She said I could come in tomorrow at 11:45 a.m."

"She won't speak with you. Not Vreeland. She'll put you off onto some assistant. Diana Vreeland *does not* give interviews. Certainly not to tyros like you who work at trade magazines," Lynda added grandly.

"Then why did Ralph tell me to call her?"

"He expected you to *not get* through to her. And you won't."

"Why would he... You mean he expects me to fail?" I asked. It was my turn to be astounded. On the other hand, he must have known she had left one magazine for the other years before. Why had he hidden that fact?

"Of course, he expects you to fail. He keeps giving you feature stories to write that he doesn't think you can do? Right?" she asked.

By then I knew that Lynda was engaged to be married and was resigning and heading off in the fall. Also that while she did her work expertly, she and Ralph never socialized at all. Meanwhile she had thawed a bit to me; probably because I seldom bothered her. In addition, I'd begun to see that all the jolly aspects Ralph had displayed the first few weeks I was there, were countered by days of anger and depression—but over what I didn't know: his wife, his family, his health, his work? I'd learned to keep away from him those days, small as the office was.

So I could actually understand Lynda saying that Ralph was giving me stories to do that I couldn't possibly do: undermining me from the inception. I'd watched my father do that to me, when he'd thought I gotten too smart too fast. I'd left home as soon as I realized that. Later on, I would see another superior do it to me, when he began to fear me, baselessly. But here I was sure that I acted like I didn't at all care about the job, which I didn't. So, the bigger and next question was: "But why would Ralph do that?"

"Don't you see he's jealous of you?" Lynda declared.

"Why?" I naively asked, but her phone was ringing and that ended the conversation.

I could answer my question myself: because I was young, in full use of my limbs; because I was good looking; because I was free enough to have co-written bad movies in Rome; because I could quit the job with few real consequences.

Ralph was quiet the next morning when he came in—probably a not so good report on his health. But I had to report to him at 11:35 am and say, "Okay, I'm off on that interview for the feature story."

"With Diana Vreeland?" he asked, brightly, smiling.

I could see Lynda turned around in her chair staring at me, making a face I couldn't decipher but which I guessed to be saying: "See! He knows you won't even get to talk to her."

"Right. That's the one. See you after lunch," I said, and as I left and waited for the elevator down in the corridor outside the office, I could all but hear him humming, even chuckling to himself with glee, as he envisaged my failure and humiliating return.

I remember thinking, "I've got to ask Joe Mathewson if he can help me find another job."

Δ

Felice Picano

The office was huge, three stories at least, approached by two sets of ajar French doors. Her desk was in the middle at the back. Two tall narrow windows flanked it. A rich carpet with what looked like a good living room set of furniture upon it, but none of that was really visible as it was all covered with swatches, dozens and dozens of swatches.

When her assistant, a pretty young woman a few years older than me, brought me in, I saw that there was another young woman standing at the side of the desk being given orders. During the fifteen minutes I was there, five or six of these pretty girls came and went after receiving their orders.

I stepped forward and went to the desk. I couldn't tell her size. But she was older—sixty-five or seventy, I couldn't be sure—with great character in her face, and big, sharp, penetrating dark eyes. She wore a string of pearls over a dark silk kerchief around her neck, and that over a shiny gray dress. On her head was a small black hat with one ebony feather at a jaunty angle.

She looked up at me and I introduced myself and began repeating what I had said to her assistant over the phone.

"Hmm," she mused, looking me up and down. I'd dressed as well as I could afford in those days. I was young, slim, with curly brown hair. "No! That won't do," she decided.

I thought she meant she'd changed her mind and I wasn't going to be interviewing her, but she instantly said to me, "Take a seat, please. I'll be with you in a few minutes." She waved to one assistant to bring her a handful of swatches on sticks lying on the sofa, and she rifled through those. Almost too low for me to hear, she said, "Have this made up"—she looked at me again curiously, then back down to the swatches—"No, this one. No more than three inches wide."

She waved her other assistant to her and whispered something to her. As the girl took off, she added, louder, "You know which corner I like there!"

The young women gone, I now stood and said, "I really appreciate you taking your time out for this. I know how busy you must..."

The phone rang, she held a hand out to me, and I sat down again.

The table in front of me was covered with more swatches, but also with all the daily New York City papers. I leafed through them, more or less ignoring her talking business, all of it fairly incomprehensibly to me, on the phone.

206

The two girls returned, one with something she handed to me. She urged me up and as I looked down, she lifted my chin and began removing my own tie. In minutes she had the cloth in her hands around my collar. "You know how to do the rest." She folded and stuffed my tie in my jacket pocket.

I looked into a very baroquely gilt mirror on the nearest wall, and I made it into a double ascot knot—the tie was a very soft cotton, black background and lots of little differently colored flowers; even a red backing had been sewn in. Of course, it looked perfect against my white shirt and silver Irish tweed jacket with dark brown trousers.

I turned to model it for Vreeland, and I gave her a thumbs-up. We both smiled.

She hung up the phone, and came to where I was. "Now I really don't have a great deal of time for you and your interesting project, young man. But lunch is free. I take it you're free too?"

Without waiting for my answer, she grabbed me by my elbow and propelled me out of the office. In the outside office, her assistants put on Vreeland's light coat, another handed her purse, and someone else held the elevator doors open. Soon we were on the street and the driver was opening the door to a limo and we were driving uptown.

I'd later find out the restaurant was The Colony. We were all but carried out of the limo and inside, and the *maitre d'* paid great attention to my name and face and seated us at a banquette corner.

As soon as we were settled, she ordered us dry white wine, "Unless you want something stronger," she added, but I didn't and I pulled out my notebook.

"Can you keep that down on the banquette?" she asked. I could and only occasionally made notes anyway.

Close up, Vreeland had nicely done gray hair, very little make up, and then only around her eyes and on her lips. I could now see how good the fabrics she wore were, although they were light. She briefly fingered the cuff of my jacket and I said, "The real thing. I got this in Shannon about two months ago. I bought two of them, quite inexpensively. The other one is a browner hue. Then I forgot I'd bought them when I left London to fly home and I only remembered after I had not declared them at Customs at Kennedy Airport."

She seemed intrigued. "No?! What happened?"

"Luckily the customs inspector was Irish and he noticed my two Dublin visa stamps. He asked how I liked my two weeks there and so we talked about my motorcycle trip around Ireland which was altogether great. He ended up not even *looking* in my bags."

"Lucky you! Tell me about that trip," she said.

The waiter came by and she ordered for the two of us, asking me—"Veal?" to which I shrugged sure, fine. I told her of the motorcycle tour my brother and I took, and how much we loved it, and how beautiful it was. Also how we encountered a huge storm while we were at the poet William Butler Yeats' graveside, on the far west coast, and how we had to wait out the storm a night in the closest farmhouse, an ancient black-stone place with dirt floors and peat in the fireplace, but how we were served great homemade soda bread and butter with tea before we took off the next morning. And how brisk and clear with miles of visibility it was then, motoring all the way down the Connemara coast, one of the greatest roads in the world, equal in magnificence only to the Pacific Highway at Big Sur.

Several women her age or younger came in, looked at us, and came over to the table. Later on I would discover one of them was Babe Paley and the other, Mrs. Winston Guest. Vreeland introduced me to them by name and as a "talented young writer."

More women came in and a few (made-up) older men too, but not Truman Capote, whom I would later discover lunched there regularly, and we met or she smiled and waved at many of them.

By the time our meals arrived at the table I was talking about living in Rome, almost a year, and about my last night there meeting Federico Fellini and Giuletta Masina, his movie star wife, at the premiere of his *Giuletta of the Spirits*, and what an insane scene that event had been, all the press and *paparazzi*, the scores of hangers-on, and the crazy European and American *Cinecittà* actors.

"I had wondered," Vreeland said, as we began eating, "If young people had adventures—or for that matter, fun!—anymore?"

"I do. And I intend to have much more in the future."

"I'll bet you will. With that attitude. But you realize, of course, that you cannot continue working at that magazine much longer. Not if you're to be a real artist."

I agreed and said I'd just realized that fact and that I could see how it was dragging down the editor. But how could I leave, without a source of income?

"One of these ladies might help set you up that way," she said, laughing as she glanced around the room. "If you'd allow her to, which I somehow doubt. But you've certainly been *noticed*! We both have!" And then she added in a lower voice, with a little thrill in it. "They all think you're my gigolo. Do you mind terribly"

"I don't mind. I'd prefer being thought of as a real date even if... well, you know... you're a famous person and all."

It was true and she liked that, and she touched my hand.

Slowly, during the meal, she began dropping names that she thought I might want to highlight in my article: Horst T. Horst, Richard Avedon, Irving Penn, Hiro, and several art directors who as she added, "were not impossible to work with, and even had a few good ideas."

She named specific issues she thought might have especially good art or photos and said she have them sent to my office. She knew how specialized and creative advertising had become: she named the Doyle, Dane Bernbach agency and a few other A.D.s by name and said she was pleased I'd thought a fashion magazine would be of any interest to them.

In turn I told her some of the previous articles I'd done for the magazine: on record album covers and Warhol movies, concluding: "A lot of those people are pretty old-fashioned, but I think it's up to young guys like me to show them that art is more than a Madonna and child or a still life. And that good design exists all around us, if we'd only look."

She patted my arm. "Good for you. And good luck. God knows, I've been trying for years."

I'd seen no menus and no prices nor did I ever see a bill. One moment, we were drinking little cups of French coffee, the next we were standing up and leaving.

Her limo dropped me off at *Harper's Bazaar's* office and Vreeland told me to speak to so-and-so on the eighteenth floor. He would let me go through photos to pick out whatever I needed for the magazine article.

Mr. So-And-So led me into the elevator and up another two floors into a huge shed-like atelier at the top of the building, all but shuttered against the sun but with enough light filtering down, a sort of open storage shack, empty except for thousands of photos simply tossed on the floor. I rummaged there for at least an hour and collected maybe fifty, mostly from differing periods. Downstairs, he gave me big envelopes to hold them.

I arrived back at work at 3:05 p.m., in a great mood, eating jelly beans one by one.

Lynda met me in the outer office.

"Where *were* you? Ralph thought you quit."

"She took me to lunch." I said.

"Who?"

"That editor. Vreeland."

Lynda's mouth opened in a silent scream—just like that fellow in Munch's painting.

"She let me interview her at lunch and let me have all these photos and she's having some other stuff sent over."

Lynda's eyes nearly turned up into her head. She rushed out of the office into the corridor where I knew the restrooms were located.

Ralph was standing in the doorway to the editorial offices. He'd heard what I'd said.

"I know I'm late," I said. "I was going through the atelier collecting all these photos for the feature article I'm writing. There were so many to choose from." I pulled out handfuls to show him.

He spun around on the tip of his cane into the office. Before the door slammed shut, I could hear the cane's tip clunking hard on the wooden floor.

I also went to the restroom. By the time I got back to my cubicle, a thick package from *Harper's Bazaar* was waiting for me on my desk: the promised issues.

Neither Lynda or Ralph said a word to me the rest of the day.

The next day he was out until noon and Lynda quizzed me for most of that time. She couldn't believe what I was saying, and her hand went up to her mouth, until I thought she might be laughing.

"Do. Not. Say. A word of this. To Ralph," She warned.

"I'll have to if he asks. No?"

Lynda threw her hands up and twirled them, and then sat down and phoned someone. I guess her fianceé.

Naturally I phoned *Vogue* and thanked Vreeland for lunch and for her help and for the magazines, speaking to one assistant or another. I promised to get her the story as soon as it was printed.

I handed in the feature article five days later, with photos and captions. It had been a cinch to write: Given Diana Vreeland's confidence in me, the article just flowed out of me.

Ralph returned it to my desk the next morning. He'd scarcely put a red pencil to it. I brought it to Austen's office and we discussed layouts. He was short of art for the next issue and saw what I had as a godsend windfall. He wanted to make the feature four full pages long. If he got away with it, it would utterly dominate that issue.

I knew he and Ralph had arguments over it. But somehow or other, Austen prevailed. When the article "Harper's Bazaar—a Century of American Art and Photography" was printed it was gloriously laid out, with two half-page sized pieces of art, and six smaller ones, It looked like a real feature in a real magazine, and it would later on be nominated for an award.

I mailed two copies of it to Vreeland at *Vogue*, again thanking her, and asking if she wanted the tie back.

A few days later I got a thank you card from her. "Well done. You're going to go far as a writer!" She added: "The tie is yours!"

I worked at *Art Direction* the remaining month of that year and a new News Editor was hired whom I trained, and I became the Assistant Editor and we all settled into a routine. But early that spring I came down with a case of mononucleosis so bad that I had to use my week vacation and my week of sick days to recover.

I was still too weak to work even when those were used up. Ralph held my job a month, then one day he called and said I'd have to come in or resign. Without a thought, I felt so sick, I resigned—and then I went back to sleep for another nine- or ten-hour stretch. I was ill for another two months.

I intended to do art when I got healthier, which took even longer. But Destiny had other plans in mind for me and it would be another twenty years before I did any art at all—and then it was art directing—this time for my own publishing companies SeaHorse Press and Gay Presses of New York.

Δ

I never saw nor spoke to Diana Vreeland again, and I never told anyone else about the encounter, which had presented an utterly different woman from the one everyone else discussed and knew.

To this day I don't know why she was so nice to me. Maybe she was attracted to me. Maybe she wanted to show me off to all the other Movers and Shakers and Jet Setters.

Or maybe she just wanted to be someone else than Diana Vreeland— "monster editor"—for an hour and a half, and naïve and egotistical me and my dumb little writing project let that happen.

But the best part is—I still have that tie!

Me & Tennessee

Tennessee Williams

From hanging out in the Mallory Pier hotels I also began meeting tourists to bed. I'd rapidly grown bored with the small inbred gay scene in Key West, and had gotten bored with often seeing "straight" construction workers, so I sometimes haunted late night Friday and Sunday hotel dances.

As a rule the men I met were in Key West with a friend or lover, who would be dead asleep in the next bed in the hotel room as I *shtupped* his horny partner. One night I met a striking and statuesque Angeleno who said he was staying at a compound on the other end of town from the pier hotel. I followed his car on my bike and we got in at two a.m. and had a good time together. Enough so he wouldn't let me leave the next morning, and insisted I stay for one more bout of lovemaking and then breakfast.

The minute I was fully awakened, showered, and dressed in the previous night's togs, I looked around and realized I'd ended up at one of the very few places in Key West where I'd never wanted to spend the night.

The property consisted of a large house and two tinier ones. The guest rooms, including the one I'd slept in, had at one point been slave quarters—complete with wall shackles for punishment. These varied structures had been cleverly reorganized around a little garden and a nice-sized swimming pool through the use of decking, with several outdoor sitting areas, some screened in, others not, some freestanding, and others more or less attached to the rambling main house.

I had passed by this compound on several occasions and had been invited to visit over the past weeks by one or more of its denizens, a group of mostly gay male writers a decade or more older than myself, most of whom I'd heard of, a few of whom I'd admired, none of whom I wanted to particularly socialize with—for no really good reason.

James Kirkwood was the leader of this group, author of the "beloved" novel, *There Must Be a Pony*, the novel and play, *P.S. Your Cat is Dead*, and the Broadway hit musical, *A Chorus Line*. Others in the group included James Leo Herlihy, who'd written the play *Blue Denim*, and the movie *Midnight Cowboy*, and the allegedly heterosexual Texan writer, William Goyen, although I don't remember meeting his actress wife, Doris Roberts.

Stuck in this den of, if not iniquity then at least of tumultuous gossip, I rather ungraciously allowed myself to be paraded outdoors by my beau of the night and plopped down at a huge breakfast table where much was made of me—Kirkwood to my Angeleno—"You must have *drugged* him. We've been trying to meet him for *weeks*." They of course hadn't failed to notice the unfamiliar bicycle outside his little house when they got up in the morning and knew their West Coast guest had "gotten lucky."

I ate and mumbled replies and drank coffee and was just about to make my escape when more people showed up: a small, thin fellow with bangs of dark hair over a face I would later describe to Andrew Holleran as "resembling a very pouty twelve-year-old placed in a corner for misbehavior"—i.e., the poet James Merrill; with him, his tall, muscular, handsome blond-bearded lover, David Jackson (who would later on under the table casually place one of my hands on his erection and kept it there a while for a little *sub mesa* fun). Also present a lovely, tanned, light-blonde woman fresh out of the woods of Montana or the corn fields of Nebraska, who turned out to be another writer, Alison Lurie.

My guy for a night, alas, left the next night and we only had a brief late afternoon tryst before never seeing each other again. But now that they knew my name, Kirkwood and company weren't about to let me go quite so easily. "Richard published your poems," one of them told me, referring to another member of their extended New York crew, poet-translator Richard Howard, who indeed had published two of my poems in an early version of *Out* magazine. That and the fact that in Manhattan I lived a block from their other pals—John Ashberry, his lover Philip, the painter Lowell Nesbitt, et al.—meant I was also to be considered part of the group. But I pleaded a complete fabrication—to avoid socializing more with them—and said I had a friend from New York staying with me in Key West who knew no one in the place, and who was really just too shy to be brought along.

Somehow the crew or one of their many minions found out where I was staying and one day a bright little envelope and card was shoved under my door with Kirkwood's excited message—"Join us for Dinner and Bridge. Don't say no. We know you both eat dinner *and* play bridge. P.S. Tennessee said he'd come!"

Now *that* was an invitation I couldn't refuse. At the time, Tennessee Williams was one of my idols. At the age of eleven and twelve, as part of a New York City Schools theater outreach program, I'd seen dozens of first run Broadway productions, including most memorably, Williams' *The Night of the Iguana*, the first Wednesday matinee after it had opened, with Bette Davis, Margaret Leighton, and Patrick O Neal, and I had been blown away by it. Those had been specially-priced student-rush tickets, and since then I'd only managed to see one more of his plays, the closing night of *The Milk Train Doesn't Stop Here Anymore*, an evening my friend Ken Lydon took me too, insisting that "every queen of any importance in the city will be here tonight."

What an event that had turned out to be. Tab Hunter, running around shirtless—and at times pantless—most of the night onstage. Mildred Dunnock as the Witch of Capri, but above all the inimitable Tallulah Bankhead, unceasingly camp for the ninety-five percent queer audience as the dying old millionairess. Her character, Cissy Goforth, has a longish speech, and I recall Bankhead stepping forward as the rest of the actors froze in tableau behind and the house lights pinned her at the very edge of center-stage to deliver that speech. From two rows behind us, someone tossed onto the boards an ampule of Amyl Nitrate, unmistakable in its yellow meshwork. La Bankhead stopped, peered down at it, picked it up, held it up to the light for verification, snapped it open under her nose, inhaled, closed her hand over it, every once in a while reopening it for a sniff, and continued her monologue, high as the proverbial kite—and by the way, flawless.

That was the late Sixties. Since then Williams had published and I had read cover to cover, his 1975 *Memoirs*, which had corroborated several facts for me about Tennessee, all of which validated for me the likelihood that I was, at least in part, the basis for one of the two characters in his 1972 play, *Out Cry*. This fact was to become much more fully established the night of the dinner and bridge party at the Kirkwood-Goyen-Herlihy compound.

I arrived on bike to find Tennessee already ensconced at the dinner table along with a few people I didn't know. The usual crowd was present, Merrill staying only till dinner was over, but David remaining to play cards. I know I was introduced to Williams before dinner, but he was busily chatting with others and paid me little attention and even sort of waved me off. So it was only once we were seated for bridge in what turned out to be three tables full plus onlookers, and I was seated to William's left side, that he looked at me fully for the first time full of curiosity and asked, "What did you say your name was again?"

When I told him, he said, "I have an old friend named Felice. Felice Orlandi. Lovely fellow. Unfortunately 'unbent' as too many handsome Italians tend to be. What's the chance of knowing two Felices in a lifetime?" he asked the room rhetorically. I remember thinking he looked like a rather squarish Cheshire Cat, or maybe like an old teddy bear, possibly because his clothing was all black and white, and also he was mischievous: during the evening, there were constant complaints of "Tay—nn! You can't do that!" during cards. But even though he drank constantly and his eyes shone with the unmistakable allure of pharmaceutical usage, he was a sharp bridge player, seldom if ever misplaying. After the game—he and his partner trounced us soundly—we changed tables. I was just getting up when Williams put a hand on my forearm and said, "Incidentally, you're not Felice from Greenwich Village?"

I confirmed that I was in fact Felice from Greenwich Village. "Ah," Williams said. "I sort of wrote you up some years ago." Before I could ask about that, he held me in a tighter grip, and with more urgency demanded, "And William T. Williams? That specimen of American masculine pulchritude? Was his male member as large as I always imagined it would be?"

"Larger!" I replied. Which earned me a satisfied smile and another pat on the forearm.

Needless to say the entire room of maybe fourteen became an ice-sculpture tableau during this brief exchange. The dialogue over, I moved to another table, and the room unglued. Although Williams and I met again in other restaurants in Key West over the next few weeks and chatted more, and I would later see him back-stage after the opening of his play *Small Craft Warnings* in Manhattan, where he played the on-stage narrator to Cherry Vanilla's brilliant impersonation, I never revealed to anyone how it was that Williams "sort of" wrote me up without ever having met me.

Here's the story. When I returned from Europe and moved back into the West Village studio that I'd sublet to my college friends Ruth and Tom Cleary, I was pretty much alone and at loose ends. In a few weeks I would meet Bob Herron and the entire Jane Street Gang who would become my social set for the next few years. But on those strangely balmy late nights of that first autumn that I lived in the Village, I would wander about this new neighborhood of mine getting to know it a little. One of those nights, a few doors away from where I lived, I met a six-foot three, red-headed, bearded, beautifully built man maybe five years my senior, named William T. Williams, and took him back to my place for sex.

The sex was—in a word—spectacular, partly because of the above alluded-to male member. But also because this gorgeous man was horny and accomplished and I was exactly his type. W.T.W. worked nearby and he was free Thursday nights. He asked me to keep some open for him, and so I invited him back. That winter we saw each other maybe a half dozen times. Afterward, or, rather in between doing it again and as guys often do, we would talk about ourselves and our lives. In this way I got to know that W.T.W. was a Southerner, from Arkansas or Missouri, I think; that he was a highly trained, highly paid male nurse; and that he now only worked in situations where there was, in his own delightfully accented words, "a high need for discretion."

Meaning what exactly, I asked? Meaning, that he tended a woman with a troublesome gun shot wound, where the bullet remained lodged in her torso months afterward, causing her pain and worry, and needing to be drained often. It was his job to bathe her, massage her, exercise her to the extent that she was capable, and to try to work that bullet out of the wound, a task that required close to a year. At first he wouldn't tell me who the woman was, but

I later uncovered from hints he dropped that it must be one of the Rockefeller wives, and that the obstinate bullet had been put into her by a jealous husband. While the impetus for this unfortunate occurrence wasn't ever too clear to W.T.W. or to myself, what was smashingly clear was that the entire incident had been successfully kept away from the police and the press.

W.T.W. told me a bunch of similar stories but frankly I never really knew whether he did so to titillate me, getting me ready for more sex, or even if the stories were true. Two weeks before he was about to leave his current job and move on to another patient in another state, he told me one more anecdote. For the seven or eight months he'd been in New York, he'd been working as nurse to Tennessee Williams who had recently undergone a major mental and physical breakdown and who'd been shipped to New York by his agent and friend Audrey Woods who'd put the playwright into a flat beneath hers, a few blocks from where I lived, and where Tennessee had lived in seclusion, with occasional nighttime walks to the nearby Hudson River in the company of his nurse.

Several years passed, W.T.W. was no longer in the city, and one morning I opened my copy of the *Times* and read a review of a new play by Tennessee Williams titled *Out Cry*. The review was by no means entirely favorable. I looked at the box containing the cast list and saw it consisted of two names: Clare, played by Cara Duff-MacCormick, and her brother/lover, Felice, with *Cabaret* film heartthrob, Michael York. The kind but not very generous reviewer said this new play was a rewrite of Williams' earlier play titled *Two Character Play*, written before I'd met W.T.W., that had premiered in London in 1967.

I was far too poor to be able to get a ticket to the play. And I thought it might all be a coincidence but I had to admit I was rather stunned. My name is—obviously—unusual in the U.S. It's common in Italy, where it is the same as Felix, and where a nineteenth-century writer Felice Romani, was a major figure of the Italian opera world, penning libretti to works by Bellini, Rossini, Donizetti, Spontini, and Cherubini. But I was pretty much the only male Felice around for hundreds of miles, and had been for years. So I suspected this character in Williams' new play might be connected to me. I felt an odd combination of being honored and betrayed at the same time. Then, because my life was so difficult, I simply forgot all about it.

Years later, I would find a copy of the play *Out Cry* and read it. I also read and compared it to *Two Character Play*. The playwright had changed the play and the character Felice from the first to the second versions, and there were even statements I remembered making, recognizable in the new play. I could only suppose that W.T.W. had mentioned me to Tennessee who asked more and more about this mysterious man whom his nurse spent free nights with, and that Tenn had little by little built up a character for me—at second hand. A fantasy character of course, since all real artists work from their own fantasy rather than anyone's reality. I'm guessing he'd then added this new fantasy to the fantasy of the straight Felice he already knew and whom he'd already written about.

But while I'd supposed all that, not until the moment Tennessee said, "I sort of wrote you up," it had been nothing more than a supposition. And otherwise I meant nothing at all to Williams. Months later when I saw Tennessee at the cast party after *Small Craft Warnings*, he was happy as a clam amidst the colorful denizens of Seventies Underground Punk New York, where he was fully appreciated by people like Charles Ludlam and Ronnie Tavel, Cherry Vanilla, Jackie Curtis, and Suzy Shit, folks I knew a little and occasionally hung out with, who had drawn the aging playwright into their cheerfully drugged-out, chaotic and wayward hearts. Unsurprisingly on that occasion, Williams barely recalled who I was, and I didn't bother reminding him. For by then I myself had begun using fantasies of real people for my own writing.

Even so, I felt he and I had established some connection, no matter how tenuous, and I was horribly shocked by his senseless and grotesque death. Williams had been so vibrant a figure. He'd been haphazard true, drifting, erratic, and at times liquored and drugged up, but despite that, quite vibrant. And after all, he was, and remains, the greatest playwright America ever produced.

As a sidelight, once I'd moved to California, I also got to meet the other Felice, the one Williams had once lusted after when they were both younger men. He was at a party given by Betty Berzon and Terry di Crescenza. Felice Orlandi was married to the actress, Alice Ghostley, and was still quite handsome in his late sixties, although quite ill at the time I met him. And now I understood those rumors that had circulated at the Tennessee Williams

Festival in New Orleans a few years earlier, and told Felice about them. He was equally amused. We spoke a little about Tennessee Williams, and he said to me, "Too bad, Tenn didn't meet you in 1966. He needed someone badly then, and I'm almost certain you would have saved him."

"Saved him from what?" I had to ask.

"Who knows?" Felice said. "From himself? From his demons? Isn't that what they say about all of you writers? That you have demons?"

Alas, today Felice Orlandi, his wife, Alice Ghostley, and even Betty Berzon have passed away…

"…And I only am escaped to tell thee."

Acknowledgements

Many thanks to Donna Lieberman, Susan Moldow and Rob Arnold for their support when I was writing certain pieces in this collection.

About the Author

Felice Picano

Felice Picano is the author of more than twenty-five books of poetry, fiction, memoirs, nonfiction, and plays. His work has been translated into many languages and several of his titles have been national and international bestsellers. He is considered a founder of modern gay literature along with the other members of the Violet Quill. Picano also began and operated the SeaHorse Press and Gay Presses of New York for fifteen years. His first novel was a finalist for the PEN/Hemingway Award. Since then he's been nominated for and/or won dozens of literary awards. Recent work includes a collection of stories, *Tales: From a Distant Planet*, and a history and memoir of his early gay life in New York, *Art & Sex in Greenwich Village*. Picano teaches at Antioch University, Los Angeles.

LaVergne, TN USA
01 February 2011
214860LV00001B/107/P